THE BROTHER OF
JESUS

THE BROTHER OF
JESUS

*The Dramatic Story & Meaning of
the First Archaeological Link
to Jesus & His Family*

HERSHEL SHANKS & BEN WITHERINGTON III

HarperSanFrancisco
A Division of HarperCollinsPublishers

THE BROTHER OF JESUS: *The Dramatic Story & Meaning of the First Archaeological Link to Jesus & His Family.* Copyright © 2003 by Biblical Archaeology Society. All rights reserved. Printed in the United States of America. No part of this book may be used or reproduced in any manner whatsoever without written permission except in the case of brief quotations embodied in critical articles and reviews. For information address HarperCollins Publishers, Inc., 10 East 53rd Street, New York, NY 10022.

HarperCollins books may be purchased for educational, business, or sales promotional use. For information please write: Special Markets Department, HarperCollins Publishers, Inc., 10 East 53rd Street, New York, NY 10022.

HarperCollins Web site: http://www.harpercollins.com
HarperCollins®, ✦®, and HarperSanFrancisco™ are
trademarks of HarperCollins Publishers, Inc.

FIRST EDITION
Designed by Joseph Rutt

Library of Congress Cataloging-in-Publication Data
is available upon request.
ISBN 0–06–058117–4 (pbk.)

04 05 06 07 08 RRD(H) 10 9 8 7 6 5 4 3 2 1

Contents

Introduction to the Revised Edition

On June 18, 2003, the Israel Antiquities Authority announced at a press conference that the inscription "James, son of Joseph, brother of Jesus," on the bone box, or ossuary, of James was a modern forgery.

On July 21, 2003, Oded Golan, the owner of the ossuary, was arrested, presumably for forging the inscription with tools found in his workshop.

So the jig was up. Everything in the first edition of this book—at least the first part, which I wrote—was either wrong or irrelevant. I had been taken in by a forger and made a fool of.

But that is not really the end of the story. As a matter of fact, the end of the story cannot yet be written. At the present time we still don't know for sure whether the inscription—perhaps the most startling artifact ever found from the time of Jesus—is authentic or a modern forgery. Nor do we know for sure whether the owner of the ossuary, Tel Aviv collector Oded Golan, is a forger.

What we do know for sure is that the Israel Antiquities Authority (IAA) has not proved its case. Maybe it will do so in the future as more and more people study the inscription and the ossuary and, despite the failings of its study, find the inscription a forgery. But at this time, the IAA has not even bothered to defend its study. We can only speak about what we know now and what we do not know now. At this time, whether the inscription is authentic is an open question. I can no longer state with such confidence, as I did in the first edition, that it is "virtually certain that the James ossuary and its inscription are authentic artifacts." But I am by no means convinced that it is a forgery either. In short, the question has been raised but not answered.

As for Oded Golan, the fact is that he has never been charged—either with forgery or any other wrongdoing. True, the IAA and the Israeli police have been assiduous—to say the least—in their effort to obtain a confession from him. Even though there was no danger that he would flee, the police handcuffed him in front of his parents and took him to be mugged and fingerprinted at the local police station. They put the cuffs on unnecessarily, the chief fraud investigator for the IAA told me, because they wanted to "pressure him." Later, they came to his home at night and team-interrogated him for nearly thirty hours, well into the following evening. When, finally, they came to arrest him, they arrived in the middle of the night, as if he were a potentially violent criminal who would endanger the police if he were awake when they arrived. *But they did not charge him with a crime.* Instead, the police convinced a judge to allow him to be held, under Israeli law, for four days for questioning, after which they would have to charge him with a crime or release him. When the four days had elapsed, they released him *without charging him.* Yet, almost everyone knows only that he was arrested (and thus presumes he is guilty).

By the time you read this, perhaps Golan will have been charged. But, just as I made the decision to print in *Biblical Archaeology Review* Professor Lemaire's original article about the inscription on the basis of what we then knew (after getting confirmation from leading epigraphers and linguists as well as the scientific judgment of geologists at the Israel Geological Survey), I can speak now of the case against Oded Golan, the owner of the ossuary, only on the basis of what we know at this time.

I can report that IAA officials have told several people, including me, that there is a group of forgers operating in Israel and that it includes an "honored Israeli archaeologist." This is extremely hard to believe. Yet it is also hard to think that this kind of information would be given out by the IAA if it didn't have the evidence to back it up.

Further, since I last wrote, Golan's association with another controversial artifact has been made public: the so-called Jehoash inscription, which mentions the biblical king Jehoash, who ruled over Judah from about 835 to 801 B.C. Golan denies ownership of the inscription, but it was in his apartment when the police seized it. Unlike the ossuary inscription, the Jehoash inscription has been deemed a "demonstrable forgery" by several distinguished paleographers who have analyzed the script and linguistics. While some other scholars are, as they say, on the fence, the weight of the evidence at this time is clearly that the Jehoash inscription is a forgery. It was this inscription that led the IAA to suspect Golan and to appoint committees to examine both the Jehoash inscription and the ossuary inscription. The IAA committee that examined the Jehoash inscription found it also to be a forgery.

But sometimes these authorities play dirty. They may still be trying to pressure Golan to confess. A case in point: after the IAA completed the study concluding that the ossuary inscription is a forgery, the ossuary was returned to the owner. By this time, he was famous and he was fearful that it might be robbed from his middle-class apartment in Tel Aviv. So he wrapped it in bubble wrap, then placed it in a cardboard box and wrapped this cardboard box in cloth. Then he took it to the only place in his apartment building where he thought it would be safe. On the roof was a small old room that hadn't been used in decades. It contained a toilet that no longer had a seat, so he took a board and placed the box on top—and locked the door. When the police came to arrest him, they wanted to take the ossuary too, so they asked him where it was. He took them to the roof where he had hidden it. The police proceeded to take off the outer cloth, open the cardboard box, remove the ossuary from the bubble wrap, place it back on the toilet, take a photograph of the ossuary on the toilet, and release the picture to the newspapers. Voilà. Now they had "evidence" of the disrespect the owner was showing to the ossuary.

Which is not to say that Oded Golan is not a forger, simply that the case hasn't been made yet.

But what of the inscription itself? Is it authentic, or is it a forgery? Whether or not Oded Golan is a forger, there is no question that he has many authentic and important pieces in his collection—and the ossuary with its inscription may be one of them, even if he is a forger.

The IAA declaration that the inscription is a forgery, reprinted in chapter 15 of our new part 3, is based on the findings of two committees, a Writing and Content Committee and a separate Materials and Patina Committee. In chapter 17, André Lemaire analyzes the work of the Writing and Content Committee and convincingly demonstrates that it is deeply flawed. As he shows, no confidence whatsoever can be placed in its conclusions, especially in light of the other world-renowned paleographers who find no reason to question the authenticity of the inscription based on the shape and form of the letters (paleography). The members of the Writing and Content Committee who studied the ossuary do not even discuss the paleography of the letters, though it seems this should have been a critical aspect of their examination. The committee's conclusions are simply impressionistic. And the ossuary committee, as Lemaire points out, did not include anyone identified by the appointing committee as a paleographic expert.

One member of the Writing and Content Committee candidly admitted that he was convinced only by the conclusion of the two relevant scientists—geologists—on the Materials and Patina Committee. Otherwise, he would have found the inscription authentic. It is clear that the geologists' judgment—and their judgment alone—guided the conclusion of the committee as a whole. Yet each of the two geologists explicitly states that his individual statement on the ossuary is not a final report or a proper scientific explanation of his position. Instead, both say they will publish a proper scientific report in a professional journal sometime in the future. Hence, it is impossible for other geologists—and I have talked to many of them—to review the work of the two geologists on the IAA committee.

But that is not the worst of it.

After the ossuary was displayed in November and December 2002 at the Royal Ontario Museum (ROM) in Toronto, a team from the museum did its own scientific study of the ossuary and its inscription. Like the original team from the Israel Geological Survey, the ROM team found nothing suspicious or modern about the inscription and declared it authentic. Perhaps both the ROM team and the team from the Israel Geological Survey were mistaken. But at the very least, the IAA committee should explain, as a professional courtesy, why it believes these other studies erred, why these scientific tests failed to reveal the forgery.

Tellingly, neither of the two geologists on the IAA committee uses the word *fake* or *forgery* in his statement. The summary of the individual statements released by the IAA (and printed in chapter 15) contains the following sentence by one of the geologists: "The inscription was inscribed or cleaned in a modern period." Everyone has acknowledged that the inscription was indeed cleaned in modern times—several times, roughly, and with a sharp instrument. But the IAA committee never bothered to consider this alternative in its own statement.

Moreover, even the IAA committee found ancient patina in some of the letters of the inscription. One of the members of the Materials and Patina Committee stated, as quoted in the summary, "The end of the inscription 'brother of Jesus' appears authentic; in some places there seems to be remains of old patina." If this statement is correct, it is highly unlikely that the first part of the inscription is a forgery.

Perhaps in the end the inscription will be proven to be a forgery. But that hasn't happened yet.

Many scholars are asking how the IAA got involved in this matter in the first place. After all, its job is not to assess the authenticity of questionable artifacts. It has never done so in the past. When questionable artifacts surface, scholars write a variety of analyses in professional journals until a consensus is reached or the two sides have reached an impasse and each individual scholar is then free to adopt the analysis that seems most convincing. Many scholars believe that is what should have happened here: let scholars from a variety of scholarly subdisciplines express their views, and let those who wish to counter them do so. The IAA committee is not a judicial authority empowered to make a definitive decision like a court. But that is how the IAA has acted here. Many scholars, both within Israel and outside of it, feel the IAA has overstepped its proper bounds.

I spoke with one member of the IAA committee who conceded that he was uncertain about the committee's conclusion, even though on balance he felt the committee's conclusion was correct. Based on our discussion, I told him that I would describe him as concluding the inscription was a forgery with a confidence level of only 75 percent. Well, he said, maybe 80 percent. But not 100 percent. The committee, of course, announced its conclusion without reserve. I then told another committee member about this, and he explained that the committee had decided that it must "reach a firm conclusion."

Few things in scholarship—especially ancient history—are 100 percent certain. But for some reason, the IAA committee decided that it must "reach a firm conclusion." This is hardly a scholarly way to proceed.

The original edition of this book describes the situation as it developed from the time of the inscription's discovery by Professor Lemaire in 2002 until January 2003, when I wrote the introduction to the first edition. This revised edition brings the story up to date to the time of this writing, October 2003. That has been done by this introduction and, more specifically, by the chapters in the new part 3 of this revised edition: the IAA's summary of its decision; an article I wrote for the *Jerusalem Post* stating my own position; André Lemaire's trenchant analysis of the IAA committee's report, reprinted from the November/December 2003 *Biblical Archaeology Review;* articles from *Christianity Today* written by the coauthor of this book, Ben Witherington III, and a discussion of the ossuary and the debate by Edward J. Keall, senior curator at the Royal Ontario Museum in Toronto and curator for the James ossuary exhibition there in 2002.

Needless to say, we all await further developments. At this time, we know only that the final chapter cannot yet be written.

Hershel Shanks
Washington, D.C.
October 2003

Introduction

T his book is about what may be the most astonishing find in the history of archaeology—an inscription that many scholars believe is the first attestation of Jesus of Nazareth in the archaeological record, carved into a limestone chest that once contained the bones of Jesus' brother James, the leader of the Jewish Christian community in Jerusalem.

Many Jews in Jerusalem in Jesus' time buried their dead in long niches in cave tombs. After a year, when the flesh had desiccated and fallen away, the bones of the deceased would be collected in limestone chests called ossuaries. The small stone boxes were just large enough to accommodate the longest bone of the body, the thighbone. Sometimes the name of the deceased would be inscribed on the outside of the box. On the ossuary that is the subject of this book, the inscription reads: "James, son of Joseph, brother of Jesus."

This ossuary has only recently surfaced—from the collection of an antiquities aficionado in Israel. The owner failed to recognize the significance of the inscription until he showed it to a specialist in ancient Semitic inscriptions from the Sorbonne. Since then, the ossuary has taken the world by storm, appearing on the front page of almost every newspaper on the globe, including the *New York Times,* the *Washington Post,* and the *International Herald*

Tribune. It has been featured on radio and television as well as in magazines like *Time.*

But the initial excitement has been followed by a barrage of questions. Where did it come from? How did the collector get it? Is it a fake? How do we know that it refers to Jesus of Nazareth? Did Jesus have a brother? Who, really, was James, and why is he so significant in understanding the earliest forms of Christianity?

And what are the theological implications of this extraordinary find? Does it cast doubt on the doctrine that Mary was a perpetual virgin? Does it challenge the Roman Catholic identification of James as only a cousin of Jesus?

These are some of the questions Ben Witherington and I address in this book. Sometimes we express our own views—quite strongly. On other matters, we present both sides of issues on which scholars disagree. As to these matters, readers will have to make up their own minds.

As you weigh the evidence and decide whether the Jesus of the inscription is indeed the Jesus we know from the New Testament, there is much to learn and enjoy along the way. You will learn about the subculture of the antiquities market and why attitudes toward this sometimes shady bazaar bitterly divide the scholarly community. You will learn about the Jewish world in which Jesus lived. You will learn about the strange custom of *ossilegium,* or secondary burial. You will learn how scholars date and authenticate ancient inscriptions by the shape and slant of the letters. You will learn what is known about the family of Jesus. You will learn how one of Jesus' brothers came to head the Jerusalem community of believers who gathered in his name. And you will learn how this brother healed a fundamental breach among factions within the community of believers.

Above all, you will be transported to life two thousand years ago within a community of Jews who were just beginning to learn what it meant to be Christian and who constituted the mother church of a movement that would become arguably the most significant religious tradition the world has ever witnessed.

Our book is divided into two parts, the first written by me and the second by Ben. As editor of *Biblical Archaeology Review,* I supervised the publication of the article announcing the inscription. I have been intimately connected with documenting the inscription's authenticity and arranging for the inaugural exhibit of the ossuary at the Royal Ontario Museum in Toronto. Ben Witherington is a professor at Asbury Theological Seminary, a leading New Testament scholar with more than twenty books to his credit, and a columnist for the popular *Bible Review.* His part of this book provides the background on James as the brother of Jesus and how that relationship was seen over the centuries by Christians. He also assesses the movement of believers in Jesus that James led and considers some of the theological implications of the ossuary inscription for various Christian traditions.

We think that the evidence for the inscription's authenticity is compelling, as do leading experts in the field. We also present the exciting evidence for evaluating the inscription and the debate surrounding it. Does this inscription indeed refer to Jesus of Nazareth? Did this stone chest once hold the bones of his brother James? You be the judge.

Hershel Shanks
Washington, D.C.
January 2003

Foreword

"I am always interested in seeing new inscriptions." That is the answer I gave to an Israeli collector in April 2002 when he told me that he probably had a few things that might interest me. We made an appointment, and a few days later I met him in his flat in Tel Aviv. Of the pieces in his collection, he was particularly interested in showing me an inscription engraved on an ossuary, or bone box, in cursive Aramaic that he could not decipher. (Indeed, it later took me several days to decipher it.) But before taking me to this ossuary, he showed me pictures of a few others, one with an inscription that he had already read, likely with the help of Israeli paleographer Ada Yardeni. The full inscription read: "Ya'akov son of Yosef brother of Yeshua." Yardeni probably helped the owner to read the difficult Aramaic words *achui d'* (brother of). Otherwise, there is no problem reading this inscription. It was very well written in classical script. The owner said he thought the inscription was especially interesting because there was only one other inscription in Rahmani's *Catalogue* (the standard catalog of Jewish ossuaries) mentioning a brother in a similar way. With this remark, he was about to show me the undeciphered inscription that he had initially invited me to see. But I stopped him.

"Wait! This inscription seems interesting to me because 'Ya'akov son of Yosef brother of Yeshua' could be 'James son of Joseph brother of Jesus,'" I said. "James is a very important person in the history of early Christianity." The Israeli collector, however, quite obviously had never heard of this person. I had to explain to him who James was, that he was mentioned in the Gospels, the Acts of the Apostles, and in the letters of Paul, as well as in the works of the first-century Jewish historian Josephus and by the fourth-century church father Eusebius of Caesarea. I explained that James was the leader of the community of Christian Jews in Jerusalem before the First Jewish Revolt against Rome (A.D. 66–70). At the same time, I told him also that this identification was not certain because the inscription contained no defining phrase such as "James the Just" or "James the Righteous," as he was commonly known, or "Jesus the Messiah" or "Jesus of Nazareth." The names Joseph, Jesus, and James were common among Jews in the first century, the period when ossuaries were primarily used in Jerusalem and, of course, the time of Jesus and the earliest Christians, including his brother James. "The identification is, therefore, a question of probability to be studied in more detail," I told him. The collector became quite interested and reminded me that, to determine the popularity of these names, it would be necessary to take into account the size of the population of Jerusalem at that time. Then he gave me a photograph of the inscription. I told him I would write to him after checking the references to James in the literary tradition and estimating in a preliminary way the probability that this inscription referred to these figures from the New Testament.

During the next few days, I took a break from my research on biblical Hebrew in its Northwest Semitic setting, which I was studying with a team of scholars from the Institute for Advanced Studies (at the Hebrew University of Jerusalem). I checked the New Testament, Josephus and Eusebius, read three recently published books about James, and started to work out the probability, taking into account the frequency of the three names in the onomastics (name lists) of this period as well as the archaeological estimate of the population of Jerusalem. I used two excellent libraries, the Jewish National Library, close to my office in Givat Ram, and the library of the French École Biblique, where I was a student thirty-four years ago.

This preliminary study proved very encouraging. So I wrote a few lines to the collector, asking whether it would be possible to check the inscription on the ossuary itself, even though I had a good feeling about the authenticity of the inscription even from the photograph. We fixed a time for a second appointment. This time I saw the ossuary itself in his apartment and could examine with my magnifying glass the inscription and how it was engraved. I saw nothing suspicious about it. So I asked the owner for permission to publish a study of the inscription, which—as I explained again—probably designated an important personage of the early church and his close relationship with Jesus of Nazareth. He agreed to the publication as long as his name was not mentioned. He also said he preferred that the article appear in an English publication, since he was not fluent in French. I mentioned the possibility of publishing it in *Biblical Archaeology Review.* It is in English, and it uses excellent color pictures. I knew from an e-mail I had received a few days earlier that the editor was coming to Jerusalem shortly and I could meet with him. The collector readily agreed.

On May 22, I had dinner with Hershel Shanks, Bezalel Porten, and Robert Deutsch. Toward the end of a lovely meal, I discreetly mentioned to Hershel the possibility of an article about an inscribed ossuary mentioning "James the brother of Jesus." Apparently he did not realize on the spot to whom I was alluding, but he told me to send him my manuscript. So the adventure began.

In the article, published in the November 2002 issue of *Biblical Archaeology Review,* I present the evidence and the analysis that have led me to conclude that the ossuary and the inscription are indeed authentic and that the inscription does most likely refer to the James, Joseph, and Jesus of the New Testament. There has already been a great deal of scholarly discussion of the ossuary and its remarkable inscription, and I am delighted to report that I am even more confident about my conclusions. I have found it

most encouraging that the leading experts in the field corrobo-
rate in verifying the discovery's authenticity. And I do not find the
arguments against, let alone rumors about, its authenticity at all
serious, especially since they have been advanced by people with
no experience in Aramaic epigraphy (writing and inscriptions) of
this period.

The reader can now read Hershel Shanks's own story of en-
countering this exciting inscription, but before letting him speak,
I may perhaps add a word or two explaining why I, personally,
thought at once about a possible identification with James the
brother of Jesus. Many years ago, I earned my doctorate in religious studies at the École Pratique des Hautes Études (in the Sorbonne, in Paris) under the tutelage of Professors Oscar Cullman
and Pierre Nautin. My research project concerned the origins of
the early church. This became my first book: *Les ministères aux
origines de l'Église* (1971). No wonder that the role of James in the
Jewish and Christian history of the first century is of great interest
to me. A decade later, in a small, popular book on ancient Israelite history (*Histoire du peuple hébreu,* 1981, sixth edition 2001),
I mention the death of James, head of the community of Christian Jews in Jerusalem. Much more can be learned about James in
this book, which I strongly encourage the reader to peruse.

André Lemaire
The Sorbonne, Paris
January 2003

THE BROTHER OF
JESUS

Part I

THE STORY OF A REMARKABLE DISCOVERY

HERSHEL SHANKS

I

OH, NO!

It's shortly after 10 A.M. on Friday, November 1, 2002, when the call comes. It is Dan Rahimi, director of collections management at the Royal Ontario Museum in Toronto, where the now world-famous ossuary, or bone box, bearing the startling inscription "James, son of Joseph, brother of Jesus" is to be exhibited in two weeks.

"I'm sitting here with Ed Keall," Dan says. Ed is the museum's senior curator of Near Eastern and Asian civilizations, and I had previously talked with him about various aspects of the exhibit. But Dan ominously continues. "Joel Peters, vice president for marketing, is also here." I start to worry. I'd had a run-in with Joel the previous day when he suggested local television stations could film the arrival of the ossuary in Toronto. We had previously agreed to grant exclusive television rights to an award-winning documentary filmmaker. He had told Joel that he would make his film footage available without charge to local television stations. So I blew my stack at Joel's suggestion. Was this dispute resurfacing, I wonder?

Dan goes on: "We're in the office of Meg Beckel, chief operating officer of the museum." Now I really begin to get scared. "William Thorsell, director of the museum and chief executive officer, is also here. I have some terrible news."

Oh, my God, I think. They're canceling the exhibit because the ossuary is "unprovenanced" (the professional archaeological term for discoveries whose origin is unknown and that were not professionally excavated). The ossuary, privately owned by an antiquities collector in Israel who wished to remain anonymous, had been purchased on the antiquities market from an unidentified Arab antiquities dealer. We don't know exactly where it was found or when or by whom. This had become an issue over the past few days as ethical questions were being raised. The leading American professional organization of Near Eastern archaeologists, which was about to meet in Toronto during the scheduled Royal Ontario Museum exhibition, would have nothing to do with the ossuary. The organization's policy is not to publish articles on, exhibit, or even professionally discuss objects that were not professionally excavated for fear that this will enhance their value.

But this isn't the problem. It's something worse. "We have opened the shipping crate, and the ossuary is full of cracks," Dan continues. I suddenly feel a rush of blood to my head. Dan goes on to describe how they carefully unpacked the ossuary only to find serious cracks, even fissures, in the soft limestone box. It had been poorly packed, he says. Small chips of stone have fallen off. He is sorry to say that one large crack goes straight through the inscription.

A press conference to reenact the opening of the ossuary crate has been scheduled for 2 P.M., less than four hours away. The museum needs to have the owner's instructions. It is already after 5 P.M. in Israel, the beginning of Shabbat, the sabbath. They cannot show the ossuary to the press in this condition, Dan says. He proposes calling off the press conference. As we talk, however, we quickly decide that the only thing to do is to be candid. While we cannot display the ossuary in this condition, there is no way to prevent the press from coming and asking questions. We must tell them that the ossuary has been damaged. In the end, the only question facing us is whether the press should be given a picture of the ossuary with its cracks. Painfully, we agree that the press should be given the picture. Will the owner of the ossuary agree?

At the time, we still refer to the owner as "Joe" to protect his anonymity. The museum does not know his real name. All dealings requiring Joe's agreement are made through his lawyer, but the lawyer's office is closed for Shabbat. So I am the intermediary. I know Joe. I know his real name, and I have even been to his apartment in Israel, so I know how to get in touch with him. I track him down in Tel Aviv.

When I tell him what has happened, he is momentarily speechless. He insists that he had the ossuary packed by the best packers in Israel, a firm that does packing for many museums. The transportation itself was handled by the world-famous Brinks. He obviously feels helpless and frustrated.

We have a number of conference calls with the museum group in Meg Beckel's office. Though they don't know Joe's name, they know his voice well; we have talked a number of times before. It is almost noon, and we are told that the cameras will begin arriving at the museum within an hour for the conference. In the end, Joe agrees with us that there is nothing to do but be candid with the press—and to give them a picture of the damaged ossuary.

The museum carefully photographed every detail of the private unpacking that took place the day before. They e-mail the pictures to Joe and to me, but I do not see them until the press conference is well under way. The photos nearly make me sick to my stomach. I had thought that Dan Rahimi might have been exaggerating the damage just to emphasize the seriousness of the situation. Instead, he had tried to put as good a face on it as he honestly could. The cracks were terrible.

The silver lining is that the Royal Ontario Museum has an excellent conservator on its staff, Ewa Dziadowiec, who specializes in stone restoration. She can conserve the ossuary in a matter of days.

Just before I am ready to sit down to Shabbat dinner with my wife, a fax from Dan comes through at my home—a copy of a fax he is sending to Joe, with an attached protocol for conservation of the ossuary. "Dear Joe," the letter begins. It urges Joe to authorize the museum to undertake the conservation as soon as possible.

My eyes immediately drop to the protocol. There I read for the first time: "The box of the ossuary has been broken into five pieces." For a moment, my heart stops.

I turn back to the letter: "Ewa proposes to remove the five fragments, clean them of dust or any other contaminant and glue them back together, using an additive like poly-vinyl acetate mixed with textured filler material and pigment. This treatment is totally reversible and can be easily dissolved with acetone. We do not propose to paint over the repair. Rather, the pigmented filler will come close to matching the colour of the ossuary. The cracks will be slightly visible."

That's the best we can do. Indeed, that's the best that can be done when what may be one of the greatest archaeological finds of all time lies in pieces.

2

AN AMAZING DISCOVERY

To say that André Lemaire is always on the prowl doesn't sound very scholarly. But it's true. A former priest, Lemaire specializes in Semitic epigraphy—the study of Hebrew, Aramaic, and other ancient Semitic inscriptions. He lives in Paris and teaches at the Sorbonne, but he is frequently found in Jerusalem, prowling the shops of antiquities dealers and consorting with antiquities collectors when he is not researching some recondite subject at the library of the École Biblique et Archéologique Française—recognized as the finest biblical library in Jerusalem.

Establishment archaeologists—particularly the prestigious Archaeological Institute of America (AIA) and the American Schools of Oriental Research (ASOR), the principal organization of Near Eastern archaeologists, which met in Toronto when the ossuary was on display at the Royal Ontario Museum—are officially opposed to what he is doing. He studies and publishes important inscriptions that come from the antiquities market. ("Publishing an inscription" is the scholarly shorthand for publishing the initial report announcing the discovery and interpretation of an ancient inscription or artifact.) In the world of scholarship, as we indicated earlier, such artifacts obtained through the antiquities market are called unprovenanced. No one, except the initial seller and perhaps the antiquities dealer,

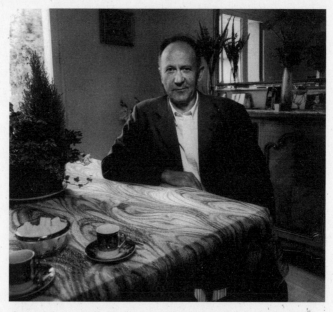

One of the world's leading experts on ancient Semitic scripts, André Lemaire is the director of studies at the École Pratique des Hautes Études, History and Philology Section, in the Sorbonne, in Paris. *Laurent Monlau/Rapho*

knows where they come from. They have not been scientifically excavated by a professional archaeologist. They have "no context," as the charge has it. They were found by accident or looted or pocketed by some worker at a legitimate excavation before the find could be registered. To publish studies of such artifacts only encourages the looters, the argument goes. Therefore the AIA and ASOR will not publish a study of an unprovenanced artifact in their scholarly journals, the *American Journal of Archaeology* and the *Bulletin of the American Schools of Oriental Research* (*BASOR*). A scholarly paper analyzing an unprovenanced inscription or artifact cannot be presented at meetings of American archaeologists that the AIA and ASOR annually sponsor.

Which is not to say that Lemaire is not admired and respected. He is. So are other leading Semitic epigraphers, such as Frank Moore Cross of Harvard, P. Kyle McCarter of the Johns Hopkins University in Baltimore, and the late Nahman Avigad, who taught at the Hebrew University of Jerusalem. (Oddly, both Cross and McCarter are past presidents of ASOR.) They all recognize that they simply cannot ignore the important pieces that have come on the market. The prime example is the Dead Sea Scrolls. The first scrolls were found accidentally in a cave by Bedouin shepherds. The scrolls were subsequently purchased through Arab antiquities dealers. That started a race between the Bedouin and professional archaeologists to locate other caves with scrolls. The Bedouin almost always beat the archaeologists. And when they did, the scholars wisely arranged to purchase them through Arab antiquities dealers who had no scruples about looting. In the end, fragments of nearly nine hundred different scrolls were acquired.

It would have been far better if professional archaeologists had excavated the scrolls in the caves. But between having looted scrolls or no scrolls at all, the choice seems obvious.

André Lemaire has made some remarkable discoveries, in addition to the many inscriptions he has studied and published that have been found in legal, scientific excavations. Almost two decades ago, he saw in the shop of an antiquities dealer the only artifact that might have come from Solomon's Temple. I say "might have" because very few things are certain in archaeology. (This is true even when they come from a scientific excavation.) The object is a tiny ivory pomegranate inscribed around its neck, "Holy to the priests, belonging to the Temple of [Yahwe]h." Yahweh is the personal name of the Israelite God. The part in brackets has been chipped off; only the last letter of the last word has survived; the rest has been, as they say, restored. Until André Lemaire discovered it, no one recognized the pomegranate's significance because only the last letter of the personal name of the Israelite God survived. The pomegranate has a hole in the bottom indicating that, as we know from other examples without inscriptions, it was the head of a small priestly scepter. We might have a somewhat better idea whether it came from Solomon's Temple if it had been found in a professional excavation. But we might not. Conceivably, but improbably, the whole inscription would have been there, so we would know that the missing part read *Yahweh* and not *Asherah,* a pagan goddess spelled with the same last letter. But even if the word *Yahweh* had survived, we could not be 100 percent sure that it was from the Jerusalem Temple. It might have come from a temple to Yahweh other than Solomon's Temple, a temple no one knows about. And even if it had been professionally excavated, there would be questions. There are always questions. Yet it is still better to have the inscribed ivory pomegranate as it is than not to have it at all.

Why so many important finds come from the antiquities market is something of a mystery. Over 90 percent of all ancient coins, for example, come from the antiquities market. You cannot be a numismatist if you ignore unprovenanced coins.

Or take bullae. A bulla is a little lump of clay or mud about the size of a fingernail that was used to seal and ensure the contents of an ancient document. The bulla is impressed with the seal of the sender, often an important official. Bullae are extremely difficult to identify in an excavation (the documents they sealed are almost always long gone, decayed into nothingness). Only two hoards of bullae from the biblical period (Iron Age), totaling just over sixty, have ever been excavated. One hoard was found in the ancient City of David (south of the Old City) in Jerusalem and the other in a jar excavated at Lachish. But more than ten times this number of bullae have come from the antiquities market. In other words, less than 10 percent of the known biblical-period bullae have been professionally excavated by archaeologists. The bullae that have surfaced on the antiquities market bear the impression of seals of important ancient kings of Judah, like Hezekiah and Ahaz, who figure prominently in the Bible. Where were these bullae found, and how? No one, at least no one willing to come forward, knows. One story (it may be apocryphal) is that shoe boxes of dirt from the dumps of legitimate excavations are sold for pennies to Arab peasants, who with their families then carefully sift through the dirt for finds that the professional archaeologists missed.

LEMAIRE DISCOVERS THE OSSUARY

It was in this subculture that Lemaire, in the spring of 2002, accepted a social invitation from a prominent collector in Israel. Lemaire was in Jerusalem for six months as part of a group of senior scholars working on West Semitic linguistics at the Institute for Advanced Studies of the Hebrew University. At the home of the collector he met another collector whom he had not previously known. Because collectors and dealers are vilified by some members of the archaeological establishment, they often seek anonymity. I know the collector at whose home the social event took place, but I will not reveal his identity. I don't want to jeopardize my own contacts. The new collector Lemaire met at the party, who is a central figure in our story, is the man we have been calling Joe.

I divide collectors into two categories: good collectors and bad collectors. Good collectors allow scholars to study and publish their treasures and will share their collections with the public. Bad collectors keep their treasures hidden; no one knows they exist. Bad collectors simply don't want to get involved. They collect for their own enjoyment. They want to avoid the vilification of some establishment archaeologists; they don't need it, they say.

Joe is a very good collector. He is willing to allow scholars, especially André Lemaire, to study and publish reports on items in his collection, and he will even allow many of his most important pieces to be exhibited in museums. All he asks of us is that we carefully maintain his anonymity.

In the course of the discussion at their first meeting, Joe invited Lemaire to look at some of his more difficult-to-read inscriptions—that is, inscriptions that are obscure or indistinct, inscriptions that only a professional epigrapher with a good eye is likely to be able to decipher. Lemaire gladly accepted the invitation and shortly thereafter visited Joe in his apartment. Joe showed him some difficult-to-read pieces, but in the course of the conversation he also showed him a photograph of an inscription that was not at all difficult to read. It was inscribed on an ossuary—a relic of a short-lived burial practice common among

Jews in Jerusalem from about 20 B.C. to A.D. 70. Corpses were laid out in family cave tombs. About a year after the death, when the body had decomposed, the dry bones were gathered together in a bone box, or ossuary, which was left in the tomb. About 250 of the 900 catalogued ossuaries from this period bear inscriptions that identify the person or persons buried inside.

On this particular ossuary inscription, all the letters were there, carefully engraved, and, with perhaps one or two exceptions, they could easily be identified. The ossuary did not seem especially important, so Joe kept it in storage. Joe said he had bought the ossuary from a dealer in East Jerusalem. At the time, he was told it came from Silwan, an Arab village just east of the City of David in Jerusalem.

Lemaire's eyes popped. The inscription in Aramaic read: *Ya'akov bar Yosef achui d'Yeshua.* In English: "James, son of Joseph, brother of Jesus." Lemaire immediately recognized its potential significance—if it was genuine. The Jesus of the New Testament had never before appeared in an archaeological context. Neither had Joseph or James. If this inscription was authentic and actually referred to these New Testament personages, it was simply mind-boggling, an unprecedented find. And the box itself may once have held the bones of Jesus' brother James.

André Lemaire is both a quiet man and a cautious scholar. I have never seen him shout. In the world he moves in, he must be careful. And he is. "Very interesting," he said. He asked to see the object itself. Shortly thereafter, Lemaire returned to examine the limestone bone box.

When he saw it, he immediately "felt good" about it, a subjective test that almost all collectors, dealers, and epigraphers initially rely on. "With this inscription, I felt at home," he says.

A few weeks later—in May and June 2002—I was in Jerusalem and learned that André, too, was there; certainly, I thought, we must get together. When I mentioned this to Buzzy Porten (his first name is actually Bezalel), he said that he would like to get to know Lemaire better and asked to join us. Buzzy is the world expert on the Elephantine Papyri, a hoard of Aramaic manuscripts from the fifth century B.C. discovered on the island of Elephantine in the Nile River south of Luxor. The manuscripts belonged to a hitherto unknown settlement of Jewish refugees. This isolated community of Jews built their own temple on the island and had contact with the priests of the Jerusalem Temple, after it had been rebuilt by Jews who returned from the Babylonian Exile in the late fifth century B.C.

I was happy to bring Porten and Lemaire together, and while I was at it I invited an antiquities dealer turned scholar from Tel Aviv, Robert Deutsch, to join us. Deutsch is a Romanian refugee who came to Israel in 1963 and found his métier in antiquities. He began taking courses at Tel Aviv University's Institute of Archaeology and eventually earned his master's degree. He is now on his way to a Ph.D. He has already published six volumes of inscriptions from private collections (one with Lemaire as coauthor, four with Michael Heltzer of Haifa University as coauthor, and one on his own).

I was staying at the artist and author's retreat of Mishkenot Sha'ananim, overlooking the walls of the Old City, near the King David Hotel. So I reserved a table for dinner at Pisces, opposite the King David. The wine was fine, the fish excellent, and the conversation superb. I returned there recently and even remembered the table where we sat. (Alas, since then Pisces has gone out of business.) I mention all this because I talked to Porten and Deutsch after the ossuary inscription became public, and neither remembered that we had talked—albeit briefly—about the ossuary inscription at dinner that night. They simply had no recollection.

Lemaire's recollection and mine also differ. Lemaire recalls that at dinner he suggested that he write an article for *BAR* (*Biblical Archaeology Review,* of which I am the editor). My recollection is that I made a note to myself of the inscription Lemaire mentioned, with the intention of calling him later to ask him to write an article for us about it. In any event, a few weeks later, back in Washington, I received a manuscript on the inscription from Lemaire.

How is it that none of us was jumping up and down in the restaurant? How is it that the inscription did not instantly become *the* topic of conversation at the dinner table?

I recently put this question to Lemaire. "I was very cautious," he said, reflecting a common scholarly attitude. But I think something else—something perhaps akin to caution—was at work: skepticism. We were all extremely skeptical. It was simply too good to be true, too good even to be taken seriously.

I confess that it was only when I began to study Lemaire's painstaking manuscript that I felt a rush of excitement. Suddenly, I knew that this was a find of potentially enormous importance.

But there was also a danger: we could publish an article about the discovery, and our claim would fall apart. That was the nightmare scenario I also considered. What if some clever forger had produced an accomplished fake? How sure were we that the figures mentioned in the inscription were the people referred to in the New Testament? Could an attack from I don't know where undermine Lemaire's careful analysis? What would other leading scholars say about the inscription and the ossuary on which it was engraved?

Like Lemaire, I wanted to proceed cautiously. At that time I had not even seen a picture of the ossuary and its inscription. And I didn't know the collector's name. I didn't want to. It was unnecessary. It was enough that Lemaire knew him. I trusted Lemaire implicitly. I understood the collector's desire for anonymity. What I wanted was the collector's cooperation, not his name.

TAKING PRECAUTIONS

I called Lemaire and asked if the collector would allow the ossuary and the inscription to be photographed (I did not know at that time that Lemaire had originally seen a photograph). Through Lemaire, the collector supplied two excellent photographs, one of the ossuary and one a close-up of the inscription. These are the photographs we still use in publicizing the inscription (*see color insert*). But they appear everywhere without a photo credit because the collector feared that the name of the photographer might provide a vital clue to identifying him.

I have seen leading Semitic epigraphers disagree with one another before. World-famous scholars and linguists are still duking it out over whether a certain ostracon (a piece of pottery used as an ancient writing surface) is a genuine receipt for a three-shekel gift to Solomon's Temple or simply a fake. Another ostracon—this one from Qumran, potentially extremely important for understanding the people who wrote the Dead Sea Scrolls—is subject to wildly different readings from two epigraphers, one American and the other Israeli. I have seen a scholarly superstar nearly taken in by a polished fake and saved from embarrassment only when another scholar called his attention to a few suspicious letters.

That is what flitted through my mind as I studied Lemaire's manuscript. Once I had the pictures of the inscription, I decided to show them to my friend Kyle McCarter, the William Foxwell Albright Professor of Bible and Ancient Near Eastern Studies at the Johns Hopkins University in Baltimore and, like Lemaire, one of the world's leading experts on inscriptions of this period. McCarter confirmed Lemaire's judgment. The inscription is ancient, McCarter judged, although he did raise the possibility that two hands were involved—one person may have carved the first half and another person carved the second half, "brother of Jesus," perhaps as much as a century later.

Although the inscription was not difficult to read, I felt it should nevertheless be drawn. Inscriptions are customarily drawn so that they can be more easily read and studied. Obviously the drawing in this case had to be by a recognized expert. For this task we engaged Ada Yardeni, Israel's leading expert on Semitic scripts and the author of the authoritative *Book of Hebrew Script* as well as the *Textbook of Aramaic and Hebrew Documentary Texts from the Judaean Desert*. In addition to a Ph.D. from the Hebrew University, she received a diploma in calligraphy from the Bezalel School of Art. Initially she made a drawing of the inscription from the pictures, and then she examined the stone and made a new drawing. Some things could be seen more easily in the lighting used for the photograph; other things could be seen more clearly on the stone itself. Her judgment was consistent with Lemaire's: the inscription is authentic and can confidently be dated to the first century A.D. She disagrees with McCarter's suggestion that the inscription may have been created in antiquity by two different people and at two different times in antiquity. (More about this in chapter 4.)

As scripts change over time, so does language—including ancient Aramaic. Scholars often date different strands of biblical texts by differences in language, of which there are an enormous number. I wanted to be sure the language of this inscription conformed to what we would expect from first-century Aramaic. So I consulted one of the world's greatest Aramaic experts, Father Joseph A. Fitzmyer, recently retired from the Catholic University of America, in Washington, D.C. He lives with the Jesuit fathers at Georgetown University, not far from my house, and he agreed to come over one afternoon to look at the pictures.

When I showed them to him, his first reaction was, "I'm troubled." He repeated, "I'm troubled." Uh-oh, I thought. This is it. The inevitable dispute. Perhaps worse than that: he'll say it's a fake. What was troubling Fitzmyer was the word for "brother." It was *achui*, spelled *aleph, het, vov, yod*. In Hebrew, the word for brother is simply *ach*, spelled *aleph, het*. "The form *achui* doesn't appear in Aramaic until a couple of centuries later," Fitzmyer said, "and when it does, it is plural, 'brothers,' not singular."

He wanted to check himself, however, so he went to the books. There he found the form *achui* in the contemporaneous Dead Sea Scrolls, more specifically in the Aramaic text known as the Genesis Apocryphon. The same form also appears on another ossuary.[1] "I stand corrected," he said.[2] (Incidentally, we have since found this form of "brother" on another stone inscription; Frank Cross called my attention to it.)[3] Father Fitzmyer was also satisfied that the letter forms were authentic and not a modern forgery.

My conclusion: either the forger of this inscription knows Aramaic better than Joe Fitzmyer, or it is authentic!

PASSING THE PATINA TEST

My next question was whether the ossuary and its inscription could be tested scientifically. After many telephone calls I located Amos Bein, director of the Geological Survey of Israel in Jerusalem. He agreed to have his laboratories test the ossuary.

The inscription (*below*) carved into the lid of this ossuary (*above*) found on Mt. Scopus reads: "Shimi, son of 'Asiya, brother of Hanin." The Aramaic word for "brother" (technically, "his brother"), *achui* (marked with brackets below), is the same unusual term that appears on the James ossuary. *Drawing from L. Y. Rahmani,* A Catalogue of Jewish Ossuaries. *Photo: Israel Antiquities Authority*

There was one problem. The ossuary, which weighs about forty-five pounds, would have to be transported to the Geological Survey's laboratories. Would the owner allow the ossuary out of his possession? Lemaire put the question to him, and he readily agreed.

The tests were performed by Amnon Rosenfeld and Shimon Ilani of the Geological Survey of the State of Israel. They examined the stone, the dirt that still clings to the sides of the ossuary, and, most important, the patina, a film formed from chemicals that seep out of or drip onto the stone over hundreds of years as

State of Israel
The Ministry of National Infrastructures
Geological Survey
30 Malkhei Yisrael St.
Jerusalem 95501, Israel
Tel. 972-2-5314211, Fax. 972-2-5380688

מדינת ישראל
משרד התשתיות הלאומיות
המכון הגיאולוגי
רח' מלכי ישראל 30
ירושלים 95501, ישראל
טל. 02-5314211. פקס. 02-5380688

17/9/2002

To Mr Hershel Shanks Editor of **BAR** Magazine.

Re: SEM-EDS analyses of patina samples from an ossuary of "Ya'akov son of Yossef brother of Yeshua".

A chalk (limestone) ossuary was brought to the Geological Survey of Israel for studying the authenticity of its patina. The following Hebrew inscription appears on one of the outer walls of the ossuary:

יעקב בר יוסף אחי דישוע

The use of chalk (limestone) was extensive during the Second Temple period in Jerusalem, primarily for the manufacture of stone vessels and ossuaries.

Chalk is a sedimentary deposit, comprised mainly of marine microorganism skeletons made of calcium carbonate. All chalks in the Jerusalem area belong to the Menuha Formation of Mount Scopus Group sequence of the Senonian period. Generally the lower part of the Menuha Formation was exploited around Jerusalem during the 1st and 2nd centuries CE and several chalk stone quarries were discovered from that period in the Jerusalem area. The studied ossuary is made of this chalk. Based on its dimensions, this ossuary was used to store bones of an adult.

The stone and the patina were examined by magnifying lenses (binocular). We observed that the patina on the surface of the ossuary has a gray to beige color. The same gray patina is found also within some of the letters, although the inscription was cleaned and the patina is therefore absent from several letters. The patina has a cauliflower shape known to be developed in a cave environment.

Remains of soil were found attached to the bottom of the outer side of the ossuary. Six samples of the chalk, six samples of the patina from various places on the external wall of the inscription and two samples of soil, were studied with a SEM (Scanning Electron Microscope) equipped with EDS (Electron Dispersive Spectrometer).

Analytic results:

The EDS analyses of the SEM laboratory showed that the chalk of which the ossuary is composed mainly of $CaCO_3$ (97%) and contains Si -1.5%; Al - 0.7%; Fe - 0.4%; P - 0.3% and Mg - 0.2%.

The patina is composed mainly of $CaCO_3$ (93%) and contains Si -5.0%; Al - 0.7%; Fe - 0.3%; P - 0.4% and Mg - 0.2%.

The soil is composed mainly of $CaCO_3$ (85%) and contains Si -7.4%; Al - 2.5%; Fe - 1.7%; P - 1.0% and Mg - 0.7% and Ti - 1.0%.

The patina is enriched with silica (about 5.0%) relative to the original stone (about 1.5%).

The soil in which the ossuary laid is of Rendzina type, known to develop on chalks of the Mount Scopus Group.

It is worth mentioning that the patina does not contain any modern elements (such as modern pigments) and it adheres firmly to the stone. No signs of the use of a modern tool or instrument was found. No evidence that might detract from the authenticity of the patina and the inscription was found.

Sincerely,

Amnon Rosenfeld.   Shimon Ilani

Dr Amnon Rosenfeld and Dr Shimon Ilani
The Geological Survey of Israel, Jerusalem.

The Geological Survey of the State of Israel's official report on the James ossuary concludes: "No sign of the use of a modern tool or instrument was found. No evidence that might detract from the authenticity of the patina and the inscription was found."

it lies in a damp cave. The chemical makeup of the patina is thus dependent on the nature of the stone.

Biting my nails, I waited impatiently for their report.

They found the ossuary to be made of chalk limestone of the Menuha Formation of the Mount Scopus Group and noted that the lower part of this formation "was exploited around Jerusalem during the 1st and 2nd centuries CE [A.D.]" Indeed, several quarries of this particular limestone and from this period have been found in the Jerusalem area.

The scientists performed their examination with a binocular scanning electron microscope equipped with an electron dispersive spectrometer that exposed the various chemical elements of each of the three aspects of the ossuary (stone, soil, and patina). The greatest number of diagnostic tests were conducted on the

The City of David was the site of the original city of Jerusalem; by Jesus' time the city had expanded to the northwest. The dead were buried in the valleys and hills outside the city proper. The James ossuary is said to have come from the village of Silwan.

patina (the coating that builds up on an ancient artifact). The patina had a gray-to-beige color. Under a high-powered micro-scope its particles could be seen to have "a cauliflower shape known to be developed in a cave environment."

Most tellingly, the patina found inside the incised letters of the inscription was the same as the patina on the side of the os-suary. This eliminated the possibility that the inscription was a modern forgery on a genuine ancient ossuary.

The ossuary's stone consisted principally of calcium carbon-ate with traces of five other elements. The patina was consistent with this. It, too, was composed of calcium carbonate with these same trace elements, except that the patina had 4 percent less calcium carbonate and three times as large a trace of silica. As the geologists reported it, compared to the original stone the patina is enriched with silica.

Could patina have been taken from another ossuary and ap-plied to this one, both on the side and within the carved letters? The geologists considered this possibility. But they found that the patina "adheres strongly to the stone," and they found no trace of a modern adhesive.

When a metal object is used to carve an inscription in stone, it leaves microscopic metal elements in the incision. Moreover, an incision made with a modern instrument would be likely to leave a sharp edge on the stone here and there. The scientists thought of these possibilities, too: "No signs of the use of a modern tool or instrument was found. No evidence that might detract from the authenticity of the patina and the inscription was found."

The ossuary inscription, they concluded, was ancient and au-thentic. I now felt confident in publishing Lemaire's article in *BAR*. The inscription had passed every test we could devise.

But there was still a residue of caution. The few of us involved still couldn't quite believe that the discovery could really be what it clearly seemed to be—the first archaeological, physical link to the Jesus of the New Testament and his family! We are amazed at the subsequent overwhelming public interest in the ossuary. I am not yet sure how to account for this response—from print and electronic media, museums, the Internet, and even television—to our announcement of the find and to its first exhibition at the Royal Ontario Museum in Toronto, where nearly a hundred-thousand people waited hours in line to view it.

THE FIRST ANNOUNCEMENT

On September 11, 2002, before anyone outside our limited circle knew of the inscription, I flew to Toronto to appear on a television program about the historicity of the Bible produced by a Canadian television company. Another television production company heard that I was going to be in Toronto and asked to see me. I declined because I thought it improper to meet with a second company while the first one had paid for me to come to Toronto. But the people at the second company were clever: they left a message that the largest paper in Canada would like to interview me while I was in Toronto. I agreed to the interview. The interview, of course, was held at the offices of the second television production company. And of course I had to be cordial.

The people from the second company turned out to be very intelligent and engaging. The creative director, an Orthodox Jew named Simcha Jacobovici (pronounced "yah-kub-O-vich"; he's of Romanian descent), has won two Emmy awards. At the end of a long day of talking, I decided to confide in Simcha: I told him about the James ossuary. He nearly hit the ceiling.

Simcha was the first to recognize the enormous public interest that the ossuary inscription would arouse. Neither André Lemaire nor I realized it. We knew the ossuary inscription was important, but we were a bit oblivious to the worldwide sensation that would greet its public announcement. At that initial conversation in Toronto, Simcha proposed making a television documentary about the ossuary inscription—and I immediately agreed to work with him. But it was he who had faith that the public interest would justify the effort and expense of making a first-class documentary. And indeed, he put his money where his mouth is: he came to Washington with his crew to film me and Kyle McCarter and Joe Fitzmyer. He flew to Israel to film the ossuary itself and to interview André Lemaire and Shimon Ilani (one of the geologists from the Geological Survey)—all this before any public announcement of the ossuary's existence.

On October 21, 2002, we held a press conference (jointly with the Discovery Channel, with whom Simcha had arranged to produce the documentary) to present the James ossuary to the world. The next morning the ossuary appeared in color on the front page of the *New York Times*. The story was on the front page of the *Washington Post* and practically every other major newspaper in the entire world! *Time* magazine devoted four pages to the story. We were on the evening news with Peter Jennings and Tom Brokaw and Jim Lehrer. Voice of America and CNN beamed us around the globe. The excitement about the discovery was greater than I had imagined in my wildest dreams.

Within days of the announcement, my friend Professor Hannah Cotton at the Department of Classics at the Hebrew University sent me an e-mail: "Nobody, even here, talks of anything else. We here at the Institute for Advanced Studies—epigraphists, historians, philologists—are going to discuss it tomorrow afternoon (13:30 local time)." The second wave of scholarly consideration had begun.

1. See no. 570 in L. Y. Rahmani, *A Catalogue of Jewish Ossuaries in the Collections of the State of Israel* (Jerusalem: Israel Antiquities Authority, Israel Academy of Sciences and Humanities, 1994).

2. Father Fitzmyer later explained himself in more detail. The last two words in the inscription, *achui d'Yeshua*, literally mean "his brother, of Jesus." Fitzmyer wrote, "Normally, one would have expected *'aha' deYeshua'*, 'the brother of Jesus.' Instead there is the form with the pronominal suffix meaning 'his brother,' which is further explained by the *daleth* and the following name, '(that is) of Jesus.' The suffixal form is unusual, because it should have been written *'ahuhi*, the way such suffixes usually appear in first-century Aramaic. A little research, however, has shown that the syncopated form (*'ahui*) is attested in one of the Aramaic texts of the Dead Sea Scrolls . . . which [has] a very similar construction. . . . Hence, even though the Aramaic wording seems at first unusual, it merely records a popular way of writing the patronymic that was not well attested heretofore. So the inscription bears all the earmarks of a genuine ancient writing." See "Whose Name Is This?" *America* 187, no. 16 (November 18, 2002).

3. It is number 20 in Joseph Naveh, *On Mosaic and Stone* (Jerusalem: Israel Exploration Society, 1978), in Hebrew.

HOW COULD THE SON OF GOD HAVE A BROTHER?

S ome inscriptions are difficult to read. This one is not. In the right light, with the exception of two or three letters, a first-year Hebrew student can read it. (Aramaic, the language of the inscription, is an ancient Semitic language that is very similar to Hebrew and uses the same letters as the Hebrew alphabet.) And there is no difficulty in understanding the basic meaning of the inscription. It contains the oft-repeated formula of identification—"X the son of Y"—followed by a brother's name. Joe could easily read it. He is a native Israeli whose first language is, of course, Hebrew. He knew what it said. But its significance never occurred to him. I asked him why he never realized how important the ossuary might be. He made a quizzical face, raised his hands above his head, and said, "I never thought the Son of God could have a brother!"

Joe, of course, is Jewish. But I have talked to many good Christians who are also unaware that Jesus had a brother—and that the New Testament says so.

Indeed, Jesus had several brothers and sisters. When Jesus was teaching in the synagogue in his hometown, Nazareth, his fellow congregants were amazed at his wisdom: "Where did this man get this wisdom and these mighty works? Is not this the carpenter's son? Is not his mother called Mary? And are not his brothers

James and Joseph and Simon and Judas? And are not all his sisters with us?" (Matthew 13.54–56). The Gospel of Mark has almost identical language, but the order in which the brothers are
listed is slightly different: "James and Joses [a variant of Joseph]
and Judas and Simon" (Mark 6.3).

If the brothers are listed in order of their birth, then James is
the oldest in both Gospels.

Nevertheless, this leaves open the precise relationship between James and Jesus. First, there is the question of who Jesus'
parents were. Mary was surely his mother. But was Joseph his father (as the Nazareth Jewish community at the time seems to
have assumed)? Or was Jesus' father purely divine? Is Jesus literally the Son of God, without an earthly father?

Second, was Mary a virgin when Jesus was born and not thereafter? Or was she perpetually a virgin, *semper virgo*, ever virgin, as
some later church doctrine holds? If the latter, then Jesus and
James cannot be related through Mary.

Third, was Joseph previously married? Or was Mary his first
and only wife?

Finally, what does *brother* mean? If it can mean cousin or kinsman, as some traditions suggest, Jesus and James might be only
cousins.

Think of the possibilities. If both Jesus and James were sons of
Joseph and Mary, they were full blood brothers. If Jesus was the
son of Joseph and Mary, and James was the son of Joseph by a
previous marriage, the two would have been half brothers. If
Jesus was the son of his divine father and Mary, and James was the
son of Joseph by a previous marriage, Jesus and James would have
been stepbrothers; that is, they wouldn't have been blood brothers at all. This reading would leave room for belief in the perpetual virginity of Mary, as some church doctrine holds, but a
standard Bible dictionary tells us that this belief "is not a serious
option in most contemporary historical scholarship."[1] If *brother*
signifies kinsman, Jesus and James might not have been blood
brothers at all but merely cousins. This last view, traditionally espoused by western Catholic tradition, is, however, difficult to
square with the use of the term *brother* on the ossuary. Even before

James's Relationship to Jesus

1. Full brothers

2. Half brothers

3. Stepbrothers

4. First cousins

There are four popular explanations of the relationship between James and Jesus. The first assumes that Jesus was born to Joseph and Mary without divine intervention; Jesus and James are thus full blood brothers. The other three traditions, which view Jesus' father as divine, are accepted by different branches of Christianity. The second view is accepted by some Protestants; the third by Orthodox Christians; the fourth by the Roman Catholic Church, which understands the Greek term for "brother" as a general term meaning "kin." In Catholic tradition, James is often identified as the child of Joseph's brother (or brother-in-law) Clopas and his wife, Mary.

the ossuary surfaced, one leading authority on James called this reading of the biblical text "improbable."[2] (Incidentally, the word *brother* on the ossuary clearly refers to a family member, not a "brother in arms," so even if all early Christians were "brothers" in that sense, that is not the kind of brother the ossuary is talking about.)

All of these possibilities will be explored in greater detail in the second part of this book. Here we need only outline the alternatives.

JAMES AND THE EARLY CHURCH

Whatever *brother* means in the Gospels and however James was related to Jesus, James became one of the most important leaders of the emerging Christian community following the crucifixion of Jesus and the dispersion of the Twelve. Although James does not seem to have been a follower of Jesus during Jesus' lifetime, it is recorded in the New Testament that the resurrected Jesus nevertheless appeared to James (1 Corinthians 15.6). Furthermore, three years after his conversion on the road to Damascus, Paul traveled to Jerusalem, where, he tells us, he "saw none of the apostles except James, the Lord's brother" (Galatians 1.19). Does this mean that James was an apostle (although he was clearly not one of the Twelve)? Whether or not James was an apostle, he presided at a famous apostolic council in Jerusalem that successfully healed a breach between the Jewish Christian community in Jerusalem and the faction missionizing to Gentiles in the Greek world. Many members of the Jerusalem community held that anyone who became a Christian must also be observantly Jewish (since they thought of themselves as full-fledged Jews who believed that the long-awaited Messiah had come and that they must faithfully await the end times that would soon follow). Paul and his associates took the position that converts need not be required to observe the now-superseded requirements of the Torah. It was James who proclaimed the healing compromise, often referred to as the Apostolic Decree, that all the apostles and elders accepted: Gentiles in the Greek world need not be circumcised and need not follow all the Jewish dietary laws; they must only refrain from unchastity, from eating meat that has been sacrificed to idols or meat that has come from an animal that has been strangled, and from consuming blood (Acts 15).

From the first-century Jewish historian Josephus, we learn that a certain Sadducee, Anan son of Anan (Ananus the Younger), was appointed high priest for three months in A.D. 62. During his brief tenure (between the death of one Roman procurator and the appointment of his successor), Anan convened his supreme council, the Sanhedrin, and had several people condemned to death, among them James, the brother of Jesus. James was stoned to death. Josephus calls Anan "insolent" and "very rigid in judging offenders." Deeply resentful, the Pharisees prevailed upon the Jewish king Agrippa II to remove Anan from office.[3]

We learn more about James and his death from the second-century Christian writer Hegesippus, whose works are preserved (except for a few small fragments) only as quotations in the writings of the fourth-century church historian Eusebius. How much of these passages is historically reliable is much debated by scholars. Hegesippus tells us that because of his "excessive righteousness [James] was called 'the Just.'" He spent so much time on his knees praying that his knees became hard like a camel's. According to this account, James was martyred when he was thrown from the pinnacle of the Temple (traditionally identified as the southeast corner of the Temple Mount, the great platform that supported the Jerusalem Temple). He was then stoned and clubbed to death. Hegesippus tells us that James was buried on the spot where he was killed. Were his bones later placed in an ossuary?

James is the patron saint of the Armenian Church. Bishop Shirvanian of the Armenian Patriarchate of Jerusalem recently told a reporter that the bones of James had rested in a chapel in the Kidron Valley until the eighth century. When the chapel was destroyed, James's bones were removed to the Cathedral of St. James in the Old City of Jerusalem, where they still lie. "The discovery of the ossuary complements our tradition," the bishop said. He believes the ossuary that originally held the bones was discarded when its contents were removed.

If you're tempted to do a little research of your own, be careful not to confuse "James the Lord's brother" with other people named James in the New Testament. Two of the twelve disciples are also named James—James the son of Zebedee (James the Great) and James the son of Alphaeus (James the Less or James the Younger; see Mark 15.40). There are four lists of the Twelve and they do not always agree, but the two Jameses appear in all of them. There are several other Jameses, too, and it is not always clear which one is being referred to. Later developments and traditions confuse the matter still further. In later tradition James, the brother of the Lord, became known primarily as James the Just or James the Righteous. Eusebius, quoting the second-century Hegesippus, cites our James as the first bishop of Jerusalem. Infinite care is required to keep all these Jameses straight. The *Anchor Bible Dictionary*'s entry on James states, "It is unclear how many different persons bear this name in the N[ew] T[estament]. . . . We could have as many as seven individuals bearing the name."

We started this chapter by asking why Joe failed to recognize the significance of the inscription on the James ossuary. Joe was not the only one. The Israel Antiquities Authority (IAA) didn't realize it either. When Joe applied for an export license so that the ossuary could be exhibited in Toronto, he quoted the inscription in his application letter. But it didn't trigger any reaction from the IAA. Neither did the fact that Joe placed a valuation of a million dollars on the two ossuaries covered by his application.

One reason the significance of the ossuary inscription is not immediately apparent is that the names we recognize—James, Joseph, Jesus—are not the forms that are used on the ossuary. The ossuary inscription is in Aramaic. James is *Ya'akov;* Joseph is *Yosef;* Jesus is *Yeshua*. *Ya'akov* is usually translated "Jacob"; its translation as "James" would certainly be surprising to most Israelis. We will discuss in greater detail in a later chapter how this transformation came about. Here we wish only to explain why the significance of the inscription did not jump out, even to the Israel Antiquities Authority.

A final reason the ossuary's importance might have gone unnoticed is that all three names were quite common in the first century. Are the people named in the inscription the people referred to in the New Testament? We will consider that question in a later chapter.

First, we must confront the more immediate question: Is the ossuary a fake? And even if the ossuary is genuine, what about the inscription? Was it perhaps a modern addition to an authentic first-century ossuary?

1. Robert E. Van Voorst, "James," *Eerdmans Dictionary of the Bible*, ed. David Noel Freedman (Grand Rapids, MI: Eerdmans, 2000).

2. Richard J. Bauckham, "All in the Family—Identifying Jesus' Relatives," *Bible Review*, April 2000.

3. Flavius Josephus, *Antiquities of the Jews* 20.9.1.

4

IS IT A FAKE?

I was once talking about a possibly faked ostracon (a piece of pottery with writing on it) with the antiquities dealer and scholar Robert Deutsch of Tel Aviv, whom I mentioned earlier and who has one of the best eyes in the business. He said to me, "If this is a fake, I know who did it." Startled, I asked, "Who?" "Frank Cross," he replied. Frank Cross, recently retired from Harvard, is probably the most highly respected Semitic paleographer in the world. It was he who practically developed the science of studying ancient Semitic scripts. His lengthy 1961 article entitled "The Development of Jewish Scripts" is still, over four decades later, the single most widely cited bibliographic item in books dealing with ancient texts, like the Dead Sea Scrolls, which, incidentally, are contemporaneous with the James ossuary inscription. Had Cross become a forger? Of course not. What Deutsch meant was that the ostracon we were discussing was certainly genuine because only Frank Cross had the knowledge and the skill to forge it.

This story illustrates something else. I used the phrase "certainly genuine." This is technically wrong. In mathematical terms, certainty means 100 percent. We could not be 100 percent confident that the ostracon was genuine. There is always some small chance that someone as skilled as Frank Cross will be a forger. If Deutsch were to be mathematically precise, he would have to say that it is very, very, very, very probable that the ostracon is genuine. Or, even more precisely, very, very, very, very improbable that it is a fake. All that an epigrapher studying an ancient inscription can do is say that he or she has not found any sign of forgery. The question is always whether this or that factor indicates a forgery. It is not whether this or that factor proves definitively that the inscription is genuine.

Yet we live in a world of practicalities. At some point, the probability becomes so great that we no longer need to say that the authenticity of an inscription is only "very probable." In the real world, we make the leap: we say that it is genuine, even though we can think of myriad theoretical scenarios (like a conspiracy of leading epigraphers who have a secret plan to profit from their false certifications) in which somehow a forger (or forgers) fooled us.

In the end, as we shall see, we must make a judgment as to whether or not the possibilities raised by the doubters are realistic.

DATING THE LETTERS

Until now, I have been using the word *epigraphy* to refer to the study of ancient inscriptions, simply because I thought it would be easily understood. From here on, I will use the term *paleography,* which refers to a special branch of epigraphy. Paleography is the study of the shapes and forms of ancient letters to determine both their date and their authenticity.[1]

The form of letters in an alphabet develops over time, just as the style of ancient pottery does. We would all recognize the difference between a letter written in George Washington's time and a letter in modern handwriting. The matter of ancient letters is infinitely more complicated than this, but the principle remains the same: the shape and slant of letters change over time. At first, scholars develop a relative chronology. Then, when a few absolute dates are pegged to some of the examples, they can develop an absolute chronology.

To make things more complicated, there are various styles of writing, from formal to graffiti, from what we would call printed

The James Ossuary Inscription, Letter by Letter

Hebrew	ע	ו	ש	י	ד	י	ו	ח	א	ף	ס	ו	י	ר	ב	ב	ו	ק	ע	י
Letter Name	ayin	vov	shin	yod	dalet	yod	vov	het	aleph	peh	samech	vov	yod	resh	bet	bet	vov	qoph	ayin	yod
English equivalent	a	u	sh	y	d	i	u	ch	a	f	s	o	y	r	b	v	o	k	a	y

← read right to left

Drawing: Ada Yardeni

letters to highly cursive letters, with semicursive in between. The writing may be engraved on a monument or dashed off on a potsherd. Differences may depend on the material: it might be stone, pottery, papyrus, parchment, or a coin. And of course variations occur because people have different handwriting: one scribe may be less skilled than another. And ancient scribes, like other people, often made mistakes. Sometimes the writing is obscure, and modern scholars must strain to decipher one letter from another—whether, for example, a Hebrew letter is a *resh* (ר) or a *dalet* (ד), a *vov* (ו) or a *yod* (י).

Each letter has its own history—and range of differences. In an authentic inscription all the letters will cohere; that is, they will all be appropriate for the date of the inscription. That is why, by studying the inscription, a paleographer can tell not only its date but also its authenticity. But there are always some variations in what we would ideally expect to find. Frequently there are questions. Paleography is not an exact science. That is where the paleographer's "feel" comes in. For André Lemaire, who was the first to study the James ossuary inscription, this instinctive feeling was paramount. He "felt at home with it," he said. It seemed right.

But he also carefully analyzed it letter by letter.

The twenty letters of this inscription are engraved in a classical script. Sometimes a name on an ossuary is scratched with a simple nail, just to identify the person whose bones are interred inside (as on the ossuary of the high priest Caiaphas, who, according to the New Testament, presided at the trial of Jesus and turned him over to the Roman authorities). The inscription may be carelessly scrawled without even a base or ceiling line. Such inscriptions are called *graffiti* (singular, *graffito*). The inscription on the James ossuary, however, is, for the most part, a formal script, engraved with a stylus.

As is usual in ossuary inscriptions, there is no space between the words. Like Hebrew, Aramaic (the language of the inscription) reads from right to left.

Four of the letters in this formal inscription are written in cursive lettering—*yod* (Y), *vov* (U), *dalet* (D), and *aleph* (a glottal stop). These four letters helped Lemaire to date the ossuary and its inscription even more narrowly. The vast majority of ossuaries from Israel date from about 20 B.C. to A.D. 70, when the Romans destroyed Jerusalem and burned the Temple. These four letters developed in this way only during the last few decades before the Roman destruction—and that is precisely when Jesus' brother James died (A.D. 62, according to Josephus).

If you want to get a feel for the science—or art—of paleography, look at the *yod*s (Ys) in this inscription. The *yod* is the smallest letter in the alphabet. Imagine a straight apostrophe. *Yod* appears four times in this inscription. It is the first letter in the Aramaic form of each of the three names (*Ya'akov, Yosef,* and *Yeshua*). There is also a *yod* in the Aramaic word for brother. Counting from the right, the first, eighth, fifteenth, and seventeenth letters are *yod*s. The first thing to notice is that these *yod*s vary considerably. That's okay. Letters vary here just as they do today when we print or write something. Part of the paleographer's art is to know when these variations are significant and when they are not. In addition, as noted above, it's sometimes hard to tell a *yod* from a *vov*. Compare the fifteenth letter with the one preceding it (to the right). The one to the right is a *vov*. But here the *yod* seems to be as long as the *vov*. (But did Ada Yardeni draw the *yod* longer than it is incised in the stone? Magnification of the two letters indicates that she did; in fact the *vov* is longer than the *yod*.) This is okay, too. Notice that the *yod*s, more easily seen under magnification, have a small tick at the top, like a little triangle on the top of the letters. (Some of the other letters in the inscription also have these.) Lemaire identifies these *yods* simply as cursive and describes them as slightly slanted. That is what helps date this inscription to the last decades before A.D. 70 rather than earlier in the first century. For Kyle McCarter, however, these cursive forms could suggest a somewhat later date and therefore possibly a second ancient hand in the inscription, as we shall see.

You can understand why even the greatest paleographers sometimes disagree with one another, although within narrow limits. Is there room for paleographical disagreement here?

ADDING AUTHORITY

Because the Society of Biblical Literature (SBL), the American Academy of Religion (AAR), and the American Schools of Oriental Research (ASOR) were all holding their annual meetings in Toronto in November 2002, we at the Biblical Archaeology Society (BAS), publisher of *Biblical Archaeology Review,* decided to try to bring the James ossuary to Toronto for viewing at these conferences. Besides, our own Bible and Archaeology Fest, which attracts hundreds of laypeople to hear special lectures by the prominent scholars attending the academic meetings, was also being held at this time.

This was not the first time BAS had arranged a special exhibit for these annual meetings, which are always held in late November in a different city each year. In 1993, these same groups met in Washington, D.C., our hometown. At that time, we arranged for an exhibit at the Smithsonian Institution of two astounding artifacts that were loaned to us by the Israel Museum. One was the small inscribed ivory pomegranate (discussed in chapter 2), which may be the only relic from Solomon's Temple, although it dates to about a century after the Temple was first built by King Solomon. The second artifact we brought to the Smithsonian was an ossuary of a personage, like James, who also figured in the New Testament, the high priest Caiaphas, as mentioned above.

So I called the Royal Ontario Museum to see if they would be interested in exhibiting the James ossuary. I received an enthusiastic yes. The next question was whether the owner would agree to it. By this time, I had been in frequent contact with him, so I broached the question to him directly. He was more than willing.

It was also necessary to obtain an export permit from the Israel Antiquities Authority. As the owner, Joe had to apply in his own name for the permit and arrange for shipment to the ROM.

The owner knew the people at the IAA, and, as he anticipated, he had no trouble getting the export permit. He had the ossuary packed by a firm he considered the leading packers of museum artifacts in Israel (Atlas/Peltransport Ltd.). The transportation itself was handled by Brinks.

The ossuary arrived in Toronto on October 31, 2002, to great pomp and ceremony. It was even met by the press at the airport. The ossuary was unpacked privately the same day; however, the museum had arranged a press conference for 2 P.M. the following day when museum officials would reenact for the cameras the opening of the carton containing the ossuary. Even when they began to open the carton privately, however, they proceeded with guarded optimism at best. The ossuary, they immediately observed, had been poorly packed—in layers of bubble wrap and a cardboard carton rather than a wooden crate within a wooden crate separated by foam.

The ROM officials carefully took digital photographs of each step in the unpacking process. The final step revealed the ossuary itself—full of cracks!

The next morning I was brought up to date with the telephone call I described in the opening chapter of this book. It was a harrowing day, to say the least. But it was only the beginning of our troubles.

The ossuary could not be restored until the insurance company's adjuster examined the ossuary and its packing and gave the okay for the restoration. For five long days, the museum and the owner tried to persuade the insurance company to send an adjuster to Toronto. Indeed, several adjusters specializing in museum objects lived in Toronto. They apparently were not satisfac-

Just in from Tel Aviv (*left*), the ossuary is wheeled into Toronto's Royal Ontario Museum. When curators removed the bubble wrap (*below, left*), they found the box had suffered significant damage (*below, right*). *Brian Boyle, Royal Ontario Museum*

tory to the insurance company. Meanwhile, the clock was running and there was a question whether the restoration process could be completed in time for the scheduled opening of the exhibit. Finally, the insurance company's adjuster arrived from New York, examined the ossuary, and approved the restoration protocol proposed by the museum. Ewa Dziadowiec, the museum's expert stone restorer, could begin her work.

To say the restoration was done very carefully is an understatement. Even the small chips that had crumbled and fallen off at the crack lines were collected and placed in plastic bags. If you look closely at the picture of the inscription side of the ossuary, you will see a large crack that already existed before shipment from Israel, beginning on the lower right and extending to the right side of the ossuary and continuing all along this side. In the restoration process this crack was vacuumed,

The worst crack ran directly through the inscription,
through the letter *dalet* (the "of" in "brother of Jesus").
Brian Boyle, Royal Ontario Museum

and even the debris picked up by the vacuum was collected in
plastic bags.

The major restoration work, however, was fitting the pieces
together and gluing them, using PVA (polyvinyl acetate) resin in
acetone. Not only is this a very strong glue with no harmful effects, it is also soluble in water so is completely reversible. To fill
the area at the crack lines where small bits had fallen off, the restorer used a mixture of calcium carbonate (the main compo-
nent of the limestone), some dry pigments (so that the color of
the mixture would match that of the ossuary) and polyvinyl alco-
hol. This mixture, too, is completely reversible if the restoration
material ever needs to be removed.

The old crack was treated differently; after all, it was part of
the history of the ossuary. Even though the gap here was several
millimeters wide in places, it was not filled. Instead, tiny epoxy
pegs were placed intermittently inside the crack to stop it from
widening further. The ossuary was now structurally more secure
than it had been when it left Israel.

The new diagonal crack that runs through the inscription

Ewa Dziadowiec of the Royal Ontario Museum repairs the ossuary. *Brian Boyle, Royal Ontario Museum*

seems to have started at the old crack near the side of the ossuary, below the inscription.

On Sunday evening, November 24, we had a private showing of the ossuary after the museum closed for the day. In addition to André Lemaire, Kyle McCarter, Joe Fitzmyer, the Jerusalem paleographer and Dead Sea Scroll scholar Stephen Pfann, Richard Bauckham (an authority on James from England), and assorted other luminaries, we also invited Frank Cross, the unofficial dean of paleographers. It is an evening I shall never forget—watching Cross and Fitzmyer, Lemaire, and McCarter squinting over the box, calling attention to this letter or that, to this detail or that, and, in the end, agreeing: nothing in the inscription suggested a modern forgery.

CONTROVERSY MOUNTS

Yet another trend was developing. Since the discovery of the ossuary, more and more people, many of them scholars, were saying the inscription was a forgery. Some people had been saying this from the moment the ossuary announcement was made. Others, both in the United States and Israel, were now joining the chorus.

But they were not paleographers.

The first person to weigh in, almost immediately after the announcement, was an academic well known in the profession for his quixotic views and efforts to garner publicity. He wrote a book contending that the Teacher of Righteousness, mentioned in the Dead Sea Scrolls, was none other than our James, Jesus' brother. It is a one-man theory. But the author's publicist had contacted journalists and told them they really couldn't do a story on the ossuary without his client's input. Hence, this scholar appeared on television and in the newspapers frequently; his argument was simply that the inscription was a forgery because it was "too pat." Lawrence Schiffman of New York University, a leading Dead Sea Scrolls scholar, describes the media attention given to eccentric views like this scholar's as an "inversion of reality," in which these unusual views are used as a "come-on, then responsible scholars counter them, leaving the audience with the impression that these are genuinely competitive views of comparable merit."

This maverick was soon joined by someone who claimed to have paleographic expertise. On an Internet Web site, one Rochelle Altman concluded that the second half of the inscription ("brother of Jesus") was not written by the person who wrote the first half. But unlike Kyle McCarter, who regarded this as a possibility, perhaps even a probability, Altman said categorically,

> The differences between the two parts are glaring and impossible not to see. . . . [In the second part of the inscription] we immediately can see that this is a different person writing. . . . Part 2 has the characteristics of a later addition by someone attempting to imitate an unfamiliar script and write in an unfamiliar language.

She also identified another "tell-tale sign of fraud." The text of the inscription, she claimed, is excised rather than incised. That is, the area around the letters has been carved out so that the letters themselves protrude.

There are several infirmities in this analysis. The first is the certainty with which Altman makes judgments. It is strange that she is so sure of herself and able to see at a glance what apparently evades some of the world's leading paleographers. Second, she is clearly wrong (although just as confident) in contending that the inscription is excised rather than incised. She had never seen the ossuary itself, only pictures. Yet without hesitation she concluded that none of the letters in the inscription is cut *into* the stone. I am no expert. But even I can see that the letters are incised. Anyone who has seen the ossuary itself knows this.

But there is a more fundamental reason to doubt Altman's judgment. It is not simply that she is unknown to everyone in the small circle of paleographers who are experts in this field. It is not that her specialty is supposedly medieval manuscripts, as opposed to inscriptions from the turn of the era. It is, rather, that she has not published any inscriptions from this earlier period.

According to the paleographers we have consulted, no one can be an expert paleographer of this period who has not closely inspected original inscriptions of this period, translated them, evaluated the script, and then published a report on their findings in a scholarly journal or book, a so-called *editio princeps*. In fact, except for this small circle of people who work in the field, none of us is an expert. I can try to explain what the process is. A student can study with experts, but in the end the scientific proof of the pudding—the demonstration of expertise—is whether he or she has professionally published in this area. In the end, we are not making our own judgments. We must choose among experts. We must decide whether we have confidence in a Rochelle Altman or, for example, a consummate paleographer like André Lemaire.

Jeff Chadwick is an associate professor of church history at Brigham Young University. He is an archaeologist who has excavated in Israel, but he has not published anything paleographically. He, too, thinks the second half of the inscription is a modern forgery. And he is willing to step into the ring with world-class paleographers to point out where they faltered.

For Professor Chadwick, the second half of the inscription is "a demonstrable forgery." He reaches this conclusion by an analysis of the photographs in *BAR*. But he goes one step further. Based on the photographs, Professor Chadwick found the drawing made by Ada Yardeni to be "incorrect." Therefore, he made his own drawing to depict more accurately what he saw in the photograph.

The next thing Professor Chadwick observes—he says it is "obvious"—is that "the letter forms in the 'brother of Jesus' are nothing like" the first part of the inscription. The last two words, he says, were "scratched into the ossuary with the conical point of a small steel nail." The letters in the first half of the inscription, however, "were made with a tool that effected a wider angle and a deeper cut than is visible in the [second half of the inscription]."

But that's not all. Professor Chadwick also finds two different hands in the last two words of the inscription. In other words, there were two modern forgers, not one. The two *ayin*s in the inscription "were not made by the same person. Again, the evidence points to forgery. . . . Two different forgers seem to have been at work." This is remarkably complex paleography for someone who isn't an expert paleographer, especially considering that the evidence seems to have escaped the notice of the premier paleographers who analyzed the inscription not by looking at photographs but by inspecting the ossuary itself.

Chadwick doesn't stop here: "The first forger sized up the existing, ancient *Yakov bar Yosef* inscription, then . . . scratched the three Aramaic letters *alef, het,* and *yod,* forming the word *achi* (contextually "brother of"), doing a sloppy job on the *alef.*" When the forger got to the *shin* in *Yeshua,* he made a "dyslexic mishap": he began carving the *shin* backward, Professor Chadwick tells us. That is, the letter our senior paleographers see as a *dalet,* Professor Chadwick says is not a *dalet* but the beginning of a backward *shin.* When "he, or a partner looking over his shoulder, realized that a disaster was occurring," the first forger stopped. "One can almost hear the exasperated [second] forger, and any partners he may have had, looking disgustedly at the backward half-*shin* on their purloined ossuary and exclaiming, 'What do we do now?'" Based on this analysis, Professor Chadwick is able to conclude that the first forger was "probably not a native Hebrew or Aramaic speaker. His experience with Hebrew/Aramaic letters was probably to occasionally read them, but rarely to write them." Nevertheless, the second forger was able to make the necessary corrections. Professor Chadwick concludes: "An ossuary that might have once sold for five hundred dollars on the antiquities market could now bring in a potentially five million dollar windfall—thanks to the clever hand of . . . the person who forged the name of Jesus."

Sound convincing? Rather, isn't this clearly a case of amateurs taking shots in the dark? I readily admit that I am not competent to judge the paleography. But I would rather stick with the unanimous judgment of the senior scholars who have devoted their lives to this arcane art.

The choice between a Rochelle Altman or Jeff Chadwick, on the one hand, and an Ada Yardeni or André Lemaire, on the other, would seem to be easy. But a number of academics, some of them respected scholars in their own fields, have also expressed doubts about the ossuary inscription, even though they are not paleographers. As John Noble Wilford wrote in the *New York Times,* "Skeptics in growing number are weighing in with doubts about the authenticity of the inscription on a burial box that may have contained the bones of James, a brother of Jesus." Unlike Rochelle Altman and Jeff Chadwick, however, who at least address the paleographic issues, the new doubters simply ignore them, realizing that such issues are beyond their expertise.

Take the case of Eric Meyers, the Bernice and Morton Lerner Professor of Judaic Studies and Archaeology at Duke University, the editor of the *Oxford Encyclopedia of Archaeology in the Near East* and a former president of the American Schools of Oriental Research (ASOR), the professional organization of American archaeologists working in the Near East. He is also a personal friend of over thirty years. But he is not a paleographer.

On November 8, Eric and I taped a PBS television program, *Think Tank with Ben Wattenberg.* We spoke about the Bible in general, but naturally the newly surfaced James ossuary inscription was also the subject of discussion. "I think there is a high probability that it is authentic," my distinguished colleague said.

A little more than two weeks later, Eric and I appeared together on a different platform. The Society of Biblical Literature, the professional organization of biblical scholars, held a special session on the ossuary on the afternoon of Sunday, November 24, in the grand ballroom of the Fairmont Royal York Hotel at its annual meeting in Toronto. The hall was packed with nearly a thousand people, including many members of the press and the Israeli owner of the ossuary (who by that time had been outed).

This time Meyers's tone was entirely different. He excoriated the owner, who was sitting in the first row below the podium, for buying unprovenanced antiquities. Meyers suggested the ossuary inscription could very well be, indeed probably was, a fake. "He had 'serious questions about authenticity,'" read the Associated Press report the following morning. Ditto the *New York Times.* He was also quoted in the opening paragraph of the story in the *Toronto Star:* "Eric Meyers has 'a bad feeling, a very bad feeling' about the authenticity of the ossuary." And in the *Globe and Mail:* "I have misgivings about the authenticity" of the ossuary inscription.

Meyers has excavated a number of sites in Galilee. His claim to expertise in connection with the James ossuary is that he wrote his doctoral dissertation on ossuaries. He is frequently called on to comment on the James ossuary, not only because of his general prominence in the field of biblical archaeology, but also because of his dissertation. The book he published based on his dissertation was severely, not to say savagely, criticized by Israel's leading expert on ossuaries, L. Y. Rahmani, who compiled the standard catalogue of ancient Jewish ossuaries, both those excavated by archaeologists and those that have surfaced on the antiquities market. In the archaeological encyclopedia that Meyers edited, the article on ossuaries (written by a former student of Meyers) noted that Rahmani's review was "unnecessarily harsh." Be that as it may, the fact remains that Meyers is an expert on ossuaries, but he is not a paleographer, and he has not published ancient inscriptions.

What fuels Meyers's skepticism? Scholars are properly skeptical. But sometimes skepticism becomes a show of sophistication. My coauthor, Ben Witherington, calls it "justification by doubt," a wordplay on Paul's "justification by faith." Scholars should indeed question and test. This is especially the case in the field of biblical archaeology, where the stakes are so high. I serve as editor of two archaeology magazines. One is biblical and the other (*Archaeology Odyssey*) is not. The biblical one (*BAR*) is a kind of scholarly killing field, full of controversy. Everything is disputed. In *Archaeology Odyssey,* the attitude is different. Who really cares if a pagan temple in the Roman Forum is a hundred yards to the north or south? But biblical archaeologists will fight to the death over whether the Jerusalem Temple was here or a few yards north—or maybe south.

Also, the ossuary appeared on the antiquities market, not out of a professional archaeological dig. Most of us involved with biblical archaeology, of course, much prefer to deal with discoveries that have been excavated by professionals rather than those that come through the antiquities market. But we cannot ignore what comes to our attention on the antiquities market. However, as noted earlier, Meyers hates the antiquities market, since items from there come without a context. Such items are for him worthless; even if they are not fakes, they might as well be. Why Meyers didn't take this position on PBS television is another question. But his suggestion in Toronto that the ossuary inscription is a forgery clearly derives from his opposition to the antiquities market (more about this in chapter 6).

What of the claim that the inscription was incised by two different hands? This claim was made with absolute certitude by Rochelle Altman and Jeff Chadwick. It has also been entertained as a possibility by Johns Hopkins professor and leading paleographer Kyle McCarter. The difference between Altman and Chadwick, on the one hand, and McCarter, on the other, is instructive. For Altman and Chadwick, anyone who can't see that the last two words in the inscription are by a different hand from the first words is blind. McCarter recognizes the two-hand theory as a possibility, even as a probability, but, as he told me, "I wouldn't insist on it."

McCarter's doubts stem from three of the cursive letters (*yod, dalet*, and *aleph*), which he feels may not be contemporaneous with the letters in the rest of the inscription. Lemaire, Cross, and Yardeni disagree; they all firmly believe that the inscription is by one hand. Moreover, as Lemaire explained to me, it is quite common in ossuary inscriptions to see a mixture of cursive and formal letters.[2]

But there is another difference between the first and second parts of the inscription. The second part is seen by some (but not by other equally qualified experts) as rougher, not as elegantly and carefully executed. But, as Ada Yardeni has remarked, "The inscription is hand-carved and not machine-made. Most of the Aramaic ossuary inscriptions seem to have been made quite carelessly and by non-professional engravers. The James ossuary is no exception."[3] Ossuary inscriptions were made quickly with a stylus; toward the end of the inscription, the script often becomes more degraded. More important in this case, the limestone where the second half of the inscription was carved appears to be softer. In her report on the conservation of the ossuary, Ewa Dziadowiec notes that the box is made of "a very soft, chalky limestone." Another report on the ossuary's condition upon arrival at the museum observes that the stone is worn and pitted. The condition seems to be even worse—more pocked—in the area of the second part of the inscription. There is also more patina in the area of the second half of the inscription, indicating a slightly different mix of chemical elements in the stone. Under these circumstances, it may well have been more difficult to carve elegant, sharp letters. This may account for any difference between the two halves of the inscription.

THE CASE AGAINST A MODERN FORGERY

But even more significant is McCarter's conclusion that if two different hands are responsible for the inscription, the second half of the inscription is still not a forgery.[4] It was added no later than a hundred years after the first part of the inscription was carved, McCarter says. He speculates that "brother of Jesus" might have been added to the original inscription because in the subsequent years, other members of the same family bore the names "James son of Joseph," and it had become necessary to identify this James further, "the brother of Jesus." Just as nicknames were sometimes added in antiquity to a person's name to distinguish him or her from family members bearing the same name,[5] so the name of James's brother was added to this ossuary inscription to distinguish him from the other Jameses in the family. McCarter does not suggest that any part of the inscription is a modern forgery.

Another reason the last two words in the inscription are highly unlikely to be a modern forgery concerns Aramaic linguistics. If you think paleography is arcane, try studying the historical development and usage of ancient Aramaic. While some amateurs are willing to attempt paleographical analysis, no one wants to get into the ring with Joe Fitzmyer when it comes to Aramaic. But the result in this case is easily stated. It just so happens that the critical words in Aramaic are the last two words in the inscription, *achui d'Yeshua*. Although I have quoted Father Fitzmyer's analysis in a footnote in chapter 2, it is worth repeating his conclusion:

> Even though the Aramaic wording [of the last two words of the inscription] seems at first unusual, it merely records a popular way of writing the patronymic that was not well attested heretofore. [There are only two other instances.] So the inscription bears all the earmarks of a genuine ancient writing.[6]

There are three other arguments why, to my mind, the second half of this ossuary inscription ("brother of Jesus") cannot be a modern forgery.

The first is that it assumes an extremely stupid forger. It assumes that a forger came across an ancient ossuary inscribed "James, son of Joseph," and saw this as an opportunity to add a reference to Jesus. But the far simpler thing for the forger to do would be to go down to the Old City and, for a couple hundred dollars, buy a plain, uninscribed ancient ossuary on which he could forge whatever he wanted, including "James, son of Joseph, brother of Jesus." This way he would not have to try to imitate the writing in the first part of the inscription and run the risk of giving away a clue to the forgery. Also, he would not have to pay for the more expensive ossuary that already had an inscription on it. In other words, the difference between the first and second halves of the inscription speaks to its authenticity, not the reverse.

That the second half of the inscription is not a modern forgery is also demonstrated, as we saw earlier, by the presence of patina inside the letters in both parts of the inscription, as attested by the museum officials in Toronto who examined the inscription. The Geological Survey of Israel certified that this is the same patina that is found on the side of the ossuary. This suggests that the box itself, as well as the entire inscription, dates to ancient times. Some people claim that it is easy to fake patina, that is, to create a modern patina that would fool even the scientists at the Geological Survey. So far this is simply an assertion. No one, to my knowledge, has successfully manufactured stone patina that would fool an expert. And the patina on this ossuary would be particularly difficult to fake. In her report, the museum restorer Dziadowiec observes that the very soft, chalky limestone of the ossuary is "deteriorated and abraded with many layers of lime and earth deposits on the exterior and interior."

Third, forgers ply their trade for profit. They want to make money. Presumably a forger would have carved this inscription in the ossuary in order to fool people into believing that it referred to central New Testament characters, thereby increasing the ossuary's value enormously. In this case, however, there is no evidence that either the buyer or the seller realized the value of what was being bought and sold. The seller sold it for a few hundred dollars, the ordinary price for any unremarkable ossuary on the antiquities market. And, as André Lemaire recounts, the owner did not regard it as important enough to have it on display with other major items from his collection, and neither was it one of the artifacts that he invited Lemaire over to look at. If a forger had put this ossuary on the market, he would have touted the startling inscription in the hope of vastly increasing its price. Instead, the owner bought it a few decades ago and in the end put it in storage.

A journalist suggested to me that the ossuary's owner might be lying, that he himself might have forged this inscription only a few months ago. I guess this is a theoretical possibility. But if this were the case—if he were in any way involved in the forgery—he would not have allowed the ossuary to be examined by the Geological Survey of the State of Israel. The fact that he willingly and without hesitation agreed to have the ossuary tested is powerful evidence that he himself is no forger.

When I suggested to Baruch Halpern, a highly respected biblical text critic and historian, that there was no profit motive to support the addition of the second half of the inscription in modern times, Halpern opined that the forger might not have been after profit; he might just be playing a joke. I suppose this, too, is a theoretical possibility, but an unlikely one.

Even if the ossuary had been excavated scientifically, there would still be a theoretical chance that it was a forgery. A decade ago, a fragment of a victory stele (inscribed stone) with a stunning inscription was excavated by a leading Israeli archaeologist, Avraham Biran, at Tel Dan in northern Israel. The inscription mentions the "House [Dynasty] of David." This was the first reference in the archaeological record to the great Israelite king: the name of David had never before been found outside the Bible. The stele dates to about a century or so after David himself lived, according to the biblical chronology. At this time, in the early 1990s, some scholars known as biblical "minimalists" (and sometimes as biblical nihilists) were arguing that no such person as David ever lived; in their view he was entirely fictional. This new evidence from Tel Dan was a powerful refutation. Some of the biblical minimalists charged that the Tel Dan inscription was a forgery: it had been "salted," planted in the excavation by a forger or by someone acting on his behalf. This charge was made publicly and has never been withdrawn, although no one gives it credence today. Still, it remains a theoretical possibility, as does the notion that a forger has found a way to create and apply a patina to the James ossuary that fooled the scientists at the Geological Survey. There is simply no way to eliminate all the theoretical possibilities that the human imagination can conjure up. It seems that the charge of forgery will be made whenever a startling inscription like this is found—even when it is excavated scientifically.

Nevertheless, to my mind, it is virtually certain that the James ossuary and its inscription are authentic ancient artifacts. I predict that in time, any doubts about the authenticity of the inscription will dissipate.

Indeed, much of the skepticism that appears to surround the ossuary may not actually exist. Case in point: John Painter, professor of theology at Charles Sturt University in Australia and author of a much-praised book on James, was one of the panelists at the Society of Biblical Literature session in Toronto, where I received the impression that he was skeptical about the authenticity of the inscription on the ossuary. Under the headline "Experts

Disagree About Authenticity of Ossuary" in the *Toronto Star,* Painter is quoted as saying, "Nothing would delight me more than to be convinced that this was the ossuary of James. But I confess I am worried." Later, he sent me an e-mail thanking me for inviting him to the private showing of the ossuary. This led to an exchange between us in which he clarified his position for me (perhaps I had failed to listen to his presentation carefully): "None of [the problems with the ossuary and its acquisition] has led me to conclude that it has been tampered with or that it is a forgery. . . . Authenticity means that it is not a forgery, but a genuine first-century inscription on a first-century ossuary. This is a position I accept." My dialogue with Professor Painter further leads me to believe that when the dust settles, the authenticity of the James ossuary and its inscription will be almost universally accepted.

One final consideration demonstrates the authenticity of the inscription—and also leads us to a consideration of whether, even if the inscription is authentic, it refers to the personages with these names in the New Testament (the subject of the following chapter). Father Émile Puech is a Dominican priest at the École Biblique in Jerusalem and a distinguished paleographer and Dead Sea Scroll scholar. Father Puech denies in the strongest possible terms that the inscription refers to Jesus of Nazareth.[7] It is "absolutely impossible," he says, to pinpoint the date of the inscription to the "decade preceding the fall of Jerusalem." Moreover, if this were the New Testament James, it would be "expected" to be inscribed "'James the Just' or 'the brother of the Lord/Messiah,'" not simply "brother of Jesus." In addition, Puech claims that "the specific relationship of James and Jesus in our ossuary is quite simply indeterminable. . . . The term 'brother' actually concurrently meant blood brother, half-brother, husband, uncle, nephew, cousin, friend, and companion." As for the biblical text, Puech says, "It was only by popular hearsay that he [James] was thought to be the 'son of Joseph.'" For these and other reasons, the inscription, in Puech's view, cannot possibly refer to Jesus of Nazareth. But the one argument that Puech—this great paleographer—does *not* make is that the inscription is a modern forgery. Or even that two different hands inscribed it.

1. Some experts regard paleography as the study of inscriptions drawn with a pen or a brush, for example on papyrus and pottery, while epigraphy is the study of inscriptions carved into nonporous materials like stone. See the *Anchor Bible Dictionary*, s.v. "Palaeography."

2. See, for example, nos. 15, 520, and 783 in L. Y. Rahmani, *A Catalogue of Jewish Ossuaries in the Collections of the State of Israel* (Jerusalem: Israel Antiquities Authority, Israel Academy of Sciences and Humanities, 1994).

3. Personal correspondence, December 23, 2002.

4. It seems that the two-hands theory is attractive to those less experienced in paleography (although not in McCarter's case). Herbert Basser of Queen's University, Kingston, Ontario, who is an excellent scholar but not a paleographer, told *McLean's* magazine (November 18, 2002): "It seems clear to me that this is actually two inscriptions run together." Like McCarter, however, Basser sees the second half as authentic. The *McLean's* article continues: "Basser cautions, however, that this revelation does not prove or disprove the identity or lineage of the person whose bones were placed in the box. 'It could very well be that a family member who revered James wanted to add the "Yeshua" line to clarify the inscription years later,' he says. 'This does not make the second author illegitimate. If this were intended to be a forgery, it would have been done far better. That it is so obvious speaks to an intention to inform, not mislead.'"

5. See Rahmani, *Catalogue*, 14.

6. Joseph A. Fitzmyer, "Whose Name Is This?" *America* 187, no. 16 (November 18, 2002).

7. Letter to the editor, *Minerva* 14, no. 1 (January/February 2003): 4.

5

IS IT *THE* JESUS?

Establishing the authenticity of the James ossuary inscription has been relatively easy. Determining whether the three people named in the inscription—James, son of Joseph, brother of Jesus—are the three people in that relation referred to in the New Testament is more difficult. Scholars will be debating the matter for years.

The fact is that all three of these names were quite common among Jews in the first century A.D. We know this not only from literary sources (even though our earliest manuscripts of these texts are from later dates—for example, the Gospels and Josephus), but also from hundreds of surviving inscriptions from what scholars call the late Second Temple period. To find an inscription mentioning Jesus is not unusual—except this Jesus wouldn't be the man we know as Jesus of Nazareth.

To determine whether the inscription on the James ossuary is authentic, we drew on paleography (the shape and form of the letters), linguistics (contemporary Aramaic usage), geological analysis (the chemical content of the patina), and even psychology (a forger would have tried to get money; neither buyer nor seller knew what the ossuary was worth).

To determine whether the three people mentioned in the ossuary inscription are the figures from the New Testament, we must turn to another pair of disciplines: statistics (the frequency of the names James, Joseph, and Jesus) and burial customs among first-century Jews.

WHO'S WHO IN ARAMAIC, HEBREW, AND ENGLISH

But before we consider the statistical findings, we should clarify which names we are speaking about. We have been referring to them in English as James, Joseph, and Jesus. In Aramaic, however, there is no *J* sound; the same is true of Hebrew. This is our first hint that the names are different in Aramaic.

The three names in Aramaic (and Hebrew) are *Ya'akov, Yosef,* and *Yeshua.* Ya'akov requires the most detailed explanation. Its usual translation in English is Jacob, the name of the biblical patriarch. But sometimes it appears differently, translated as James. How did Jacob become James? When the Bible was translated into Latin, Ya'akov became *Iacobus* (or *Jakobus* in the Germanic spelling). From Iacobus to English Jacob is easy. In the New Testament, Jesus' brother is called Iakobus in Greek—ιακωβος— *iota, alpha, kappa, omega, beta, omicron, sigma.* But when this name was translated into Latin the *b* sound was replaced by an *m* sound. This often happens; both the *b* sound and *m* sound are bilabials, formed by pursing the lips. With the *b* sound we blow a puff of air out between the lips; not so with the *m* sound. That is the only difference. (Although the transformation of bilabials is common, no one seems to know exactly why.) Thus Iakobus in Greek became Iacomus in Latin, and from there the leap to James was short.

But why didn't the patriarch Jacob in Genesis also become James? It's simply arbitrary. For the patriarch Jacob, the church retained the Semitic form. For the brother of Jesus, the Hellenized form was adopted.

Another variation results from the fact that Hebrew and Aramaic are written almost entirely without vowels. Over time, certain consonants came to be used as vowels (called *matres lectionis*). Sometimes names appeared with vowels and sometimes not. For example, in the early books of the Bible, like the books of Samuel and Kings, David is spelled without vowels: *DVD*. In Chronicles, however, a letter is added to represent the second vowel in the name. Throughout the Bible Ya'akov is written without the final vowel. In some inscriptions, however, the name appears with this vowel.

Many Hebrew and Aramaic names appear in several forms—Jacob, Jake, and Kobie, for example, are the same name, as are Joseph, Joe, and Yossi (the last two in both cases are nicknames). In ancient times, many of the variants were not nicknames, however, but alternative forms. Thus Yosef could appear as Yehosef. Yeshua, or Jesus, has even more variants. It may be Yeshua, as it is on the James ossuary, or Yeshu or Yehoshua. The latter is the name of Moses' successor; when it refers to him, we translate it Joshua. But when it appears at the turn of the era, at the time of Jesus of Nazareth, we translate it Jesus. But the names are really the same.

Taking into consideration all the variants, we can determine how popular a particular name was at the turn of the era. We have a considerable body of inscriptions, and we know how frequently a given name appears in these. According to one study of the Gospels, inscriptions, and other ancient texts, the most popular name in Jesus' time was Simon/Simeon. Joseph was second and Jesus/Joshua sixth. Eleventh was James/Jacob.[1] The percentage of times these names appear in the archaeological record has been calculated by Israeli scholar Rachel Hachlili.[2] She finds that James appears in 2 percent of inscriptions; Joseph, the most popular of the three names in our ossuary, occurs in 14 percent; while Jesus appears in 9 percent.

Imagine a bowl with thousands of little balls bearing the names of each person living at the time. If we pick out one ball, in 2 percent of the cases it will read James, in 14 percent of the cases it will say Joseph, and in 9 percent of the cases it will say Jesus.

Our pick will display one of these three names in 25 percent of all cases (2 percent + 14 percent + 9 percent = 25 percent).

Instead of just one ball, however, let's pull out three balls with names on them. What are the chances that the first one will be

Most Popular Names Among Jewish Males of the Second Temple Period
(c. first century B.C.–first century A.D.)

Name	Frequency
Simon	21%
Joseph	**14**
Judah	10
Yohanan	10
Eliezer	10
Jesus	**9**
Jonathan	6
Matthew	5
Hanina	3
Yo-ezer	3
Ishmael	2.2
Menachem	2
Jacob/James	**2**
Hanan	2
Levi	0.2
Isaac	0.2
Gamaliel	0.2
Hillel	0.2
	100%

Based on data from Rachel Hachlili, "Names and Nicknames
of Jews in Second Temple Times,"
Eretz-Israel 17 (Israel Exploration Society, 1984).

James, the second one Joseph, and the third one Jesus? The answer is surprising. The chance that all three names will appear in this order is only 1/40 of 1 percent (0.02 [the decimal equivalent of 2 percent] x 0.14 x 0.09 = 0.000252). This is called the product rule.

We also have a pretty good estimate of the size of the population of Jerusalem at this time, based on archaeological data. (Most estimates in the *ancient* literature are obviously exaggerated and unreliable. For example, the first-century Jewish historian Josephus says the Romans killed 1,100,000 Jews when they destroyed Jerusalem in A.D. 70.) At the turn of the era, the city covered 450 acres, the most since its founding as much as three thousand years earlier. Jerusalem was a large and prosperous city in the period between the death of Herod the Great in 4 B.C. and the Roman destruction of A.D. 70. Excavations in the city over the past fifty years support this estimate of the size of the city at this time. No archaeologist has suggested that it was larger (although some say it was smaller).

Many scholars have studied the density of urban areas in ancient times—from Mesopotamia to Ostia, the harbor of Rome. According to their data, a population density of 160 to 200 people

Jerusalem's Area and Population Through the Ages

The Jebusite City and King David (c. 1000 B.C.)

Area: 10 acres
Population: 2,000

King Solomon (c. 930 B.C.)

Area: 32 acres
Population: 5,000

King Hezekiah (c. 701 B.C.)

Area: 125 acres
Population: 25,000

Return from Exile (c. 333 B.C.)

Area: 30 acres
Population: 4,500

The Hasmoneans (2nd century B.C.)

Area: 165 acres
Population: 30,000–35,000

Herod the Great (c. 4 B.C.)

Area: 230 acres
Population: 40,000

Before the Destruction of the Second Temple (c. 66 A.D.)

Area: 450 acres
Population: 80,000

Justinian (c. 565 A.D.)

Area: 300 acres
Population: 55,000–60,000

per acre is a reasonable estimate.[3] This corresponds well with the population density of ancient cities that have survived into modern times. In the first half of the twentieth century, the population density of Damascus and Aleppo was about 160 people per acre. In 1918, the population density of the Old City of Jerusalem (within the walls) was about 200.

To estimate the first-century population of Jerusalem, the area of the Temple Mount (thirty-six acres) must be deducted because no one lived there. The area of the palaces and the citadels, on the other hand, was occupied by the king's household, administration personnel, and the military. Taking into account all this data, Magen Broshi, former curator of the Shrine of the Book, where the Dead Sea Scrolls are housed in Jerusalem, estimates that the population of Jerusalem in Jesus' time was about 80,000, a figure that is widely accepted by other scholars.

André Lemaire used Broshi's findings to compute the frequency of the names James, Joseph, and Jesus, appearing as son, father, and brother. First, he halved the 80,000 population estimate to 40,000 because only approximately half the population would have been male. Then he doubled the 40,000 back to 80,000 to cover two generations of males, after narrowing the date of the ossuary to the last decades of the period between 20–15 B.C. and A.D. 70, when most ossuaries were used. In other words, this ossuary inscription can be dated on paleographical grounds to a period of close to two generations. This dating is based on the three semicursive letters in the ossuary inscription. Therefore, two generations of men form the population to which the probabilities should be applied.[4]

In short, Lemaire took a potential population of 80,000 men and applied 1/40 of 1 percent (2 percent x 14 percent x 9 percent) to this figure, which yields about 20 people who, at this time, were named James and had a father named Joseph and a brother named Jesus. Briefly during my sojourn into the world of statistics, I thought that this number should be divided by six, because there are six different combinations of the three names and only one would match the inscription. But this is wrong, as statistics experts have confirmed. The product computation includes the order in which the names appear. The chances that the names would appear in any order is six times the original number (that is, 6 x 20).

The power of these statistical conclusions is revealed when we compare the inscriptions on two other ossuaries. One of these, published by Professor E. L. Sukenik of the Hebrew University in 1931 (but purchased by the Palestine Archaeological Museum in 1926), is twice inscribed—once simply *Yeshu* (Jesus) and then *Yeshua bar Yehosef,* "Jesus son of Joseph." The single inscription on the other ossuary, published in 1981, is so clumsily scratched that paleographers cannot be sure what it says, but the best guess is *Yeshua bar Yehosef,* "Jesus son of Joseph." No one seriously suggests that either of these inscriptions refers to Jesus of Nazareth—and with good reason. Quite aside from the theological doctrine that Jesus arose on the third day, statistically the chances of this being Jesus of Nazareth are very slim. On the same assumptions we made above, over a thousand men in Jerusalem at this time were named Jesus and had fathers named Joseph (0.09 x 0.14 x 80,000 = 1,008).

In both instances, though, we are dealing with probabilities, not actual cases. That is, the actual number of people in Jerusalem named James who were sons of Josephs and brothers of Jesuses may have been 15 or 25. We can compute the level of confidence (that is, what percentage of the time we will pull these three names in this order out of the bowl) within a certain range. Imagine an infinite number of bowls with the 80,000 names in them. In 68.27 percent of the cases (1 sigma), the bowl will contain the names of between 15.5 and 24.5 people named James, the son of Joseph, brother of Jesus. In 95.45 percent of the cases (2 sigmas), the bowl will contain the names of between 11 and 29 people who qualify.

More crucial, however, is the validity of the assumptions involved in the computation. For example, it might be argued that the database we use is not large enough to conclude, definitively, that 2 percent of the men in first-century Jerusalem were named James, 14 percent Joseph, and 9 percent Jesus. As Professor John Painter, a leading James scholar from Australia, put it to me: "I don't think the database of names from that era is big enough to

The ossuary (*above*) bears two inscriptions (*top left*) on its front: one reading "Yeshu"; the other "Yeshua bar [son of] Yehosef." The inscription (*left*) scratched on the ossuary (*below*) is also believed to read "Yeshua bar Yehosef." *Drawings from L. Y. Rahmani, a* Catalogue of Jewish Ossuaries. *Photos: Israel Antiquities Authority*

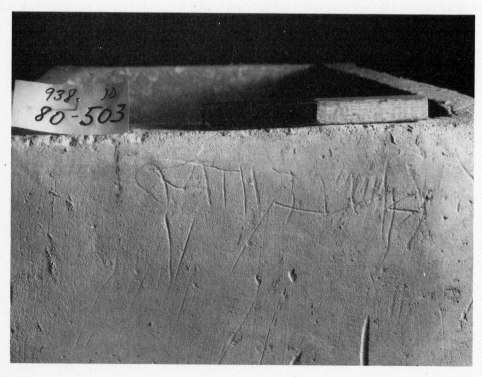

give a proper sample. It's possible, but I don't think the evidence is probable."

Moreover, it can be argued that the pool of men postulated by Lemaire is not large enough, since it is improperly confined to Jerusalem: evidence from other ossuary inscriptions shows that Jews from Latin-speaking lands were sometimes brought to Jerusalem for burial. So, too, were Jews who spoke Greek and Palmyrene. So even though Lemaire claims to have come to a conservative estimate—he assumed 200 people per acre in his computation—he may have erroneously limited his database to Jerusalem. In addition, were there not many villages within a twenty- or twenty-five-mile radius of Jerusalem that might be taken into account?

Yet other factors might significantly reduce the chances that as many as 20 people would qualify as James, the son of Joseph, brother of Jesus. For example, since ossilegium—gathering the bones of the dead into a box—was a Jewish custom, we should exclude from the pool all non-Jewish Jerusalemites. We can also exclude all children and adolescents. We know that whoever was interred in the James ossuary was an adult because the box is adult-sized. Ossuaries for children and adolescents are smaller.

Additionally, we should exclude the people who were too poor to buy an ossuary or who weren't prominent enough to have friends and patrons who would contribute to such a purchase. To further complicate the discussion, it may be argued that almost everybody could afford an ossuary because, as we explain later in this chapter, an ossuary could be bought for as little as the day's wages of a skilled artisan. But how reliable is the evidence for this? And anyway, the rejoinder might go, it is not the cost of the ossuary but the cost of the burial cave that matters. No one would be buried in an ossuary unless the ossuary could be placed in a family cave—and these were expensive indeed.

Another factor: only a small percentage of ossuaries were inscribed. In the standard catalogue of ossuaries, the figure is about 26 percent. But actually it is probably not more than 20 percent because the catalogue does not include the thousands of plain ossuaries—without decoration or inscription—that have been discovered. The fact that such a small number of ossuaries is inscribed suggests that inscriptions were added only by families that were literate. If we assume that only 20 percent of the population could read, this would drastically reduce our pool.

Actually, a professor of statistics at Tel Aviv University has made these calculations using extremely sophisticated techniques. Camil Fuchs considered the birthrates, death rates, family size, and population growth rate and assumed that no brothers would bear the same name. He also assumed that 5 percent of the Jerusalem population was non-Jewish, 50 percent of the population was rich enough to afford an ossuary, and 20 percent of the population could read, and that not all of these factors were independent of one another. Naturally, there will be debates as to whether these assumptions are valid (Could poor people afford ossuaries? Did nonliterate people nevertheless pay for ossuaries to be inscribed?); besides, the percentages are not always based on reliable statistics. For example, how do we know that 5 percent of the Jerusalem population at this time was not Jewish? Fuchs would answer that he studied all the available evidence and made a conservative estimate (just as Lemaire did when he assumed that Jerusalem was inhabited by 200 people per acre).

Some of Fuchs's estimates are even more conservative than Lemaire's. Lemaire took into account only the final two generations before the Roman destruction of Jerusalem in A.D. 70, based on the shape of several letters in the inscription. Fuchs included the period from A.D. 6 to 70 and, alternatively, from 20 B.C. to A.D. 70. Fuchs cites more than one estimate of the population of Jerusalem; 80,000 is the higher. Similarly with his estimate of the literacy rate of 20 percent. (However, he derives the frequency of each of the three names from the percentages of their appearances on ossuary inscriptions rather than their appearances in inscriptions from all sources. He thus assumes that the population of those who would be interred in ossuaries differed from the entire Jewish population of Jerusalem.)

Fuchs concludes, with a confidence level of 95 percent, that no more than four individuals (3.63 to be exact) would have the required name configuration. At a confidence level of 70 percent, no more than two individuals (1.71 to be exact) would bear the required name configuration. For Lemaire there were probably 20 men who were James, son of Joseph, brother of Jesus. For Fuchs the number is much lower—between 2 and 4.

Even taking these numbers at face value, however, we do not end up with a high probability that we have found the ossuary of the New Testament James. Using Lemaire's figure of 20, there is only one chance in 20 that we have the right James—that's a 5 percent chance. On Fuchs's calculation, the chances are much better, but still only between 25 and 50 percent.

In short, statistics alone won't do it. Yet the statistical analysis in a general way does seem to be bringing us closer to James the brother of Jesus of Nazareth.

THE BROTHER ON THE OSSUARY

But the most important factor has not been mentioned yet—the very unusual mention of the deceased's brother on the James ossuary.

The customary formula in ossuary inscriptions is to name the deceased and the father of the deceased. That is the equivalent of a person's full name in ancient times, the father's name being a kind of last name in modern terms. Of the hundreds of ossuary inscriptions that are known to us, in only one other case is the brother of the deceased named, added to the usual designation of the father.[5]

Lemaire suggests only two reasons the brother might be named in an ossuary inscription: (1) the brother was responsible for the burial of the deceased; or (2) the brother was a prominent person with whom the deceased would desire to be identified, a kind of eternal connection. The first suggestion could not apply in this case. Jesus of Nazareth could not be responsible for James's burial because he had been crucified thirty years earlier.

The second explanation, however, is pertinent. By the time of James's death, Jesus was indeed prominent; he was the inspiration for a burgeoning religious movement. Moreover, James himself was deeply involved in the movement, as head of the

Jerusalem church. The second-century Christian writer Hegesippus calls James the first bishop of Jerusalem. So the appearance of brother Jesus in this ossuary inscription is consistent with what we know about James from history.[6]

It is this factor that persuades me of the likelihood that this ossuary belonged to James the brother of Jesus of Nazareth. The evidence is not so clear that it would stand up in court in a criminal case; we have not proved it beyond a reasonable doubt. But I do think it would be enough to sustain an award in a civil suit, where the standard of proof is a preponderance of the evidence. That is, this box is more likely the ossuary of James, the brother of Jesus of Nazareth, than not.

In my opinion, therefore, it is likely that this inscription *does* mention the James and Joseph and Jesus of the New Testament. In that case, it is the first and only archaeological attestation of all three of these New Testament personages. Which means, of course, that it is the first and only appearance in the archaeological record of Jesus of Nazareth.

For Father Fitzmyer, on the other hand, the ossuary's link to the New Testament remains only a possibility, not a probability. "James of Jerusalem is never said in the New Testament to have had a father named Joseph," Fitzmyer tells us.[7] Luke 3.23 says very specifically that "Jesus, when he began his ministry, was almost thirty years of age, being the son (as was *supposed*) of Joseph [my italics]." The Greek word *adelphos,* translated "brother" when Paul calls James "the brother of the Lord" (Galatians 1.19), can also mean "kinsman" or "relative." Hence, James could simply have been a relative of Jesus, not a brother. In later Catholic tradition, the nature of their relationship was specified as that of cousin. If James was only a cousin of Jesus, his father would not be Joseph and the James ossuary inscription could not refer to this New Testament James.

Amos Kloner, a Jerusalem scholar who specializes in late Second Temple period burial customs, is also skeptical. He points out that most ossuaries with inscriptions are found in groups, sometimes as many as twenty in one cave complex. Very few have been found singly in small caves, a reflection of the fact that most cave tombs, especially those with inscriptions, are family tombs. Did James have a family in Jerusalem? Possibly, but of course, we don't know where this ossuary was found. Perhaps it was in a large cave complex. But there is no archaeological indication of this. Kloner raises another point: inscriptions were used after many generations had been buried in the cave, to identify the members of the various generations. Even if James's family settled in Jerusalem, there was not enough time between Jesus' crucifixion and James's death thirty years later to require identifying inscriptions, Kloner maintains. Perhaps, though, the early Christian community had a tradition of burying its members, presumably in a cave of its own. If the second part ("brother of Jesus") of the James inscription was indeed added at a later time, this fits nicely with Kloner's proposition that inscriptions were featured in multi-generational burials, whether family or Christian.

Other scholars have argued that if the ossuary inscription really refers to the New Testament Jesus, he would be identified as Jesus of Nazareth, or James would be called "the brother of the Lord," as he is in Galatians. Interestingly, however, a number of distinguished scholars have made what amounts to the opposite argument. There is a passage in Josephus that describes the trial and stoning of James; James is identified, in passing, as "the brother of Jesus, who is called the Messiah." The fact that James is called "the brother of Jesus," as in the James ossuary inscription, rather than "the brother of the Lord" indicates that the passage is an authentic historical reference to Jesus. So say leading scholars Father John P. Meier of the University of Notre Dame, Paul Winter, and Emil Schürer.[8]

THE ARCHAEOLOGICAL LINK TO JESUS

This reference in Josephus raises another point: How can I say that the James ossuary may be the first and only appearance of Jesus of Nazareth in the archaeological record? As a matter of fact, Jesus of Nazareth is referred to not only by Josephus, but also by the Roman writers Suetonius and Tacitus. And of course Jesus is the central figure in the Gospels and the letters of Paul.

The letters attributed to Paul were written in the mid–first century (not all of Paul's letters are by Paul, however). The so-called synoptic Gospels, Matthew, Mark, and Luke (they contain many parallels), were all written between about A.D. 70 and 100. The date of the Gospel of John is more debatable, but some scholars date it to about A.D. 100. There can be no serious question about Jesus' existence. He certainly walked this earth. We need no archaeological evidence to tell us this or even to confirm it.

But these are literary references, not part of the archaeological record. And no copies of the literary references date as early as the first century, like the James ossuary. Our earliest copy of Josephus dates to the eleventh century. Our earliest copies of the Gospels go back only to the fourth or fifth century. A small fragment of John, known as the Rylands Papyrus, dates as far back as about A.D. 125, still almost a century after Jesus' death.

The oldest surviving Gospel fragment (front and back) dates to about A.D. 125—at least fifty years after the James ossuary. Known as the Rylands Papyrus, the 3.4-inch-tall Greek fragment includes a few broken lines from the Gospel of John. *John Rylands Library, Manchester, U.K.*

It has been suggested that we might identify the person interred in the James ossuary from an analysis of the bones. However, this ossuary, like almost all ossuaries that surface on the antiquities market, was empty when it was acquired. Nevertheless, it did contain some small bone chips, the largest about a half inch wide and three inches long and resembling a small honeycomb on the inner side. The owner of the ossuary paid no attention to these bone chips until his ossuary became famous. Then he collected them in a Tupperware container, where they remain today. Whether they could tell us much is doubtful. We cannot even be sure that they are the bones of the James interred in the ossuary; ossuaries often held the bones of more than one person. But a carbon-14 test, which can be performed on anything organic, could at least reveal the age of the bones. DNA tests also could be performed on the bone chips. But this would tell us very little; after all, we don't have a sample of the DNA of Jesus' family. Moreover, given the sensitivities in Israel with regard to ancient Jewish bones—they are regularly reburied when they are discovered in archaeological excavations, to comply with Israeli laws—it is unlikely that any tests will ever be carried out.

BURIAL AMONG JERUSALEM JEWS

How does this ossuary fit into the life and customs of Jerusalem Jews at the turn of the era?

In the first century B.C. and the first century A.D., Jerusalem Jews buried their dead in caves carved out of soft limestone. Mostly these were family caves, used for generations. So many have been discovered throughout Jerusalem that we can confidently describe a typical example.

On entering a burial cave, one steps down into what archaeologists call a standing pit, where one can stand erect. Here mourners would have come to commemorate the dead. A tomb may have several rooms, or adjacent caves, carved out of the rock. In the entrance rooms and adjoining chambers are long, hollowed-out niches or recesses called loculi (singular, loculus; the Hebrew is *kokh*, plural *kokhim*). These loculi are dug about six feet

PLAN

loculi

standing pit

entrance

SECTION

standing pit

A typical burial cave plan is shown from above (*top*) and as if sliced vertically (*middle*). The loculi—deep niches carved into the walls—were used to lay out corpses and to house ossuaries. In the photo (*below*), ossuaries still remain in the loculi. *Drawings after Zvi Greenhut, Israel Antiquities Authority. Photo: Zev Radovan, Jerusalem*

deep into the rock and about a foot and half wide and high, often with a slightly arched top.

Initially a corpse was placed in a loculus, which was then closed up with a blocking stone. After about a year, when the flesh had desiccated and fallen away, the loculus was opened and the bones of the deceased were collected in a box, usually of limestone, called an ossuary. We know almost exactly when the practice of ossilegium began: the earliest oil lamps found in caves with ossuaries can be dated quite securely to 20–15 B.C. The practice came to an end when the Romans destroyed Jerusalem and burned the Temple in A.D. 70. The overwhelming number of ossuaries were used within twenty miles or so of Jerusalem. Occasionally they are found in other areas, like the Galilee, where Jerusalem Jews fled after the Roman destruction. (Galilee ossuaries were made out of clay, not stone, however.) A few ossuaries from smaller, isolated communities date as late as the end of the third century. Yet the overwhelming concentration of ossuaries is in Jerusalem spanning a ninety-year period. As one scholar has observed, "The practice developed suddenly, and just as suddenly stopped."[9]

Why ossilegium developed—and died out—is largely unknown. Many people, even scholars, think it strange that it was a Jewish custom; after all, rabbinic texts regard human bones as unclean and defiling. Yet the practice of secondary burial in ossuaries was sanctioned by the rabbis. A late first-century sage is quoted in a later rabbinic text as saying to his son, "My son, bury me first in a grave. In the course of time, collect my bones and put them in an ossuary; but do not gather them with your own hands."[10]

The customary explanation for the Jewish use of ossuaries is based on two theological doctrines: eventual resurrection of the dead and the need to expiate sin. The deceased, with his or her bones collected in an ossuary, would be ready for physical resurrection. Expiation from sin was associated with the painful decomposition of the flesh, after which the bones remained in a supposedly pure state. Since belief in the physical resurrection of the dead is known to be a tenet of the Pharisees (a famous rabbinic text states, "Anyone who does not believe in the resurrection

of the dead does not have a place in the world to come"), it is
speculated that ossilegium was primarily a Pharisaic custom. Christianity shared the belief in resurrection of the dead with Pharisaic
Judaism (see Acts 23.6–8), so it seems quite likely that James's
bones would have been collected in an ossuary by his followers, if
not by his family. (Ben Witherington will talk more about this in
part 2.)

Some have questioned whether Jewish Christians would have
practiced ossilegium. The answer is almost certainly yes. At this
time, Jerusalem Christians considered themselves Jews. It would
be more accurate, in fact, to call them Christian Jews rather than
Jewish Christians. James would have initially required all converts
to the movement to be Jews; that was the doctrine of the Jerusalem church. Paul, however, wanted to preach to Gentiles in the
Greek world. As we will see in chapter 9, a compromise was ultimately reached through James's leadership whereby Gentiles
could be accepted into the community provided that they re-
frained from fornication and desisted from eating blood or meat
that had been sacrificed to idols or animals that had been strangled.
In other words, they did not have to observe the Jewish dietary
laws (kashrut), and they did not have to undergo circumcision. But
the Jerusalem contingent of Christians continued to regard themselves as Jews and to observe Jewish law. And it is likely that one of
the last things they abandoned would have been burial customs.

A more prosaic explanation for Jerusalem ossilegium is simply that as more space was needed in Jerusalem caves for subsequent burials, the bones of people previously buried in these
family caves had to be removed. Rather than simply heaping
them up in a charnel pile (as was done in the First Temple period), people respectfully placed their ancestors' bones in a special box designed for this purpose.

Another secular reason may lie behind the popularity of ossilegium among Jerusalem's Jews. "The relatively sudden use of ossuaries may have more to do with the development of the
stone-carving industry than with theological beliefs," says Steven
Fine.[11] This industry is often associated with the gigantic project
of Herod the Great in rebuilding the Temple and associated

structures and enlarging the Temple Mount. When Herod's grandiose project was completed, a great many stonecutters were put out of work. Shortly thereafter, ossuaries as well as stone tables and vessels became popular.

Perhaps all these factors contributed to the growth of ossilegium. In any event, it would have been routine for James's bones to be collected in an ossuary a year after his death.

As previously noted, often the bones of more than one person were placed in an ossuary. Ossuaries come in various sizes, some of them so small they were obviously intended for children. Others, slightly larger, were for adolescents. Those for adults vary in size from 16 to 25 inches long. The James ossuary is about 22 inches long at the top, tapering down to 20 inches long at the bottom, a common feature of ossuaries. Minimally, the ossuary must be long enough for the longest bones, the femurs (thighbones), of the deceased. Most ossuaries are about a foot wide and a foot high.

Sometimes ossuaries have four small, low feet, but just as often they do not. (The James ossuary does not.) Ossuary lids come in three shapes—flat, as in the case of the James ossuary, arched (vaulted), or gabled. The lid either rests on the long rims (sides) of the ossuary or on small ledges cut into the rim; the James ossuary's lid rests on such ledges.

The vast majority of ossuaries are plain and uninscribed. It is easy to be misled by a too-casual look at the standard catalogue of ossuaries by L. Y. Rahmani (*A Catalogue of Jewish Ossuaries in the Collections of the State of Israel,* 1994), which lists 897 ossuaries, 233 of them—roughly 25 percent—inscribed. But the catalogue does not include plain undecorated and uninscribed ossuaries—which is the bulk of them. There must be thousands. Walk into any antiquities shop in the Old City, and you'll see several plain ossuaries for sale. A reporter researching a story on the James ossuary saw "four unadorned ossuaries gathering dust [in a shop on the Via Dolorosa], stuffed with bric-a-brac and a garden hose." The owner of the James ossuary has more than thirty ossuaries in his collection. Plain ones are not highly prized, however, because people tend not to want a bone box in their living room.

Ossuary lids are flat (*top, left*), as on the James ossuary, arched (*top, right*), or gabled (*bottom, right*). Drawings from L. Y. Rahmani, *A Catalogue of Jewish Ossuaries*

The James ossuary is quite plain, with only a line tracing a frame about half an inch from the outer edges. However, when the box was carefully examined at the Royal Ontario Museum, two rosettes, each one within two compass-drawn concentric circles, were faintly visible on the back of the ossuary. One of these rosettes was more visible than the other. Some people even thought they could see another rosette on the right side of the ossuary (when facing the inscription). Some red paint and a six-pointed star were also faintly visible on the back of the ossuary within one of the rosettes. Many ossuaries are decorated with rosettes, which can have anywhere from three to twenty-four petals. Red washes were often applied over the surface of ossuaries.

Since the rosettes on this ossuary are on the back, some people argue that this ossuary had already been used when it was purchased to contain the bones of James and the inscription added later when it was reused for James. Some ossuaries were emptied and reused. This could have happened in this case. It is consistent with the fact that archaeologists have found several ossuaries that were repaired in ancient times. Sometimes pieces of an ossuary were glued or plastered back together in ancient times; in two instances, ancient iron rivets hold the pieces together. Some of these repaired ossuaries are undecorated, so it was not only the fancy (that is, expensive) ones that were fixed.

Why are the rosettes on the back (and side) of the James ossuary so faint? The best hypothesis is that the inscribed side of the ossuary was face down for two millennia, while the other sides weathered.[12]

That some ossuaries were repaired raises the question of the price of an ossuary. From two surviving price tags on ossuaries, we learn that one plain ossuary sold for one drachma or dinar and four obols. A drachma, the term in the Hellenistic period, and a dinar, the term in the Roman period, equals $3\frac{1}{2}$ grams of almost pure silver. An obol is one-sixth of a drachma or dinar. Another, elaborately decorated ossuary sold for only one drachma or dinar more. Rahmani suggests that the price on the second ossuary was only for the decoration; the ossuary itself would have cost extra. Still, this is quite inexpensive. An ancient list of ossuary artisans gives the amount each artisan has to his credit; these figures range from one obol to four drachmas or dinars. In short, the day's wages of a skilled artisan could buy an ossuary. This has been confirmed experimentally, too. Amos Kloner took a block of limestone to a stonecutter and asked him to make an ossuary from it. He did so in four and a half hours.

Even relatively poor people, then, could have afforded ossuaries. Moreover, we cannot conclude that plain ossuaries were for poor people and fancy ones for rich people. In the same family tomb we may find elaborately carved ossuaries, ossuaries with simple rosettes, and plain undecorated ossuaries. In the famous Tombs of the Kings in Jerusalem, which belonged to the royal house of Adiabene, richly embellished sarcophagi lay adjacent to the much simpler sarcophagus of Queen Helena. "This evidence refutes the suggestion that a plain ossuary or coffin indicates parsimony or lack of care for the deceased," as Rahmani states. Thus "the choice of cheaper types [of ossuaries] should not be regarded as a sign of comparative poverty."[13]

An ossuary from the Caiaphas family cave tomb bears an
image of a Corinthian column set between two six-petaled
rosettes in concentric circles. *Garo Nalbandian, Jerusalem*

Several motifs reappear in ossuary decorations. Besides
rosettes, we often find date palms and architectural elements—
ashlar walls, doors, gates, and columns. Some architectural decorations seem to imitate a structure or building, perhaps relating
to the Temple not far away or the entrance to the cave tomb in
which the ossuary sat. They have no special meaning or significance as far as we know, however.

Most ossuary inscriptions are sloppily executed, often
scratched with a nail that was discarded on the spot. We sometimes see a letter added above an irregularly shaped inscription
because it had been omitted accidentally. By our count, only 15
of the 233 inscriptions in Rahmani's catalogue were carved with
great care, in formal script. Most, as Rahmani states, are "carelessly executed, clumsily spaced, and, often, contain spelling [and
other] mistakes. This is true even in cases of renowned families,
including those of high-priestly rank."[14] This sloppiness also char-
acterizes the decorations; on about forty ossuaries in the Rahmani catalogue, minor decorative details were left unfinished.

All this makes it very difficult to draw any conclusions from
the faint decoration on the James ossuary, the mix of formal and
cursive script in the inscription, or the degraded letters at the
end. Was this a reused ossuary, decorated with rosettes on the

An elaborate paneled doorway—perhaps resembling the entrance to the Jerusalem Temple—is carved into this ossuary. *Zev Radovan, Jerusalem/Hebrew University Institute of Archaeology*

The door frame at right resembles the entryway to a cave tomb at Akeldama (*see color insert*). On the front of this ossuary are four windows framing palm motifs and another door. *Israel Museum, Jerusalem*

front by the first user and turned around by the second user and inscribed on the clean side? Or was there only one user, who decided to place the inscription on the back? Was the family who bought the ossuary poor or rich, of high rank or low rank? Would the head of the Jerusalem church be buried in an unadorned ossuary like this one (stressing his humility and his spiritual qualities) or in an elaborate ossuary (reflecting his high station)? It doesn't matter whether the Jesus movement at this time was wealthy and powerful or weak and poor: none of these factors makes it more or less likely that the inscription on the James ossuary refers to New Testament personages.

Inscriptions have been found on the long and the narrow sides of ossuaries. Inscriptions on the ends of boxes may have been for identification purposes only, while inscriptions on the long side might have indicated a more honorific purpose. Yet we can draw no firm conclusions from the fact that the inscription on the James ossuary is on a long side. In general, little attention was paid to the placement of the inscriptions on ossuaries. Decorated sides are sometimes inscribed even when there is unadorned space available. Sometimes inscriptions are carved right through decorations; sometimes they are horizontal, sometimes vertical, and sometimes on a slant.

It may be tempting to draw inferences from the uncentered placement of the inscription on the James ossuary. Some have suggested that because the word *Jesus* is near the center, it was the only original part of the inscription; everything before it must be a modern forgery. All such speculation is useless.

Some things we can occasionally glean from ossuary inscriptions. The place of origin of the deceased may be reflected in the kind of script used, as indicated by a few Latin and Palmyrene examples. These demonstrate that even in this early period, Jews from elsewhere brought their deceased to be buried in Jerusalem. Whether this was the case with James, who spent his early life in Galilee, we cannot know.

The majority of ossuary inscriptions, however, are in what scholars call Jewish scripts—Hebrew and Aramaic. Sometimes it is difficult to tell the difference. But with the James ossuary inscription it is easy. It uses the Aramaic word for "son" (*bar*) instead of the Hebrew word (*ben*), and also the Aramaic form, instead of Hebrew, for "brother."

The most common type of ossuary inscription gives the name of the deceased and of his father. But sometimes further identifications were added to enhance the prestige of the deceased or his descendants. Thus the rank of high priest was noted on one ossuary. On another, a woman is described as the daughter of a priest. One man is identified as an elder. A famous ossuary inscription refers to one Simon (Shimon) as the "builder of the sanctuary [temple]." Nicanor is called he "who made the gates [of the temple]." All this suggests that it would not have been unusual for those who buried James to have enhanced his prestige by noting that he was the brother of the well-known Jesus. Or, as Kyle McCarter has argued, the two words *brother of Jesus* might have been added by the family to clarify who this James was after several generations had passed.

Although the James ossuary inscription is not needed to prove the existence of Jesus, it does have a tactile, visual quality that bridges the millennia in a very different way from a literary text. This plain stone box somehow transports us back almost two thousand years—to a stone burial cave in ancient Jerusalem, where the friends or family of a man named James reverently laid his bones and honored him then or subsequently by taking the extraordinary step of identifying him with his presumably famous brother, James.

אלעזר בר נהטרא טמא ד

"Simon, builder of the sanctuary," reads this ossuary inscription. Simon's family apparently added his job description so that he (and they) would always be remembered for his good work. *Israel Antiquities Authority*

1. Richard Bauckham, based on the data in Tal Ilan, *Lexicon of Jewish Names in Late Antiquity: Part I—Palestine 330 B.C.E.–200 C.E.*, Texts and Studies in Ancient Judaism 91 (Tübingen: Mohr Siebeck, 2002).

2. See Rachel Hachlili, "Names and Nicknames of Jews in Second Temple Times," *Eretz-Israel* 17 (1984): 188–211 (in Hebrew), and pp. 9*–10* (English summary).

3. See Magen Broshi, "Estimating the Population of Ancient Jerusalem," *Biblical Archaeology Review* (June 1978).

4. He also considered some additional factors, such as the fact that two brothers in the same family could not have the same name. But these factors have only a minor effect on the results.

5. See L. Y. Rahmani, *A Catalogue of Jewish Ossuaries in the Collections of the State of Israel* (Jerusalem: Israel Antiquities Authority, Israel Academy of Sciences and Humanities, 1994), no. 570, which reads, "Shimi [Shimon or Simon], son of 'Asiya, brother of Hanin."

6. An inscription on a woman's ossuary from Jericho names, not her husband, but her son—as unusual as referring to a brother. Rachel Hachlili, the excavator, explains that the "status" of the woman was "important," perhaps because she was a widow who had responsibility for raising the children. Rachel Hachlili, "The Goliath Family in Jericho: Funerary Inscriptions from a First-Century A.D. Jewish Monumental Tomb," *Bulletin of the American Schools of Oriental Research* 235 (1979): 31 at pp. 57–58.

7. From a personal conversation.

8. Cited in John P. Meier, "The Testimonium—Evidence for Jesus Outside the Bible," *Bible Review* (June 1991).

9. Steven Fine, "Why Bone Boxes?" *Biblical Archaeology Review* (September/October 2001).

10. Semahot 12.9.

11. Fine, "Why Bone Boxes?"

12. This is the suggestion of Kyle McCarter. In a conversation with Frank Cross after this book was set in type, he told me that the fact that the back of the ossuary was weathered, but the side with the inscription was not, suggested that the inscription might be a modern forgery. When I told him about McCarter's suggestion, Cross exclaimed, "The whole matter is up in the air." My own view is that the faint rosettes do not indicate a modern forgery of the inscription. A modern forger would simply use an easily available blank ossuary. He would not buy trouble with an ossuary that was already faintly decorated. The faint rosettes, therefore, are a sign of authenticity, not the reverse. In addition, the differences between the first half and the second half of the inscription (paleographically insignificant, in Cross's view; for McCarter, however, they may indicate two hands) would not be likely to appear in a modern forgery. A modern forger would not allow this, as the difference might arouse suspicion. Then, too, there is the lack of any profit motive, which would negate a modern forgery. In any event, Cross does not base his suspicions on the paleography of the inscription. For him, as for all other experienced paleographers, the inscription itself contains no sign that it is a modern forgery.

13. Rahmani, *Catalogue*, 11.

14. Rahmani, *Catalogue*, 12.

6

CAN WE IGNORE IT?

All of us involved in the discovery would love to know where the ossuary was found and whether there were bones inside when it was recovered. If so, the bones might tell us the state of the deceased's health and what he died from. Even aside from the bones, the James ossuary would answer more of our questions if it had been excavated in a professional archaeological excavation. Was the ossuary part of a family tomb? What was the burial cave like—plain or fancy? Were there other ossuaries in the burial cave? Were any of them decorated or, like this one, inscribed? What could other finds in the cave tell us about the people (the family?) buried here and the lives they led? Where exactly was the cave in relation to other burial caves and in relation to the city and the Temple Mount?

But this ossuary came to us unprovenanced. It surfaced on the antiquities market. Even if the inscription is authentic (as it almost surely is), we would know more about the ossuary and its contents if we knew where and under what conditions it was found. As it is, it is an artifact without context. Or, in the words of the critics, it has been "ripped from its context."

Yet what should we do? Ignore it?

What we do know about the ossuary, we have learned from the owner. The Israeli press sleuths managed to identify him.

We're not sure how—perhaps from the Israel Antiquities Authority, since his name was on the application to export the ossuary for exhibit in the Royal Ontario Museum. Once the Israeli newspapers learned who the owner was, they sent paparazzi on a stakeout at his apartment building, and Joe became front-page news in Israel. Weekend features soon followed, with detailed descriptions of the life and times of Oded Golan, a fifty-one-year-old Tel Aviv collector. His cherished privacy has been lost forever. He is, in a manner of speaking, a celebrity.

So now we can call him by his real name.

Oded Golan began collecting antiquities when he was eight years old. When he was nine, he discovered a cuneiform tablet overlooked by professional archaeologists when they tossed waste debris into a dump. As a youngster he developed a relationship with the illustrious Israeli biblical archaeologist Yigael Yadin, who invited the then-eleven-year-old boy to participate in Yadin's dig at Masada as the youngest member of the team.

Today, Golan is a successful engineer, entrepreneur, businessman, and near-professional pianist. A white baby grand piano, surrounded by wall cases displaying stunning ancient artifacts, sits in his apartment in a middle-class Tel Aviv neighborhood. Golan describes his collection as "most probably the largest and most important privately owned collection of its kind in Israel."

He says he bought the ossuary many years ago from an Arab antiquities dealer in Jerusalem's Old City. Now he cannot even remember who the dealer was. The dealer told him that the ossuary had been found in Silwan, an Arab village in Jerusalem just south of the Mount of Olives and in plain view of the nearby Temple Mount. It is an area of soft limestone bedrock on the flank of the Kidron Valley, which is pockmarked with burial caves that have yielded innumerable ossuaries. The Israel Geological Survey found that the James ossuary's soft limestone matches the limestone in Silwan. Ossuaries are frequently found and offered for sale in groups, but Golan says the dealer told him that this one came on the market alone.

For years, the ossuary sat on the balcony of Golan's parents'

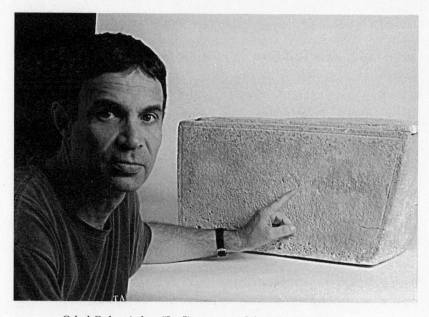

Oded Golan (a.k.a. "Joe"), a successful engineer and
entrepreneur living in Tel Aviv, points to the inscription on
the James ossuary, one of the thousands of ancient artifacts
he has amassed since he started collecting at age eight.
Associated Press

apartment, where he then lived. When he moved to his own
apartment, he took his collection with him, including the ossuary. That was about fifteen years ago. When his collection grew
so large that it could not be accommodated in his apartment,
he placed some items in storage. As he told a reporter for
Toronto's *Globe and Mail,* when he was twenty-three, it was an
important piece, but when he was forty-three "it was one of the
least important pieces and it went into storage." It was still in
storage when André Lemaire first visited Golan in his apartment
to discuss some other inscriptions. Golan showed Lemaire a
photograph of the James ossuary and its inscription, and the rest
of the story we already know.

RUMORS FLY

With the outing of Golan, the rumor mill, especially in Israel, went into high gear.

One jealous, and very prominent, collector said that he had been offered the James ossuary a year before the article about it appeared in *Biblical Archaeology Review*. At that time, he claimed, the inscription read only "James son of Joseph."

Another story was that the ossuary had been dug up illegally in an Arab village on the southeastern side of the New Testament's Hill of Evil Counsel a bare three months before it appeared in *BAR*. In this version of events, the illegal diggers sold the ossuary for $1,800 to an Arab intermediary named Abu George. Abu George, we have been told, is an unlicensed antiquities dealer (that is, a middleman for looters), who has been arrested on more than one occasion by the IAA; now, however, he may be working as an agent for the IAA. The story goes that Abu George sold the ossuary to Golan for $80,000. It is also said that the illegal diggers believe they were snookered by Abu George and may take their revenge physically. In this scenario, Golan, too, might be in jeopardy.

Invidious stories have also circulated about Golan's character. He is in it only for the money, some say. The chief investigator of the IAA, Amir Ganor, was quoted as saying, "I think [Golan] is laughing at us all the way to the bank."[1] One widely circulated rumor, originally attributed to a high-ranking museum official, alleged that Golan purposely had the ossuary poorly packed so that it would break in shipment and he could collect an enormous amount from the insurance company. Others said that Golan was not a collector but rather an antiquities dealer operating without a license.

The newspapers reported that the police were investigating Golan. The truth, though, was that the IAA had talked to him to learn more about the ossuary and how he acquired it. The police were never involved.

Then there were those who claimed they knew who forged the inscription—a certain well-known antiquities dealer, whom

Golan had paid. One well-known Israeli academic who said he knew who the forger was (but wouldn't identify him to me) remarked, "The Jerusalem forger strikes again."

With stories like these circulating, it is not hard to understand why Oded Golan wanted to retain his anonymity.

DOES EVERYTHING CHECK?

Yet it must be said that there are also problems with parts of Golan's story, inconsistencies that have fueled the rumor mill. One gray area is the date of purchase of the ossuary. It is important because it may determine whether Golan or the state of Israel has rights to the ossuary. According to Israeli law, if an object was acquired before 1978 (when this law was passed), no questions about its provenance are raised, even if it was bought from a looter. Since 1978, in a vain effort to reduce looting, Israel has required purchasers to retain a receipt from a licensed antiquities dealer, who in turn must keep a record of how he legally acquired a given artifact (from someone who owned it before 1978). If an artifact was acquired after 1978 and is unsupported by a receipt from a licensed antiquities dealer, it is subject to confiscation by the state. Everyone recognizes that this law has had little, if any, effect. People who sell to antiquities dealers naturally assure them that the item concerned has been in the family forever. At most, instead of remaining in Israel, illegal antiquities flow out of the country to Jordan or Lebanon and from there to Zurich or London. But Golan may present a unique opportunity for enforcement of the law—and possible confiscation of the James ossuary.

The law as applied is said to be quite different. But this is hearsay, oral, vague—and officially unverifiable. The antiquities market operates by its own rules. Even though the rules are undefined, the IAA knows what they are. And there is a comfortable, if sometimes antagonistic, modus vivendi among collectors, dealers, middlemen, and the IAA.

Press reports state variously that Golan has owned the ossuary for fifteen, twenty-five, thirty, and thirty-five years. Some stories say he has owned it since the early 1970s, others since the midseventies;

still others, since the early to midseventies. It was I who told the
press that he had had the ossuary for about fifteen years, based
on what I believed Golan had told me. Golan now maintains that
he gave this as the number of years he had the ossuary in his own
apartment. Perhaps, when we initially talked in his apartment, I
asked him how long he had the ossuary there. Before fifteen
years ago, Golan says, it was in his parents' apartment.

Yet in 2002, when Lemaire was first shown a picture of the ossuary, it was not in Golan's apartment but in storage.

If Golan in fact acquired the ossuary only fifteen years ago,
the state may have a claim to it. If he bought it more than twenty-
five years ago, in the mid–1970s, this would take his purchase
back before the critical 1978 date. Golan claims that many people—
old girlfriends and friends of his parents—saw the ossuary in his
parents' apartment and can testify to its being there at the earlier
date. But are they sure it was *this* ossuary they saw? The *Globe and
Mail* found Golan's explanation a bit bizarre but concluded that
"he related it with such unrestrained enthusiasm and lack of defensiveness" that it seemed entirely believable.

Another inconsistency relates to why Golan didn't recognize
the significance of the inscription. When I asked him about this,
he replied, "I didn't know the Son of God could have a brother."
Some stories in the press said that he failed to understand the
inscription because he couldn't decipher the unusual word for
brother (*achui*).

By now, I think I know Golan well. He impresses as a truth
teller. He is charming, unpretentious, intelligent, and completely
open. Yet I can understand how someone could form a very different opinion based only on the record of these inconsistencies—and the swirling rumors.

A MISGUIDED POLICY

But another fundamental issue lurks in the background of the
doubters' claims. It is the legitimacy of the antiquities market.
The American Schools of Oriental Research (ASOR), the professional organization of American Near Eastern archaeologists, has

a formal policy that its members should not undertake research on unprovenanced objects. An unprovenanced object cannot be published for the first time in its prestigious professional journal, the *Bulletin of the American Schools of Oriental Research* (*BASOR*). (However, once someone else publishes an unprovenanced object in another journal, then it is apparently acceptable to cite it in *BASOR*.) A paper concerning an unprovenanced artifact cannot be delivered at ASOR's annual meeting. That is why ASOR, meeting in Toronto in 2002 at the same time as the Society of Biblical Literature (SBL), officially ignored the ossuary. In contrast, SBL held a special session on the ossuary that drew a huge crowd.

The effect of ASOR's policy is only to drive the market underground; we simply don't hear about important unprovenanced artifacts. Golan tells of many important finds that collectors keep to themselves because they do not want to be vilified and excoriated by professional archaeological associations like ASOR and the Archaeological Institute of America (AIA), which has adopted a similar policy.

How to deal with looting is a major question in the profession. Whether ASOR's and AIA's policies are the best way of dealing with it is a contentious issue that is widely discussed. All of us despise looters; yet looting is admittedly worse than ever. ASOR's and AIA's policies have abysmally failed to stop, or even reduce, looting. It is time to take a look at market-based solutions that might at least stem the illegal trade and reveal treasures now hidden from public view. The low-level looting of pots and oil lamps, which sell for less than a hundred dollars, could be rendered unprofitable if governments would sell off some of the thousands of duplicates of these items that lie gathering dust in overstuffed archaeological storerooms. Who would buy a looted pot (even from a licensed antiquities dealer) that may be a fake if he or she could buy instead a government-authenticated object with a valid export permit?

Sometimes the authorities know that an important site is being looted, yet they seem powerless to stop it. In such a case, archaeologists could hire the looters, often poor villagers who have no other way of earning a living, to excavate the site under professional supervision. This, incidentally, is what Père Roland de Vaux did when he caught Bedouin looters excavating caves containing Dead Sea Scroll fragments. It was, and is, no secret that Tell Beit Mirsim in the West Bank and Bab edh-Dhra and Qazone, both in Jordan, were and are being looted. At the first two sites it is primarily pots; at Qazone it is inscribed tombstones. Tell Beit Mirsim cannot be saved (the looters have pretty much destroyed the site), but at Bab edh-Dhra and Qazone, the looters could be hired as workers. To finance the excavation, some of the proceeds from the sale of the duplicate finds (after they have been recorded and photographed) could be used. Whatever disadvantages this may have, it is better than having the sites looted.

When important artifacts come to light, we should make sure that the finders are fairly compensated. To some extent this may mean getting into bed with looters, just as investigators do when they pay ransom in kidnapping cases. Different situations require different strategies. Sometimes you must deal with looters, as archaeologists did in the late 1940s to recover the Dead Sea Scrolls.

Collectors who rescue important objects from the market should be honored. There seems to be no way that archaeologists can locate these truly high-end objects, such as, for example, seal impressions of kings of ancient Judah. That is why most of the bullae (seal impressions) we know to have survived have come from the antiquities market. The same goes for coins. It must be frustrating for professional field archaeologists to find themselves upstaged by looters. But it is unreasonable to claim, as some scholars sometimes do, that we can place no trust in the authenticity of anything that surfaces on the antiquities market.

Furthermore, we should draw a distinction between looted objects and objects that were accidentally found. Many artifacts are discovered by accident—in the course of plowing, digging for an extension to a house, or laying a new pipeline or highway. Admittedly, it is not always easy to determine whether an object was found rather than looted, just as it is often impossible to tell how long someone has owned an object. But we must do the best we can and adequately reward the finder who turns in his find to the authorities rather than selling it on the antiquities market.

The problems are difficult and varied, and the solutions uncertain. What is certain, however, is that present policies are ineffective and, if anything, result in our not knowing about important finds. The suggestions outlined above may not solve the problem, but at the very least they would seem to be worth a try. Perhaps they could be developed or modified. And in the meantime, it is high time to stop vilifying Oded Golan for acquiring the James ossuary on the antiquities market.

This, then, is the story of the James ossuary so far as it is known at the present time. The remaining questions are now the proper province of New Testament scholars. Who was James, what was his relationship with his brother Jesus before and then after the crucifixion, what role did the family of Jesus play in the emergence of Christianity, and what are the implications for Christianity of realizing that the mother church of the movement in Jerusalem was a community of Jews, distinguished by their belief that the Messiah had come in the person of Jesus?

To these questions my colleague Ben Witherington now turns in part 2.

1. Quoted in the *Toronto Star,* November 8, 2002.

Part II

—

THE STORY OF JAMES, SON OF JOSEPH, BROTHER OF JESUS

BEN WITHERINGTON III

Introduction

IN HIS END,
A BEGINNING

As I write this, thousands of people are lining up to see the ossuary of James on display at the Royal Ontario Museum in Toronto. Why all this interest in a first-century burial box of modest proportions and simple design that has a one-line inscription? Certainly, the consuming interest in this discovery is because of the person mentioned in the last word of the ossuary inscription—Jesus. North America, like much of the Western world, is a society in which Jesus is virtually omnipresent, while at the same time the population is largely biblically illiterate. There is a seemingly inexhaustible fascination with Jesus but widespread ignorance about what the Gospels and the rest of the New Testament actually say about him, his family, and the early Christians. Even serious believers tend to operate with only a sketchy sense of what the Bible actually says. My hope is that this discovery prompts people to discover a fuller picture of Jesus' life and legacy.

The further appeal of the ossuary, I believe, is that it promises for the first time the opportunity to "touch" Jesus, to experience a physical connection with him through the inscribed burial box of his brother James, a pivotal early Christian leader who has been hidden in the shadows of history. Now, in this simple inscription, the Gospel figures of Jesus, Joseph, and James—until now known only through texts—become arrestingly tangible. In an age that demands compelling evidence for claims of faith and history, the world now has something concrete to see, examine, reflect on, and respond to.

The discovery especially encourages us to rediscover and reconstruct what we can know about the figure of James. James was a monumental figure in the first centuries of Christianity. He was the first head of the Christian church in Jerusalem, the mother church of the Jesus movement, and he—along with members of his community—was at the same time a faithful and Torah-observant Jew. He was the pioneer of Jewish-Christian reconciliation. The revival of his legacy would be eye opening and most beneficial today.

Ben Witherington III
Lexington, KY
Hanukkah/Christmas 2002

7

FROM BROTHER
TO FOLLOWER

The discovery of the ossuary may well be the most significant biblical archaeological find of our time and the first-ever physical link to the historical Jesus of the New Testament.

But who was this James, "brother of Jesus"? And why is he so important in understanding the family of Jesus and the early Jesus movement that eventually developed into Christianity?

As we will see, James played a very large role. In fact, if one asked members of the first-century church who were their top leaders, they might mention three, maybe four, names: Peter, John, Paul, and James, the brother of Jesus. In fact, they would probably mention James first.

However, as Christianity developed into the dominant religion of the Roman Empire and eventually of the Western world, it became primarily the Church of Peter and Paul. The ossuary brings back to the fore the importance of the church of Jerusalem, which was centered around James and the family of Jesus and was much more traditionally Jewish than the other Christian communities emerging in Rome and elsewhere in the empire. (Our word *church* translates the Greek word *ekklesia*, which means simply "assembly" and hence is cognate with *synagoge* or "synagogue.") Unfortunately, the Jerusalem church faded in

importance with the violent Roman suppression of the Jewish revolt in the latter half of the first century and beyond.

The ossuary thus opens the door on a story and an authentic
form of earliest Christianity that has been largely lost to us but
may well be most closely linked to the person and the religious
way of Jesus.

JESUS HAD A BROTHER?

When the ossuary first appeared many people were surprised that
Jesus could have had a brother. Wasn't Mary always a virgin?

The Roman Catholic Church has taught officially that the
family members mentioned in the Bible were Jesus' cousins. The
Eastern Orthodox Church calls them half-brothers and -sisters
(arguing that Joseph was a widower who had children from a
prior marriage). Protestants, however, since they do not accept
the doctrine of the *perpetual* virginity of Mary, believe that Jesus
had brothers and sisters who were the children of Mary and
Joseph. In other words, they see Mary as a virgin who gave birth
to Jesus but who did not remain a virgin as she continued her life
as the wife of Joseph. Still, even among Protestants, that Jesus had
brothers and sisters is not emphasized.

What is the evidence for suggesting that James was indeed
Jesus' brother rather than, say, a cousin or a half brother? Let's
see what terminology the Bible itself uses.

In the first place, James's and Jesus' other siblings are always
called his brothers and sisters in the Gospels. When Jesus comes
to Nazareth to preach, the hometown folk are perplexed about
what to make of him and so try to place him among his family
members: "Is not this the carpenter's son? Is not his mother
called Mary? And are not his brothers James and Joseph and
Simon and Judas? And are not all his sisters with us?" (Matthew
13.55–56)

There was indeed a word for cousin in Greek, *anepsios,* and it is
never used of James or the other siblings of Jesus. It is interesting
how the second-century Christian writer Hegesippus distinguishes

between those who were cousins of Jesus (*anepsioi*), and James and Jude, who are called brothers of Jesus (cited in the fourth-century historian Eusebius, *Hist. Eccl.* 4.22.4; see 2.23.4, 3.20.1). The two terms clearly do not mean the same thing in Greek.

Second, the story of Mary's virginity (told in Matthew and Luke) seems limited to Jesus' birth. When Joseph learns that his fiancée is pregnant, he first decides to break off their engagement quietly, but an angel appears in a dream to tell him to continue the union: "When Joseph awoke from sleep, he did as the angel of the Lord commanded him; he took her as his wife, but had no marital relations with her *until she had borne a son*" (Matthew 1.24–25; emphasis added). The most natural way to read this Greek sentence is that it implies strongly that he did have a sexual relationship with Mary after the birth of Jesus.

Third, in the context of Jewish culture during that time, it was considered a duty, not merely an option, for a married couple to fulfill the commandment to be fruitful and multiply, so long as one was not somehow blemished or physically impaired.[1] If Joseph and Mary were devout Jews, and the evidence suggests they were, it is highly likely they would have obeyed the Law in such a matter, especially when marriage was viewed as a vehicle to sustain a family line and maintain an inheritance within that family line.

Fourth, we now evidently have an Aramaic source, the inscription found on the ossuary of James. It tells us that James was Jesus' brother, and here, as elsewhere, there is no attempt to qualify the term *brother* in some way. It is an argument from silence to suggest either that Joseph had been married previously, for no New Testament source implies this, or to claim that the brothers and sisters were really cousins, for no New Testament text suggests this either.

The issue here is not whether it is theoretically possible that Mary could have made a vow to lifelong virginity. This is possible. But that she would have done so as a Jewish woman already betrothed and prepared to have a child, namely Jesus, seems most unlikely. The idea of the perpetual virginity of Mary probably

first arose in a second-century Christian text called the Proto-
Evangelium of James. We will say more about this text when we
discuss the traditions about James that arose in the era after the
New Testament was written.

The notion of the perpetual virginity of Mary is not to be confused with the idea of the virginal conception of Jesus, sometimes
called the virgin birth. The belief in the perpetual virginity of
Mary is a further development of the belief in the virginal conception. The virginal conception is mentioned in Matthew 1 and
in Luke 1–2 and has to do with the Gospels' proclamation that
Jesus was conceived in Mary's womb without sexual intercourse
with a man. The perpetual virginity doctrine is the belief that
after Mary gave birth to Jesus she remained a virgin for the rest of
her life. In fact, the doctrine typically includes the notion that
Mary remained a physically intact virgin after giving birth to
Jesus, the birth itself as well as the conception being viewed as
miraculous and in no way affecting Mary's body so far as her virginity is concerned.

The idea that the perpetual virginity of Mary was a necessary
Catholic doctrine arose in the sixteenth century. Catholics and
Protestants then differed on whether the birth of Jesus was actually miraculous or not. Luke 2.22 ("When the time came for their
purification according to the law of Moses, they brought him up
to Jerusalem to present him to the Lord") seems to suggest that
Mary and Joseph both went through a period of purification after
the birth of Jesus before they took him up to the Temple to dedi-
cate him to the Lord. This text then suggests that Mary and
Joseph saw the birth of Jesus as a normal one that required a certain time and perhaps certain rituals of purification.[2]

Finally, Eusebius, the fourth-century church historian who
quotes from an earlier second-century historian, Hegesippus,
says that James became the first bishop of Jerusalem in part *because* he was the brother of Jesus. (James also became a leader
because he had one of the marks for being an apostle: the risen
Lord personally appeared to him after the resurrection—see
Paul's listing of eyewitnesses to Jesus' resurrection in 1 Corinthians 15.5–8.)[3]

WHAT'S IN A NAME?

Now let's turn to James himself. His name was *not* James—as Hershel Shanks explained earlier—it was Ya'akov in Hebrew, the English form of which is Jacob.[4] In fact, all the people in the New Testament called James actually are named Jacob. The Greek *Jakobus* was rendered in Latin as *Jacomus*. When the Latin was translated into Spanish the form *Jaime* was used. The earliest English translators often relied the forms of the names in Latin or other European languages. Translators are famously conservative, and because the King James Version in 1611 rendered the name as James, it has been James ever since in English translations.

But the original name, Jacob, is important. In the genealogy for Jesus listed at the beginning of the Gospel of Matthew, there are only two Jacobs or Jameses mentioned: the patriarch (1.2—grandson of Abraham, son of Isaac, father of the twelve tribes of Israel) and James's grandfather (1.16—"Jacob the father of Joseph the husband of Mary, of whom Jesus was born, who is called the Messiah"). It is clear that the family of "James" was proud of its Jewish patriarchal heritage and was naming its son after one of the great figures in the book of Genesis and after the child's grandfather.

But the Gospels are full of people named James. There is James the son of Zebedee, brother of the apostle John; James the son of Alphaeus, another disciple; James, the father of Judas and Thaddeus, and so the father of two of Jesus' disciples; and then there is James who is called the brother of the Lord. All of these figure into the Gospel narratives. How can we tell who is who when there were no last names in that era?

The answer is apparent from the above list. The people in the first century had to distinguish between like-named people just as we do. They used four strategies for naming a person: patronymics (the phrase "son of . . ." followed by the first name of the father: "James, son of Joseph"); nicknames (Peter is called Cephas, equivalent to our "Rocky" or "Rock"); descriptive epithets ("the little one"); or geographical designations of the hometown ("of Nazareth"). Fortunately, there are enough of these sorts of clues in the Gospels so that we can usually tell the players even without a program.

Historically, the James/Jacob we are studying was distinguished from other people of the same name in three ways: (1) he was called the brother of the Lord (by the apostle Paul in Galatians 1.19); (2) he was called James the Just (in the noncanonical Gospel of Thomas, Eusebius, and elsewhere); and (3) now we have the inscription of the ossuary calling him both the son of Joseph and the brother of Jesus. The association of James with his father, Joseph, is implicit but nonetheless clear in Matthew 13.55 (the villagers' questioning of Jesus: "Is not this the carpenter's son? . . . And are not his brothers James and Joseph and Simon and Judas?"), and whenever Jesus' brothers and sisters are listed, James is always listed first (see also Mark 6.3, Matthew 27.56).[5] In fact, there was only one James who could safely and regularly be called James without further explanation or ambiguity, and it was James the brother of Jesus. The James we are referring to, then, is mentioned in the Gospels of Matthew and Mark by name and also in the Acts of the Apostles, and the letters of 1 Corinthians, Galatians, James, and Jude.

While James was Jesus' brother, he was probably not one of Jesus' disciples during Jesus' lifetime. In John 7 we read:

> Now the Jewish festival of Booths was near. So his [Jesus'] brothers said to him, "Leave here and go to Judea so that your disciples also may see the works you are doing; for no one who wants to be widely known acts in secret. If you do these things, show yourself to the world." (For not even his brothers believed in him.) (John 7.2–5)

Here it is quite plain that Jesus' brothers did not fully believe in or follow him before his death. So when we talk about James's "early years," we will not be talking about his role as one of the twelve apostles but rather his life growing up in early Judaism, to which we now turn.

GROWING UP WITH JESUS IN NAZARETH

What sort of life and upbringing would someone like James have had as a Jew in Galilee in the first century A.D.? Eastern Orthodox tradition portrays James as Jesus' oldest half brother from Joseph's alleged first marriage. But there is simply no evidence in the New Testament for this. In fact, it is an argument from silence to suggest that Joseph was a much older man than Mary when he married her. This idea apparently arose because Joseph seems not to be around by the time Jesus began his ministry (see Mark 6.1–3; we'll say more on this later).

On the contrary, what the birth narratives suggest in Matthew and Luke is that Joseph, being a righteous man who followed the Law, was betrothed to his intended wife Mary at the normal age (which would have been about sixteen for a Jewish man and twelve to thirteen for a woman). Both of these Gospels begin with the story of the birth of Jesus and only later mention the brothers and sisters of Jesus. So in terms of narrative logic, these evangelists strongly imply that the brothers and sisters came along after the birth of Jesus, not before.

Notice that in Luke 2.41–52, where Joseph and Mary take twelve-year-old Jesus to Jerusalem, our only biblical story of Jesus as a youth, there is no mention of other brothers or sisters going up to Jerusalem to the festival with them, which surely they would have done if they were older than Jesus. This is especially significant when we see that "his mother and his brothers" and sometimes "his sisters" are almost always mentioned together later in the narratives (see Mark 3.31–35, Mark 6.1–3, and John 2.12). We will take it as a working hypothesis, then, since the New Testament gives no contrary evidence, that James was Jesus' younger brother and grew up in the same home with him.

Many of our impressions of life in New Testament times are shaped by our understandings of Jerusalem, the cultural and spiritual center of Jewish life. But life in Galilee, a province to the north of Jerusalem, differed from life in Judea. Politically, Galilee was ruled by a client king named Herod Antipas rather than by direct Roman rule, as in Judea. What we know about Herod

Antipas is that he was an Idumean—not a full-blooded Jew but still a Semite. He was also a Hellenizer, a promoter of Greek culture and customs, building cities based on Greek models, like Sepphoris just outside of Nazareth.[6] This no doubt would have annoyed many Jews in the region, and not just John the Baptist. In fact, Jesus himself called Herod Antipas "that fox." So political life in Galilee had its tensions, especially if you were part of a devout family.[7]

How do we know that James's family was devoutly Jewish? First, notice the names of Joseph and Mary's sons. Besides Jesus, there were James and Joseph, named after famous patriarchs, and Judas and Simon, named after Jewish Maccabean war heroes (Mark 6.3). It is clear the family was proud of its Jewish heritage and, in particular, the heritage they had as a free people following God's will.

Second, we see that the family followed the Jewish religious custom of making repeated trips up to Jerusalem for the Jewish festivals. In Luke 2.41 we read, "Now every year his parents went to Jerusalem for the festival of the Passover." Also in John 7.3 we find Jesus' brothers encouraging him to come with them to Jerusalem for the festival of the booths.

Third, there is the evidence that Jesus' family attended synagogue services. Why else would Jesus so often place himself in this context after he began his ministry? "On the sabbath he began to teach in the synagogue" (Mark 6.2 and others).

Fourth, the story in Luke 4.16–30 indicates that Jesus could read the Hebrew scroll in the synagogue. When he returned to Nazareth after his ministry had begun, Jesus "went to the synagogue on the sabbath day, as was his custom. He stood up to read." This suggests he had training in the home or in the synagogue to do so, since Aramaic and not Hebrew was the family's spoken language.

Fifth, both Matthew (1–2) and Luke (1–2), independently of one another, depict Joseph and Mary as devout Jewish people who have religious visions, dreams, and even encounters with angels. They are clearly portrayed as holy people. Equally important, Luke 2.41–52 tells us that Mary and Joseph trained their children in their faith, for it is surely no accident that we are told that Jesus was taken up to the Temple when he was at the proper age to become a "son of the commandments" (*bar-mitzvah*), and there is a strong emphasis on Jesus' own ability to convey his faith and its teachings; on that trip to Jerusalem we find the twelve-year-old discoursing with the Jewish teachers.

Amid a devoutly Jewish family life, Joseph practiced a respectable trade: carpentry. According to Mark 6.3 Jesus himself was a carpenter, a worker of wood; and according to Matthew 13.55 so was his father. Joseph probably passed on the family trade to his sons, and so we may envision James as being trained in this trade as well.

Woodworking was viewed as a clean or ritually unobjectionable trade—unlike, for example, tanning hides, which meant one touched animal carcasses and became ritually unclean. It is possible that Jesus' family was involved in building some of the structures in Sepphoris, a town near Nazareth that was being turned into a grand Roman-style city during this time. There is both archaeological and literary evidence of the manufacturing of furniture in this vicinity.[8] While carpenters certainly did not rank at the high end of the social structure of society, neither were they on the low end; tenant farmers and day laborers were certainly poorer, as were shepherds and agricultural workers. Jesus should not be called a peasant. Furthermore, if there was a good deal of building going on nearby in Sepphoris, even a woodworker who simply built furniture might expect to make a living that could support the family.

We know that different Galilean villages specialized in different trades and that the wheat of Sepphoris was famous (Jerusalem Talmud Qam. 6D). It is thus possible that some of Jesus' family was involved in agricultural pursuits. Certainly both the parables of Jesus and some of the wisdom teaching found in the book of James strongly indicate that these men were familiar with various kinds of farming.

In sum, James was raised as the second oldest son in a religious family, in a region politically governed by a Greek-loving client monarch, with a father trying to make a living building furniture.

Family life in Jesus' day was quite different from what it is today. For one thing, almost all ancient Jewish marriages were arranged. In essence, marriage was a property transaction meant to secure the future of one family through an alliance with another. The society was heavily patriarchal, which meant that the marriages were arranged by the two male heads of their families. There was no dating or romance or courtship in the modern sense, but there was a formal betrothal, as was the case with Mary and Joseph. Betrothals carried a legal status: a formal action was required to dissolve one. In Jewish culture, unlike in the Greco-Roman world, all extramarital sexual activity was seen as immoral or sinful, especially in the case of women. Not only did the Jewish tradition strongly emphasize limiting one's sexual activity to the confines of marriage, it also stressed honoring one's parents (as we know from the Ten Commandments).

Keeping these values in mind, we appreciate the fine line Jesus walked in Luke 2.41–52:

> Now every year his parents went to Jerusalem for the festival of the Passover. And when he was twelve years old, they went up as usual for the festival. When the festival was ended and they started to return, the boy Jesus stayed behind in Jerusalem, but his parents did not know it. Assuming that he was in the group of travelers, they went a day's journey. Then they started to look for him among their relatives and friends. When they did not find him, they returned to Jerusalem to search for him. After three days they found him in the temple, sitting among the teachers, listening to them and asking them questions. And all who heard him were amazed at his understanding and his answers. When his parents saw him they were astonished; and his mother said to him, "Child, why have you treated us like this? Look, your father and I have been searching for you in great anxiety." He said to them, "Why were you searching for me? Did you not know that I must be in my Father's house?" But they did not understand what he said to them. Then he went

down with them and came to Nazareth, and was obedient
to them.

This story shows the strains of being a prophet and religious
trailblazer in one's own family setting, especially a family that
seems to have been quite traditionally observant. Still, in the end,
the account affirms that Jesus did try to obey his parents while
honoring God's call on his life.

Family could also include extended family, and it is interesting
that in his famous saying about prophets being without honor in
their own country Jesus mentions an increasingly narrow circle in
which that seemed to be true—in their hometown, among their
relatives, and within their own home (Mark 6.4). Jesus apparently
had relatives in Nazareth, but notice that he distinguishes them
from those within his own home. This probably suggests Jesus and
James did not live in an extended family situation involving other
married siblings or slaves within the household.

JAMES IN JESUS' MINISTRY

What would happen to a family in which the eldest son, who was
the chief or primary heir, decided not to continue in the family
business and support the family but instead embarked on a career as an itinerant teacher and preacher? Note that Jewish teachers at that time did not generally take their teaching activities on
the road. Jesus was a maverick in this regard, and it affected his
family. He may have followed John the Baptist's example. Also
note that Jesus made Capernaum, not Nazareth, his home base
during the ministry, which also would have affected his family. We
seldom dwell on the family Jesus left behind when he started his
ministry. The social structure of Jesus' family would have had to
change dramatically, especially if Joseph died before or during
the time of Jesus' ministry (the last time he is mentioned is
when Jesus is twelve). What would Jesus' departure have meant
for James?

Since James was probably the next oldest son in the family, responsibility for the welfare of the family would have fallen to him,

which might not have been entirely welcome. With this in mind, let's look at the story in Mark 3.20, 31–35:

> When his family heard [that Jesus was healing the sick and casting out demons], they went out to restrain him, for people were saying, "He has gone out of his mind.". . . Then his mother and his brothers came; and standing outside, they sent to him and called him. A crowd was sitting around him; and they said to him, "Your mother and your brothers and sisters are outside, asking for you." And he replied, "Who are my mother and my brothers?" And looking at those who sat around him, he said, "Here are my mother and my brothers! Whoever does the will of God is my brother and sister and mother."

This story shows that within the family there was very serious concern about Jesus' behavior. Indeed, the concern was so serious that, as the story goes, they came out apparently to take Jesus away from the crowds and back home because the family thought Jesus was "beside himself."

In a traditional culture in which honor and shame are dominant concerns, this is an important matter; for if some member of the family is bringing shame on the family, it becomes the family's responsibility to deal with the matter. When we couple this story with the statement in John 7.5 that the brothers didn't believe in Jesus, and the evidence of Joseph's apparent absence from the family at this point, then some interesting issues arise for someone like James. James becomes the de facto head of the family, along with his mother, and a good-faith effort is made to bring the potential stigma under control by bringing Jesus back into the family circle. Jesus, however, is having none of it. He says his primary family is the family of his associates and followers.

If James's views are reflected in John 7.3–5, where Jesus' brother goads him to make his miracles known in Jerusalem, it appears that James saw Jesus as something of a self-seeking messianic pretender. The situation seems to be similar to the sibling rivalry we find in the story of Joseph the patriarch and his brothers in Genesis 37. Notice in John 7.3–5 that Jesus does not go with his brothers up to Jerusalem but does then turn around and go to the festival without them. We see also that the brothers do recognize that Jesus is capable of performing miracles and doing remarkable things and also that he is someone with a following and indeed is seeking a following.

But if there was some distance between Jesus and his family during his ministry, how is it that James became leader of the Jerusalem church apparently from the outset? In Acts 1.14 we find Jesus' followers gathered together just prior to Pentecost: "All these were constantly devoting themselves to prayer, together with certain women, including Mary the mother of Jesus, *as well as his brothers*." Esteemed Bible scholar F. F. Bruce puts the issue well: "It might have been expected that the disgrace of his execution would confirm in their minds the misgivings which they had felt about him all along."[9] What happened to turn the brothers around?

If we need more proof that Jesus was somewhat estranged from his siblings, we need look no further than what happened at Jesus' death, when by all accounts he was not buried by his family or his inner circle of disciples, even though his mother may have been present at his death (see John 19.25–27). I suspect the issue of shame is primary here. If Jesus was perceived to have shamed the family during his ministry, the fact that he died in the most shameful way possible in the ancient world would possibly have been the final straw severing his siblings' ties to Jesus, unless something dramatic happened to rectify the matter afterward. Notice, too, that according to all the Gospels Jesus was buried not in a family plot but in the tomb of Joseph of Arimathea. This suggests there was no family plot in Jerusalem, which is no surprise since the family was only visiting Jerusalem during festival times while still residing in Nazareth.

This raises some interesting issues with regard to the burial box of James and his burial in Jerusalem. Presumably his would have been an isolated, not a family, burial, a burial by the Jewish Christians in Jerusalem. Perhaps in the end, James, like Jesus, had come to see the family of faith as his primary family. Notice as well that in all the accounts of Jesus' entombment, he is not buried in the ground but is laid out in a tomb (see Matthew 27.57–61). This is important, for it suggests that the practice of reburial in an ossuary was going to happen to Jesus once the flesh was no longer on the bones (though the Gospels proclaim that the process never got that far). There was then a potential precedent within the family for James's being laid out in a tomb and then his bones being transferred to an ossuary.

JAMES AND THE RESURRECTION OF JESUS

According to Acts 1.14, both Mary and the brothers of Jesus (but where were the sisters?) were present in the upper room praying at Pentecost when the Holy Spirit fell upon the followers of Jesus. How had it happened that James was present on this occasion when in fact he had not been a follower of Jesus during Jesus' earthly ministry? The answer to this question is found in Paul's first letter to the church in Corinth, which provides us with the earliest list of those who saw the risen Jesus.[10] Paul writes,

> I handed on to you as of first importance what I in turn had received: that Christ died for our sins in accordance with the scriptures, and that he was buried, and that he was raised on the third day in accordance with the scriptures, and that he appeared to Cephas [Peter], then to the twelve. Then he appeared to more than five hundred brothers and sisters at one time, most of whom are still alive, though some have died. Then he appeared to James, then to all the apostles. Last of all, as to one untimely born, he appeared also to me. (1 Corinthians 15.3–8)

This listing of those to whom Jesus appeared seems to be placed in chronological order, for Paul uses the Greek words for *then* and *afterward* more than once and concludes the list with himself using the qualifier "last of all." Paul is probably quoting an old witness list from Jerusalem, just as the traditions mentioned in verses 1–4 ("For I handed on to you as of first importance what I in turn had received," v. 3).

Paul first mentions an appearance to Peter, and then an appearance to the Twelve (which actually were the Eleven at that juncture, with the demise of Judas Iscariot), then an appearance to more than five hundred believers at once, most of whom are said to be still alive in the early 50s. Then there is mention of an appearance to James, then to all the apostles, and then finally to Paul. The list contains many interesting features, not the least of which is that the only names mentioned are Cephas and James. The main question here, then, is whether the James mentioned in this list is James the brother of Jesus or another James.

The list should be compared to what Paul says in 1 Corinthians 9.5: "Do we not have the right to be accompanied by a believing wife, as do the other apostles and the brothers of the Lord and Cephas?" If the apostle James, son of Zebedee, were meant by Paul when he says "James" in 1 Corinthians 15, there would be no reason to single him out from the other members of the Twelve. No, in this case Paul is talking about three appearances to individuals (Peter, James, and Paul), and also appearances to groups of people (the Twelve, the five hundred, the apostles). The Gospels do not mention the story of a resurrection appearance to James, but then the individual appearance to Peter/Cephas is not recounted either but only mentioned in passing in Luke 24.34.

If this list is in chronological order, then it is possible that the appearance to James came later, possibly in Galilee. Then again, if James was in Jerusalem for Passover, more likely it happened in Jerusalem. We do not know. But it is noteworthy that James is distinguished from both the Twelve and the apostles when it comes to appearances, which suggests he was not originally part of either group. Since James the brother of Jesus is the only James Paul mentions elsewhere in his letters, the reference here is surely to the person Paul calls a pillar of the Jerusalem church in Galatians 1 and the "Lord's brother."

It appears that James, like Paul, was a convert to the Jesus movement because at some juncture he saw the risen Jesus, for nothing prior to Easter can explain his having become such a follower of Jesus, much less a leader of Jesus' followers.

CONCLUSIONS

The true name of James is Jacob, and he was named after his grandfather and the patriarch of a much earlier era in Jewish history. James is listed among the brothers and sisters of Jesus and is always associated with Mary in the Gospels. He is identified as James the brother of the Lord by Paul.

James grew up in a devout Jewish family in Nazareth. James is never singled out from his siblings in the Gospel accounts, and we have no special stories in the New Testament about his individual accomplishments prior to the death of Jesus. What is notable is that wherever we have a list of Jesus' siblings, James is always mentioned first, which suggests he was the oldest of these other brothers and sisters and so the one most likely to be viewed as the head of the family, along with Mary, if Joseph and Jesus were both absent or deceased. The important story in John 7.3–5 indicates that Jesus' brothers were not among his disciples during his lifetime, though they seem to have believed he could work miracles and had messianic intentions. James's family could be called an ordinary working-class family, whose trade was woodworking or carpentry, and so they were certainly not peasants. The fact that Mark 6 shows that Jesus was literate and could read Hebrew suggests that the family, or at least the men in the family, had some education. The fact that they regularly attended festivals in Jerusalem speaks volumes about their devotion to their Jewish faith.

In all probability, it was the appearance of Jesus to James, probably in Jerusalem at the Passover in the year 30, that led to his not only becoming a follower of Jesus but also leader of the Jerusalem church. We find him in the company of the disciples prior to Pentecost (Acts 1.14). This suggests that he, like Mary and James's siblings, had been in Jerusalem when Jesus died, even though the account in John 19.25–27 mentions only Mary observing the crucifixion, and the synoptic Gospels (the first

three Gospels—Matthew, Mark, Luke—which contain many similar stories) do not show any of the family present at the cross.
Something dramatic must have happened to James after the
death of Jesus to account for his being included in Acts among
the disciples and later named as leader of the Jerusalem church.
It seems clear that it was Jesus' appearance to him that mainly accounts for his conversion to the movement and his rise to prominence.

1. See the discussion in Ben Witherington, *Women in the Ministry of Jesus*
(Cambridge: Cambridge University Press, 1984).

2. Of course, the normal birthing process involves blood and the delivery of
the afterbirth, and it is understandable how from an early Jewish point of view
this might be seen as making the mother temporarily ritually unclean.

3. This list dates to at least within twenty years of Jesus' death, while there
were still eyewitnesses alive, for Paul wrote 1 Corinthians in the early 50s.

4. Just as the name Jesus is a rendering of the Hebrew Yehoshua and Aramaic Yeshua (i.e., Joshua), by way of the Greek, which is Iesous.

5. The Mary, mother of James, of Luke 24.10 is surely not the mother of
Jesus, as the mother of Jesus is always identified in connection with Jesus. This
means the James in question in Luke 24.10 is also not Jesus' brother.

6. The term *Hellenizing* means trying to imitate Greek culture, customs, and
language. The term *Idumean* comes from the region of Edom. In the Old Testament, Jacob and Esau were sibling rivals, and in due course there was a rivalry between the nation of those who descended from Esau, called Edomites and then
Idumeans, and those who descended from Jacob. The term *Semite* is applied to a
wide range of Semitic peoples, including both Israelites and Edomites.

7. Both John the Baptist and Jesus were angry at Herod because they saw
him as polluting or destroying the biblical faith of the Jews. They were not
merely irked by his grandiose building efforts. Herod Antipas is not to be confused with Herod the Great, his father, who ruled all the land at the time of
Jesus' birth, sometime around 4–5 B.C. The land was divided between Herod the
Great's three sons, and Herod Antipas got Galilee and ruled there until late in
the A.D. 30s, or well after the death of Jesus in the year 30.

8. See J. F. Strange, "Galilee," in *The Dictionary of New Testament Background*,
ed. C. A. Evans and S. Porter (Downers Grove, IL: InterVarsity Press, 2000), 394.

9. F. F. Bruce, *Peter, James, and John* (Grand Rapids, MI: Eerdmans, 1979), 87.

10. The vast majority of scholars agree that Paul's letters are chronologically
the earliest New Testament documents, even though the Gospels generally
record earlier events than the events mentioned in Paul's letters.

8

FROM FOLLOWER TO HEAD OF THE JERUSALEM CHURCH

History, it is said, is written by the winners. We can understand, then, why there has been so much neglect of a figure like James, the brother of Jesus. His form of the early Christian movement waned and for the most part died out by the fourth century. The Petrine form of Christianity (derived from Peter) became dominant in the West and led to Roman Catholicism. In the East there remained pockets of something like Jewish Christianity, in Syria and elsewhere, but basically various forms of the Orthodox tradition (Coptic, Armenian, Syrian, Russian, Greek) arose and dominated the landscape.

In neither of these major streams of tradition did James play a dominant role, though in the Eastern Orthodox traditions he received more prominence than in the West. As if that were not enough, the sixteenth-century Reformation, which began in Germany and spread to Switzerland, England, Scotland, and elsewhere, embraced a form of Christianity largely shaped by Paul's views. In none of these forms of Christianity was James given his due. In fact, Reformer Martin Luther called the letter of James "an epistle of straw."

But in the world of the first-century church, the leaders of the new Christian movement were certainly Peter and Paul, but also James, the brother of Jesus and revered leader of the movement's "mother church" in Jerusalem, who was regarded by many as pre-eminent.

JAMES THE JUST

The apocryphal Gospel according to the Hebrews gives a fuller account of Jesus' postresurrection visit to his brother. It says that James took an oath to eat no bread until he saw the risen Jesus. When Jesus did finally appear to him, "He [Jesus] took bread, gave thanks, and broke it, and then gave it to James the Just, saying to him, 'My brother, eat your bread, because the Son of Man has risen from those who sleep.'"[1]

This document seems to come from the late second century, and from some Jewish Christian community that sees itself in continuity with James and the earliest Jewish Christians. While this story is legendary, it may well preserve several historical kernels about James that need to be considered. The trick is to figure out what is grounded in history and what reflects later Christian interests.

From the historical record, a few key attributes of James stand out. First, both within the Christian tradition and in first-century Jewish historian Josephus's work, James is presented as someone with a reputation for deep piety and righteous character. James is known as an "ascetic." Asceticism is the practice of abstaining from certain things, chiefly food and drink but sometimes also sexual activity and even all contact with other human beings, in an effort to purify one's life. This is why James came to be known as James the Just or James the Righteous.

This reputation means, among other things, that James took very seriously the importance of being faithful to both the Law and various Jewish traditions not specifically recorded in the Law. This tradition about James, in fact, matches what we learn of him from Paul's letter to the Galatians and from Luke's account of the early church in Acts 15, as we shall see.[2]

James was concerned with maintaining continuity with early Judaism, which meant continuing to keep the Law. He was at least in sympathy with the Pharisaic Jewish Christians. The Pharisees were a particular stream or sect of early Judaism who were noted for their concerns to maintain a clear sense of the boundary between Jewish and non-Jewish identity and practices, hence the emphasis on circumcision, sabbath keeping, ritual purity, and the like. Those Pharisees who became followers of Jesus took the position that new Christians had to keep the Law. While in the end James turned out to be a mediating figure between the Pharisaic Jewish Christians to his right and Paul and those interested in a Law-free gospel to his left James nevertheless did not allow concerns about inclusion of Gentiles in the church to dictate how Jewish Christians ought to live.

In addition to keeping the Jewish Law, James is also known for embracing ascetical practices. The Gospel of the Hebrews account mentioned earlier suggests that James followed a time-honored ascetical practice—fasting—in order to be able to see the risen Jesus. The decree in Acts 15, which James orchestrated and which resolved a dispute about how to incorporate Gentiles into the church, reflects a concern about food, and in particular where Gentiles should not eat, namely in the presence of idols in pagan temples. An ascetic Jew would have been very troubled by such a practice. Yet one should not push the ascetical reading of James too far, for Paul strongly implies in 1 Corinthians 9.5 that James and the other brothers of Jesus, unlike Jesus, were married.[3] Yet James was "Torah true" and believed in righteous deeds as an important part of being a follower of Jesus.[4] This is the meaning behind the famous utterance of James found in the New Testament letter of James 2: "faith without works is dead!" (vv. 14–26)

James's asceticism may have been shaped by his following of Old Testament teachings about Nazaritic vows, which did not require celibacy but did involve abstaining from some foods and normal practices, such as cutting one's hair (see Numbers 6). In Acts 21.24 James and the leaders in Jerusalem ask Paul to undertake a Nazaritic vow. Hegesippus, a church historian from the second century, and perhaps the Gospel of the Hebrews seem to confirm that James was a Nazarite or took on Nazaritic vows from time to time. This might explain why James got a reputation for spending time in the Temple, for Nazarites were to remain present in the vicinity of the Temple (Numbers 6.18–20). This theory could also explain why James stayed in Jerusalem and is never said to travel.[5]

Besides showing James as a Law keeper and an ascetic, the story from the apocryphal Gospel has another interesting feature. Jesus refers to himself as "the Son of Man." Paul never calls Jesus the Son of Man, and indeed outside the Gospels and one reference in Acts, this is a title applied to Jesus nowhere else in the New Testament, except in allusions to chapter 7 of the book of Daniel in the book of Revelation. It seems clear that because the title Son of Man did not mean to the Gentiles what it suggested in the book of Daniel, namely, that Jesus was both a human and divine figure, this title was soon abandoned in the Gentile mission.

Still, the term is the most common form of self-identification found on Jesus' lips in the Gospels. This suggests something important. Jewish Christianity, which continued well beyond the New Testament period, maintained continuity not only with its Jewish heritage but also with the heritage Jesus passed on to his followers, including the way that he spoke of himself as Son of Man.

LEADER OF THE EARLIEST CHURCH

James and the disciples of Jesus did not see themselves as Christians. They saw themselves as Jews who followed the Jewish Messiah. It needs to be kept squarely in view that these people did not view themselves as founding a new religion. When we talk about James as the head of the earliest church, we are not talking about the church as a separate religious entity. In the key debate in the Jerusalem church over whether Gentile Christians should have to follow the Law (including circumcision and dietary restrictions), James quotes from the Hebrew Bible (Amos 9) to make his point that the kingdom of God was always meant for the Gentiles as well as the Jews. James views the gospel message as a case of Old Testament promises to Jews being fulfilled, and of Gentiles joining a Jewish messianic movement centered on Jesus, not of Jews joining some new religion.

James and the earliest Jewish Christians need to be viewed as promoting a sectarian form of early Judaism, not unlike the Qumran sect did. (The Qumran sect, also called the Essenes, produced the Dead Sea Scrolls. The group was highly ascetic and served as a renewal movement within Judaism during Jesus' day. A significant number of its members lived at the Dead Sea apparently and sought to prepare for God's final intervention and judgment on the corruption in Israel.)

New Testament scholar Craig A. Evans puts the matter helpfully as we try to locate James and his church in the context of early Judaism:

> In sum, we could say that if we drew three circles to represent the Judaisms of Qumran, the Rabbis, and James, the circles would overlap. But the centers of these circles, centers which represent the essence of the respective Judaisms, would not. We would have three overlapping circles, but three distinct, separate centers. The Judaism of Qumran is focused on the renewal of the covenant, with great emphasis on cultic reform. The Judaism of the Rabbis is focused on studying and obeying the Torah, the key to life in this world and in the world to come. The Judaism of James is focused on faith and piety centered on Messiah Jesus.[6]

The early church saw itself as a Jewish sect. This is confirmed when we see that the language used on the inscription on the ossuary of James is Aramaic, not Greek, which would have been spoken in a Gentile or even a mixed gathering of Jews and Gentiles. Even in the decade of the 60s the Jewish character of this form of the Jesus movement was still dominant in Jerusalem. Because most Christians see their history as coming through the Gentile branch of the church, they are used to thinking of the Jesus movement as a largely Gentile affair dominated by Gentile concerns and customs by the A.D. 60s, which is to say, by the time Paul was concluding his missionary efforts. But that was not true of the mother church in Jerusalem. There was more than one strain of early Christianity, and the discovery of the ossuary reminds us of this in a powerful way.

But how did James so quickly become the leader of the Jerusalem church? We have already noted how James joined Jesus' followers soon after the resurrection but before Pentecost (Acts 1.14). But how soon after the founding of the church in Jerusalem (which occurred at Pentecost) did James assume its leadership?

Part of the answer is implied in Acts 1.14 itself. Why would the writer of Acts (Luke) mention "the brothers of Jesus" unless they were destined to play a leadership role?

We next encounter James in Acts 12, which begins with the story of the other main figure named James, the son of Zebedee and brother of John.[7] It seems King Herod Agrippa had become angered by the Christians and had "James, the brother of John, killed with the sword" (v. 2). Next he arrested Peter with the same goal in mind: "When he had seized him, he put him in prison and handed him over to four squads of soldiers to guard him, intending to bring him out to the people after the Passover" (v. 4). But while in prison, Peter got a visitor:

> Suddenly an angel of the Lord appeared and a light shone in the cell. He tapped Peter on the side and woke him, saying, "Get up quickly." And the chains fell off his wrists. The angel said to him, "Fasten your belt and put on your sandals." He did so. Then he said to him, "Wrap your cloak around you and follow me.". . . After they had passed the first and the second guard, they came before the iron gate leading into the city. It opened for them of its own accord, and they went outside and walked along a lane, when suddenly the angel left him. (Acts 12.7–10)

He experiences a humorous reunion with the local believers, who don't believe it is Peter at the door because they know he is in prison. Before leaving town to hide in Caesarea, Peter tells the assembled what happened and to "tell this to James and to the believers" (v. 17).

Notice the urgency of telling James. This suggests James already was an important leader at that time, which must have been in the A.D. 40s. John Painter has suggested that Acts 12 should be read as a flashback indicating how James the brother of Jesus came to leadership in the Jerusalem church, namely because Peter had to go elsewhere and the other James had been executed.[8] There is probably some truth in this assessment, but it is doubtful he rose to leadership simply by default. In fact, Eusebius, the fourth-century father of church history, does not recognize the leadership of Peter at all in the Jerusalem church. Indeed, in his *History of the Church (Historia Ecclesia)* he quotes Clement of Alexandria as saying that Peter, James, and John after the ascension of Jesus chose Jesus' brother James as the first bishop of Jerusalem (*Hist. Eccl.* 2.1.3). Allowing for the use of the later Christian term *bishop,* this tradition could well be grounded in fact. Eusebius has his own view, which is that when Stephen was martyred James became the leader (2.1.2).

Whatever the method of ascent, it seems clear that James was clearly a prominent leader in the Jerusalem church, if not its head, a decade after Jesus' death and resurrection.

DEBATING PAUL

The Epistle to the Galatians is one of Paul's earlier letters. It may well be his very first letter, written in about the year 49, before the major Jerusalem council mentioned in Acts 15.[9] In any case, it is a genuine Pauline letter that recognizes at an early date the great importance of James, as well as of Peter and John.

In the letter, Paul strongly opposes those who want to force Gentiles into becoming Jews in order to become Christians (by getting circumcised and following the Law). To set up his arguments he recalls his own journey from almost two decades before:

> I was violently persecuting the church of God and was trying to destroy it. . . . But when God . . . was pleased to reveal his Son to me, so that I might proclaim him among the Gentiles, I did not confer with any human being, nor

did I go up to Jerusalem to those who were already apostles before me, but I went away at once into Arabia, and
afterwards I returned to Damascus. Then after three years
I did go up to Jerusalem to visit Cephas and stayed with
him fifteen days; but I did not see any other apostle except James the Lord's brother. (Galatians 1.13–19)

We can date this meeting with Peter and James rather precisely. Paul says this visit transpired three years after his Damascus
road experience. This would certainly place the event in the 30s,
perhaps as early as the year 37.[10] This text, then, suggests that
within a few years of Jesus' death (which likely took place in 30)
James was already a recognized leader in Jerusalem of the Jesus
movement. Notice, too, that in this very earliest reference to
James in the New Testament (in that Galatians was one of the first
New Testament books to be written), he is distinguished from
other Jameses by being called "the Lord's brother." It appears
that the one label that was constantly applied to this James—
early, middle, and late in his life—is that he was the brother of
Jesus. So it is not at all surprising that he would be identified this
way on his ossuary as well.

Paul goes on to mention James again in connection with
Paul's second visit to Jerusalem, which happened about 48:

Then after fourteen years I went up again to Jerusalem
with Barnabas, taking Titus along with me. . . . When
James and Cephas [Peter] and John, who were acknowledged pillars, recognized the grace that had been given to
me, they gave to Barnabas and me the right hand of fellowship, agreeing that we should go to the Gentiles and
they to the circumcised. They asked only one thing, that
we remember the poor, which was actually what I was
eager to do. (Galatians 2.1–10)

This was the famine relief visit mentioned briefly in Acts
11.30, but it was also an occasion on which Paul had a private
meeting about his gospel and missionary work with the "pillars"—

James, Peter, and John. Keep in mind that Paul is being polemical in Galatians 2 and somewhat defensive about his gospel to the Gentiles. So when he refers to these men as "reputed to be leaders" (v. 2) or "reputed to be pillars" (v. 9), it is not because there was any doubt about their leadership. Rather, it reflects Paul's concerns about his own status and whether his mission to Gentiles would be recognized as legitimate. It also reflects the fact that early Jews placed importance on people's honor ratings, as in fact was common throughout the Greco-Roman world.

Notice also that in Galatians 2.9 James is listed first among the "pillars." What are we to make of this terminology?

The Greek term *stuloi*, "pillars," suggests that these three men—James, Peter, and John—are seen as the main supporting columns in the promised future temple or tent currently under construction by God through the gospel.[11] The word frequently occurs in the Greek version of the Old Testament (called the Septuagint or LXX) to refer to the supports of the Tabernacle, and later the columns of the Temple (1 Kings 7.15–22; 2 Chronicles 3.15–17). The earliest Christian leaders are thus seen as the supporting columns of the future, or "eschatological," people of God. (The term *eschatological* comes from the word *eschaton*, which means "end things." People in the first century believed that God's final saving and judging activity was already transpiring in their time.) The idea of leaders as the supporting columns appears also in Revelation 3.12: "If you conquer, I will make you a pillar in the temple of my God; you will never go out of it. I will write on you the name of my God, and the name of the city of my God, the new Jerusalem that comes down from my God out of heaven, and my own new name."

In early Judaism there was a great deal of speculation about the destruction and rebuilding of the Temple and about the people of God,[12] and Jesus himself had some things to say about this matter (Mark 14.58; see also John 2.19; Acts 6.14), as did Paul (1 Corinthians 3.16–17; 2 Corinthians 6.16). It is not surprising, then, that the earliest Jewish followers of Jesus believed that God was rebuilding his people as his new Temple and that James was one of the pillars in that reconstruction. It is thus all the more significant that James himself speaks about the rebuilding of God's people in Acts 15.16–17, under the metaphor of re-erecting David's tent (quoting from Amos 9). James believes that in the future God will rebuild the Jewish tent, which will in turn cause Gentiles to come into it.[13]

We see also in Galatians 2.9 that Paul mentions being given "the right hand of fellowship." He had expressed a fear of working in vain, unless the pillars approved his mission and gospel. This makes perfectly clear the degree of importance and authority that James and the Jerusalem leaders had not only in Paul's eyes, but also in the eyes of the church at large. The phrase "give the right hand" is the gracious gesture of a person in a superior position (see Josephus, *Ant.* 18.328–29). This tells us that already in the decade of the 30s James is a major leader of the Jesus movement. And there is even more to be learned about James from Galatians.

Paul goes on to relate an incident in connection with Peter that transpired in Antioch in the mid–40s:

> But when Cephas [Peter] came to Antioch, I opposed him to his face, because he stood self-condemned; for until certain people came from James, he used to eat with the Gentiles. But after they came, he drew back and kept himself separate for fear of the circumcision faction. And the other Jews joined him in this hypocrisy, so that even Barnabas was led astray by their hypocrisy. (Galatians 2.11–13)

There was obviously a problem with regard to Jewish and Gentile believers eating together in Antioch. Paul tells us that James sent some men from Jerusalem to check out the situation. According to Galatians 2.12, Peter withdrew from fellowship meals with Gentiles when these men from James arrived. This in itself suggests that James was the recognized head of the Jerusalem church, such that even Peter deferred to his judgment. Notice that it does not say the men came from the Jerusalem church but rather that they came from James himself.

We see in the three references to James in Galatians 1–2 the gradual ascendancy of James over the Jerusalem church. Peter is mentioned first in the earliest reference in Galatians 1.18, but thereafter James is mentioned first and seems to be in control of things. This impression is confirmed in Acts 15 at the famous council meeting. There Peter and Paul confer, but James is the one who concludes the matter. We will say more about this crucial meeting in the next chapter.

Let us be clear about what Acts and Paul, and not just later Christian tradition, suggest about James as leader in the Jerusalem church. First, the book of Acts does not use the term *bishop* to refer to him. The leaders in Jerusalem are called elders in Acts 11.30 in continuity with the Jewish tradition, and in Acts 15.2 they are called apostles and elders. First Corinthians 9.5 speaks of the other apostles and the Lord's brothers, but there the Lord's brothers and the apostles are distinguished. And as we have seen, Galatians suggests that James is a pillar, indeed apparently the chief pillar, of the Jerusalem Christian community, which was viewed as the reconstituting of God's people in the eschatological age.

No one ever suggests that James was an itinerant apostle. He apparently never traveled. Rather, he was always in Jerusalem; people came to see him, and he sent out emissaries and messages to other communities. Perhaps this is why he is not usually called an apostle in Christian tradition, for the term *apostolos* refers to one sent out, to be an agent or a missionary. Neither, for that matter, is James later called pope. He is, however, certainly listed in the earliest lists of bishops of Jerusalem in two early Christian sources: Eusebius (*Hist. Eccl.* 4.5.3–4; 5.12.1–2) and Epiphanius (*Pan.* 66.21–22).[14]

No honorific title is applied to James on the ossuary. Such titles were not uncommon in grave inscriptions in the first century, but there is none on James's ossuary. He is simply the "son of Joseph, brother of Jesus." This is consistent with the letter James wrote that is included in the New Testament. He begins it simply as "James, a servant of God and of the Lord Jesus Christ" (James 1.1). There is no evidence that he insisted on some exalted title.

What Paul says in Galatians 2 is that he is reputed to be a pillar, which implies someone else's way of giving James an honor rating. Nevertheless, both Galatians and Acts make very apparent how important James was. If an independent-minded missionary apostle like Paul felt he needed James's support for his work not to be in vain, and if Luke portrayed him in Acts 15 as the one who resolved the major crisis prompted by the Antioch incident, James was clearly a central figure in early Christianity.

This bears emphasizing precisely because, of the "big three"—Peter, James, and Paul—it is almost always James who gets neglected in the discussion. It makes sense since Paul wrote or is said to have written some 40 percent of the New Testament. The success of Paul's Gentile mission pushed Christianity in an increasingly Gentile direction as the first century progressed. Of course, Peter is a major figure in the Gospels and Acts, and two letters attributed to him are included in the New Testament. He later took on enormous significance for the church in Rome and the Roman Catholic tradition. James has labored long in the shadow of these two towering figures. Yet it is James that both Peter and Paul answer and defer to, according to Galatians 1–2 and Acts 15.

TROUBLE IN ANTIOCH

We have already spoken of the fact that Galatians 2 records an incident in Antioch that transpired around the year 48 that involved tensions between James, Peter, and Paul and more broadly between Jewish and Gentile Christians. In the early days of the Jesus movement, Antioch was the most important city after Jerusalem, and possibly Damascus, in terms of winning followers among both Jews and Gentiles. The third largest city in the Roman Empire, Antioch now bears the name Antakya in modern Turkey.

According to Luke, Antioch is the city where Jesus' followers were first called *Christianoi,* or "Christians," which literally means those who belong or adhere to Christ, and *Christ* of course comes from *christos* in Greek, which means "the anointed one" or, in Jewish terms, the messiah (Acts 11.26). A significant number of Gentiles came to Christ in that city, and those conversions raised the issues of table fellowship and also the more serious matter of whether Gentiles would be required to conform fully to the Mosaic Law in order to be followers of Jesus, including whether they were to be circumcised.

There is no doubt that a good number of Jewish followers of Jesus in Jerusalem believed that Gentiles must become Jews in order to be followers of Jesus, indeed, in order to be saved. Was this James's view as well?

Some scholars have thought so and have imagined a major split between James and Paul on this issue. The evidence, however, does not really support this conclusion.

The mention in Galatians 2 of men coming "from James" to Antioch and causing a disturbance should be coordinated with what Luke says in Acts 15: "Then certain individuals came down from Judea and were teaching the brothers, 'Unless you are circumcised according to the custom of Moses, you cannot be saved'" (v. 1). In Galatians Paul says that even Peter and Barnabas stopped accepting Gentile hospitality because of their teaching. But the teaching also brought Paul and Barnabas into sharp dispute with these representatives of the Jerusalem church. When the dispute was brought back to Jerusalem, Luke says that "some believers who belonged to the sect of the Pharisees stood up and said, 'It is necessary for them to be circumcised and ordered to keep the law of Moses'" (15.5).

It is natural to conclude that the group that went to Antioch belonged to the Pharisaic Christians in Jerusalem. This might well explain why Paul exploded about this matter in Galatians 2. After all, Paul had left his Pharisaic loyalties behind when he gave his allegiance to Jesus. He believed that the Mosaic Law should not be imposed on Gentile converts, viewing it as neither necessary nor sufficient for their salvation. From Paul's viewpoint, some in Jerusalem did not understand the radical implications of a gospel that proclaimed salvation by grace through faith in Jesus as a means of entering the community of God's people. Paul accused these Pharisaic Jewish Christians of trying to "Judaize" his converts, not just in Antioch, but also in Galatia. Indeed, this very matter is what prompted him to write his letter to the neophyte Galatian Christians.

The crucial question became: How then should believers live as Jews and Gentiles in Christ? Would there be separate communities for each kind of Christian? But how then would that fulfill the prophecies about the reconstruction of God's people, including the incorporation of Gentiles into that people? No issue was more crucial to the Jesus movement in the middle of the first century A.D. Standing right at the heart of the matter with Peter and Paul was James, and it was he who would resolve the matter, as we shall see in the next chapter.

CONCLUSIONS

It is clear James was a crucial early leader of the Jesus movement, known for his Jewish piety and faithfulness to the Torah. Indeed, he gained a reputation early on for being something of an ascetic. This aspect of his faith should not be exaggerated since, unlike his brother Jesus, he was married.

James is viewed in Paul's letter to the Galatians as a pillar of the new church, understood as the "eschatological" or future Temple known as the people of God. It is clear that at least by the time of the events recorded in Acts 12, he was the leader of the Jerusalem church, which is further confirmed in Acts 15 and Galatians 2. Others conferred, but James concluded. Others evangelized or acted as apostles or missionaries, but James authorized. It was James who wrote the encyclical letter to the Gentile Christians according to Acts 15, and it was James who wrote the encyclical letter to Jewish Christians that we call the letter of James in the New Testament. James stood at the center of things; missions and messengers went out from him and came back and reported to him. Even in the late 50s, Paul was still gathering money to take to James and the "saints" of the Jerusalem church in hopes of cementing the union of Jew and Gentile (see Romans 15).

But what kind of leader was James? Was he a partisan for hard-line Jewish Christianity that would make it difficult for Gentiles to follow Jesus? Or was he more of a mediating figure?

1. One of the more helpful recent treatments of our subject is John Painter's *Just James* (Columbia: University of South Carolina Press, 1997).

2. Lest we think James is the only one who had such tendencies among the earliest Jewish followers of Jesus, Paul tells us that in Rome there were Jewish Christians who did not eat meat and abstained from wine as well; see Romans 14.2, 21.

3. This is an important text, and not to be lightly dismissed. It shows that the later extremely ascetical portrait of James is likely to be an exaggeration.

4. *Torah* refers to the Old Testament in general, or more specifically to the Pentateuch, the first five books of the Bible attributed to Moses, and even more narrowly to the Law within those books.

5. The vows of the Nazarite are discussed in Numbers 6. This text says that if someone wants to vow to be "separate" to the Lord in a special way they must abstain from wine and wine vinegar and grape juice and grapes or raisins. They must abstain from shaving the hair on their heads, and they must never go near a corpse. This vow is normally seen as a temporary one, for the same chapter specifies that when the vow is over they are to shave their heads and offer sacrifices. On the theory of James being a Nazarite, see Bruce Chilton, "James in Relation to Peter, Paul, and the Remembrance of Jesus," in *The Brother of Jesus* (Nashville: Westminster/John Knox, 2001), 146–47. I am also indebted to Richard J. Bauckham's forthcoming essay on Acts 21 and James's last meeting with Paul.

6. Craig A. Evans, "Comparing Judaisms: Qumranic, Rabbinic, and Jacobean Judaisms Compared," in *Brother of Jesus,* 182.

7. Acts 12.2 and 12.17, once compared, make very clear that one should never make the mistake of identifying James the son of Zebedee and James the brother of Jesus. On the historical reliability of this and other traditions in Acts, see Ben Witherington, *The Acts of the Apostles* (Grand Rapids, MI: Eerdmans, 1998).

8. Painter, *Just James,* 43.

9. See the discussion in Ben Witherington, *Grace in Galatia* (Grand Rapids, MI: Eerdmans, 1998).

10. See the discussion in the appendix in Ben Witherington, *The Paul Quest* (Downers Grove, IL: InterVarsity Press, 1998).

11. See the fine essay by Richard J. Bauckham, "For What Offense Was James Put to Death?" in *James the Just and Christian Origins,* ed. Bruce Chilton and Craig A. Evans (Leiden: Brill, 1999), 199–231.

12. See Ezek. 40–48; Jub. 1.17–28; 1 Enoch 90.28–29; 11QTemple; Test. Ben. 9.2.

13. See the essay by Richard J. Bauckham, "James and the Gentiles (Acts 15.13–21)," in *History, Literature, and Society in the Book of Acts,* ed. Ben Witherington (Cambridge: Cambridge University Press, 1996), 154–84.

14. See the discussion in Richard J. Bauckham, *Jude and the Relatives of Jesus in the Early Church* (Edinburgh: T & T Clark, 1990), 71–72.

9

JAMES, MEDIATOR BETWEEN JEWS AND GENTILES

Nearly all scholars agree that Acts 15 provides us with Luke's perspective on one of the most important of all early church events, the so-called Jerusalem Council. Luke's perspective would also represent Paul's view, since Luke was a close associate of Paul. Unlike the meeting Paul refers to in Galatians 2, which was private, this was the most public and potentially volatile of all early church meetings. Had Paul been describing the same meeting in Galatians 2 as we find in Acts 15, he certainly would have cited the Jerusalem Decree to his Galatian converts, for it meant they were not required to undergo circumcision. (The silence of Galatians with regard to the Jerusalem church's deciding Gentiles did not have to be circumcised is deafening.)

At the midpoint of the first century, in about the year 49, James presided over the first major turning point in early Christian history. Doubtless there would not have been a council at all if there had not been considerable success in the Gentile mission, indeed so much success that it threatened to overwhelm the original Jewish Christian flavor of the Jesus movement and turn it into something else altogether. According to Luke, Paul's first missionary journey (mentioned in Acts 13–14) coupled with the crisis in Antioch (mentioned in Acts 12) had made it necessary to address the issue of whether Gentiles could be accepted as followers of Jesus without becoming Jews (or at least proselytes or God-fearers).

But another important factor was at work here. Earlier that same year, 49, the emperor Claudius expelled Jews and Jewish Christians from Rome because of a row over Christ.[1] On any showing, A.D. 49 was a tumultuous year, and one can well imagine that Jewish Christians in Jerusalem, especially the Pharisaic ones, were feeling on edge and possibly worried about a reaction throughout the empire as the Jesus movement emerged from the synagogue and took on a life of its own. What would happen if it became the generally received opinion in the empire that the Jesus movement was not just another form of early Judaism, which had established itself with Rome as a respected ancient religion, but rather a new superstition not protected by Roman tolerance for ancient and indigenous religions of various peoples such as the Jews?

In general, Romans allowed conquered peoples to keep their native religion but required them to add to it the Roman cults, particularly the cult of the emperor. Jews were a special case since they were monotheists and would not accept the worship of additional deities. Romans tended to be accepting of ancient religions, which had a long pedigree, but not new ones, especially if they came from the East and threatened to disrupt the political stability of the region. When the Christian movement began to emerge from within Judaism, it no longer was perceived as an ancient and lawful religion. It was therefore subject to close scrutiny and potential prohibitions, and its practitioners would be expected to venerate the emperor as well. This problem became acute from the time of Nero's persecutions in the 60s, and the fall of Jerusalem in A.D. 70, onward.

Nerves were undoubtedly on edge when Paul and Barnabas came to Jerusalem for this meeting. The Jerusalem church perhaps rightly felt that Jews would not be attracted to the Jesus movement if they thought that Jesus' followers were not expecting their converts to remain faithful to the Mosaic Law in some way. But how to adjudicate this matter without compromising the heart of the gospel preached to Gentiles and Jews, namely, salvation by grace through faith in Jesus? Who constituted the people of God, and on what basis? What place did Gentiles have within the people of God? Crucial issues were at stake.

Here is how Luke sets up and records the proceedings:

> When they [Paul and Barnabas] came to Jerusalem, they were welcomed by the church and the apostles and the elders, and they reported all that God had done with them. But some believers who belonged to the sect of the Pharisees stood up and said, "It is necessary for them to be circumcised and ordered to keep the law of Moses."
>
> The apostles and the elders met together to consider this matter. After there had been much debate, Peter stood up and said to them, "My brothers, you know that in the early days God made a choice among you, that I should be the one through whom the Gentiles would hear the message of the good news and become believers. And God, who knows the human heart, testified to them by giving them the Holy Spirit, just as he did to us; and in cleansing their hearts by faith he has made no distinction between them and us. Now therefore why are you putting God to the test by placing on the neck of the disciples a yoke that neither our ancestors nor we have been able to bear? On the contrary, we believe that we will be saved through the grace of the Lord Jesus, just as they will." The whole assembly kept silence, and listened to Barnabas and Paul as they told of all the signs and wonders that God had done through them among the Gentiles. (Acts 15.4–12)

As we can see, Peter enters the discussion by taking the Pauline view of the matter. This is appropriate since the first Gentile convert came through Peter (see the account of Cornelius's conversion in Acts 10). Paul and Barnabas simply recount the miraculous signs and wonders God did among the Gentiles when they were on their missionary tour.

The next person to step up to address the meeting was James.

THE SPEECH OF JAMES

The Pharisaic Christian position did not prevail because James did not agree to require circumcision of Gentiles. Neither did James simply echo Peter's speech. James was a mediator, and he took a mediating position on these volatile issues. James's speech followed immediately after Paul and Barnabas gave their report:

> After they finished speaking, James replied, "My brothers, listen to me. Simeon [a variant of the Hebrew Shimon, translated into English as Simon and referring here to Peter] has related how God first looked favorably on the Gentiles, to take from among them a people for his name. This agrees with the words of the prophets, as it is written, 'After this I will return, and I will rebuild the dwelling of David, which has fallen; from its ruins I will rebuild it, and I will set it up, so that all other peoples may seek the Lord—even all the Gentiles over whom my name has been called. Thus says the Lord, who has been making these things known from long ago.'" (Acts 15.13–18)

James picks up where Peter left off. He seems to be providing scriptural support for Peter's argument that the Gentiles should not be required to keep the entire Mosaic Law.[2]

We can find many verbal similarities between this speech (especially 15.13: "My brothers, listen to me. Simeon has related how God first looked favorably on the Gentiles, to take from among them a people for his name") and statements in the letter of James (see 2.5: "Listen, my beloved brothers and sisters. Has not God chosen the poor in the world to be rich in faith and to be heirs of the kingdom that he has promised to those who love him?"). Both of these passages speak of the action of God in choosing a people.

This is the only time in Luke and Acts (both written by Luke) that Peter is called Simeon, the literal Semitic form of his name. This suggests that James was speaking in Aramaic when he gave this speech. In any case, Luke is highlighting the Jewishness of James's language by using this form of the name.

As we now have it, James's speech is in Greek. And, as is the case throughout Acts, the Septuagint, or Greek version of the Old Testament, is cited, probably because it was the only version Luke had access to and knew.[3] But would Aramaic-speaking James have used the Septuagint to make his point?

The case that James makes is based on the Greek rendering of Amos 9.12 rather than on the Hebrew version of that verse, which is a bit different. The Hebrew text speaks of possessing "the remnant of Edom, and all the nations that bear my name." The Greek Old Testament, however, reads, "So that the remnant of Adam [that is, "people"] and all the nations that bear my name may seek the Lord."

We see here two significant changes: (1) *Edom* becomes *Adam,* so that the verse refers not to Israel's rival but to all peoples descended from Adam, presumably with the exception of the Jews; (2) the idea of "possessing" does not appear in the Septuagint, replaced by an added clause about the pagan nations being able to seek the Lord.

James is clearly quoting an edited version of the Septuagint text. As Richard Bauckham, an expert in early Jewish and Jewish Christian ways of handling Scripture, has shown, it was exceedingly common to use the version of a scriptural passage most likely to support the point to be made.[4] In this case, using the Septuagint was all the more apt since it was the version most used in the Diaspora (the areas outside Judea where Jews lived) and likely to be known by Gentile God-fearers and proselytes (Gentile converts to Judaism).

In fact, in his Scripture citation it appears that James is combining Amos 9.11–12 ("On that day I will raise up the booth of David that is fallen, and repair its breaches, and raise up its ruins, and rebuild it as in the days of old; so that they may possess the remnant of Adam and all the nations who are called by my name, says the LORD who does this" LXX) and Zechariah 2.11 ("Many nations shall join themselves to the LORD on that day, and shall be my people; and I will dwell in your midst. And you shall know that the LORD of hosts has sent me to you").

The point of this biblical citation is to show that God would rebuild David's fallen tent and that Gentiles would then be included in the people of God. James seems to be an early advocate of restoration of Israel theology. The Lord returns to rebuild Israel's tent *so that* all other peoples may seek the Lord. James's point is that no one should be surprised at the influx of Gentiles in the present eschatological time (time of fulfillment) since it was prophesied long ago. It appears that this speech is meant to prepare the audience to hear James's support for including Gentiles in the Jesus movement without requiring that they simply become Jews and keep the entire Mosaic Law. What, then, was the nature of the compromise James offered the divided Christian body on that day?

THE DECREE

After James quoted the prophet Amos, he continued:

> Therefore I have reached the decision that we should not trouble those Gentiles who are turning to God, but we should write to them to abstain only from things polluted by idols and from fornication and from whatever has been strangled and from blood. For in every city, for generations past, Moses has had those who proclaim him, for he has been read aloud every sabbath in the synagogues. (Acts 15.18–21)

When he finished speaking, the decree was presented in written form:

> Then the apostles and the elders, with the consent of the whole church, decided to choose men from among their members and to send them to Antioch with Paul and Barnabas. They sent Judas called Barsabbas, and Silas, leaders among the brothers, with the following letter: "The brothers, both the apostles and the elders, to the believers of Gentile origin in Antioch and Syria and Cili-

cia, greetings. Since we have heard that certain persons who have gone out from us, though with no instructions from us, have said things to disturb you and have unsettled your minds, we have decided unanimously to choose representatives and send them to you, along with our beloved Barnabas and Paul, who have risked their lives for the sake of our Lord Jesus Christ. We have therefore sent Judas and Silas, who themselves will tell you the same things by word of mouth. For it has seemed good to the Holy Spirit and to us to impose on you no further burden than these essentials: that you abstain from what has been sacrificed to idols and from blood and from what is strangled and from fornication. If you keep yourselves from these, you will do well. Farewell." (Acts 15.22–29)

After these two versions of the decree, we see it referred to again in another encounter involving James and Paul in Acts 21.25: "But as for the Gentiles who have become believers, we have sent a letter with our judgment that they should abstain from what has been sacrificed to idols and from blood and from what is strangled and from fornication."

Unfortunately, there are slight variations in these versions of the decree. The version that is likely the earliest, providing an explanation for the later modifications, is the version that names abstention from the following items: (1) meat sacrificed to idols (*eidolothuton*), (2) blood, (3) things strangled, and (4) fornication (*porneia*). If Gentiles avoid these items, then fellowship with Jewish Christians is possible.

But what is the import of these items for Gentiles, and what is James really asking? Is James actually imposing on Gentiles the food laws in Leviticus (for example, 17.10: "If anyone of the house of Israel or of the aliens who reside among them eats any blood, I will set my face against that person who eats blood, and will cut that person off from the people")? Or is he perhaps quoting the restrictions given to Noah by God in Genesis 9.3–4 ("You shall not eat flesh with its life, that is, its blood")? The latter is often how the decree has been interpreted, but there are problems with this view.

For one thing, Genesis 9.3–4 is about abstaining from meat with blood in it, and nothing is said about "idol meat" or associations with pagan worship. Furthermore, the restrictions in Genesis 9 were regarded in early Judaism as applying to Gentiles living in Israel, not to Gentiles living in the Diaspora. Nothing is said about sexual immorality in this Genesis text.

What then of Leviticus 17 and 18? Is James appealing to this text and applying it to Gentiles? Again, these are rules for Gentiles living within Israel, not for the Gentiles being addressed in the letter that the Jerusalem church sent out. Leviticus 17.10–14 prohibits the eating of blood but nothing more. Nothing in the text mentions anything about food eaten in the presence of idols. Nor is anything said about things strangled, nor is the term *porneia* (fornication) used, a term that describes sexual aberrations occurring between people too closely related by blood. Are these Levitical restrictions really what James wanted to impose on Gentiles? It seems unlikely, especially since there is another, and much more likely, explanation of the decree.

Let us suppose that the decree was as much about venue as it was about eating and sexual immorality. Then we might ask, Where would Gentiles regularly encounter and be tempted by these four items? What would be the most basic requirements that God requires of people? Obviously the Ten Commandments suggest that a person must give up idolatry and immorality to properly worship the God of the Bible. This is most likely what James is requiring in the decree, by saying, in effect, "Stay away from pagan temples where there is idol worship involving idol meat and blood and things strangled and sexual immorality."[5]

James is requiring, then, that Gentiles forsake their pagan past, with its idolatry and immorality, and give up attending the worship and banquets found in pagan temples. Temples, priests, and sacrifices were the essence of pagan religion in antiquity. Often the sacrifices were performed ritually in the context of festivals and feasts. Pagan temples became like some modern clubs, with guilds and associations and groups and individuals socializing and conducting business with their friends. For Gentiles to stop going to pagan temples did not mean just refraining from participating in pagan rituals. It meant giving up a large part of their social networking.

James is not imposing food laws per se on Gentiles. If Gentiles would consistently do what James requests, it would be a witness to Jews in the empire that the heart of the Ten Commandments was being honored. We know from a text like 1 Corinthians 8–10, which discusses the very matter of attending idol feasts, that Gentile Christians were tempted to continue following that social practice even after their conversion, and we know that Paul warned that it was scandalizing Jewish Christians, as well as Jews in Corinth. In my view, Paul is implementing the decree in that instance.

The implications of this interpretation of the decree are important for our understanding of James. James is not imposing on Gentiles a modicum of food laws from the Old Testament. He is rather urging a hard-and-fast break with their pagan past, especially with pagan worship and dining practices in temples. In this regard, James and Paul are by no means far apart.[6]

Where James and Paul apparently differed was on whether Jewish Christians, not Gentiles, should be required to continue observing the Mosaic Law. Paul's answer was no, it could be a blessed option but was not required (see 1 Corinthians 9). James's answer apparently was yes, it was required that Jewish Christians continue to be observant, not least because of the hope of winning more Jews to the following of Jesus.

The divide would come, then, over what Jewish Christians would be expected to do to have fellowship with the ever-increasing majority of Gentile Christians. Some Jewish Christians would be willing to become temporarily unclean through dining with Gentiles and then go through ritual purification. Others would not be willing to do this, and so a stream of strongly Jewish Christianity would go its own way, having very little contact or fellowship with Gentile Christians. What then of the letter to Gentiles in the Diaspora?

THE LETTER TO GENTILES

The peaceful tone of the letter found in Acts 15.23–29 is immediately apparent. It mentions that the Jerusalem church recognizes that some went out from them and upset the Gentiles, doing so without authorization. This is why they sent two representatives of the Jerusalem church, Judas and Silas, with Paul and Barnabas to convey or interpret the sense of the letter and the decree it contained.

There is also a concern about burdening the Gentiles (15.28), an issue raised by Peter in his speech (15.10). Beyond the few items listed in the decree, nothing was to be added. Judas and Silas are described as prophets, that is, people in tune with the Spirit inspiring them to present the decree faithfully.

Notice that Paul and Barnabas are not entrusted with the letter's delivery or interpretation. Those are the responsibilities of the representatives of the Jerusalem church. So Paul and Barnabas could be accused of slanting the decree in a direction the Jerusalem church would not necessarily endorse. This shrewd maneuver avoided that possible obstacle.

Overall, the picture of James is of a compromiser who was flexible enough not to stifle the Gentile mission. And if the test of good leadership is that the leader does not take the easiest way out but rather chooses the option that is best for all concerned, then James meets that test. This will become apparent in the next account that refers to James, namely, the story of James's final meeting with Paul, recorded in Acts 21.

JAMES AND THE ARREST OF PAUL

Paul was on any showing a controversial figure, and his statement in 1 Corinthians 9.20–21 that he could become the Jew to the Jew and the Gentile to the Gentile, because he was no longer under the Mosaic Law but rather under the Law of Christ, was bound to raise many eyebrows among Jews in Jerusalem and elsewhere.

In Acts 21 we find an example of this pragmatic approach to Jewish customs. Paul is asked by James to demonstrate that he

James, the brother of Jesus, holds a scroll in this late-thirteenth-century gilded portrait by an Italian artist remembered only as the Master of Saint Francis. Called a "pillar of the church" by Paul, James led the Jerusalem church after Jesus' death.

"James, son of Joseph, brother of Jesus" reads the Aramaic inscription incised into the side of this 20- by 10- by 12-inch limestone box, called an ossuary. Of the roughly 900 catalogued ossuaries from this period, 250 bear inscriptions, most of which simply identify the deceased and his father. The addition of the brother's name is highly unusual; we have only one other example.

Photos © Oded Golan, Drawing: Ada Yardeni

◀── read right to left

Jesus	of	brother	Joseph	son of	Jacob (James)
Yeshua	d	achui	Yosef	bar	Ya'akov
ישוע	ד	אחוי	יוסף	בר	יעקוב

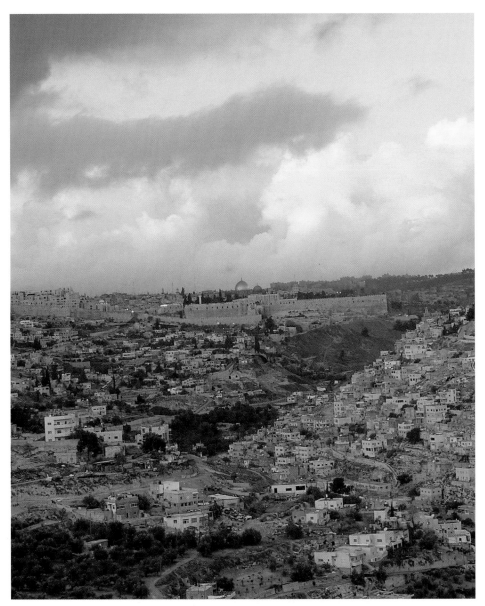

In this view of Jerusalem from the south, the golden Dome of the Rock is visible on the Temple Mount, the walled platform that supported the Jewish Temple until it was destroyed by the Romans in A.D. 70. The low ridge just south of the Temple Mount is the City of David (center), the site of the earliest Jerusalem settlement. The Kidron Valley separates the City of David from the Arab village of Silwan, on the hillside at lower right. The James ossuary was allegedly discovered in Silwan, an area pockmarked with ancient burial caves.

Garo Nalbandian, Jerusalem

An elegant entrance leads to a family burial cave in Akeldama, a burial ground just southwest of the City of David, where the Kidron and Hinnom Valleys meet. Although the New Testament identifies Akeldama as the potter's field where Judas hanged himself after betraying Jesus, the first-century A.D. graves found here are far too grand to have been used for poor strangers.

Garo Nalbandian, Jerusalem

A monumental rosette decorates the ceiling of one of Akeldama's most magnificent tombs. Arched niches carved into the cave wall originally held corpses and ossuaries. Called *kokhim* in Hebrew, the niches are typically 2 feet tall, 1.5 feet wide, and 6 feet deep.

Garo Nalbandian, Jerusalem

Masterfully decorated with swirling rosettes and palm fronds, this ossuary contained the remains of six people, including a sixty-year-old man believed to be Caiaphas, the high priest who presided over the trial of Jesus.

Photo: Garo Nalbandian/Collection Israel Antiquities Authority

The Aramaic inscription "Joseph son of Caiaphas" is roughly scratched on the side and the back (not shown) of the ossuary. Although the New Testament identifies the priest simply as Caiaphas, the first-century A.D. Jewish historian Josephus calls him "Joseph who was called Caiaphas of the high priesthood."

Israel Antiquities Authority Drawing: Ronny Reich

⟵ read right to left

Qafa	bar	Yehosef
Caiaphas	son of	Joseph

Mary tenderly embraces Jesus as they flee Bethlehem and King Herod's threat to slay any babes born there (Matthew 2:16). Joseph gazes back in concern, while a young boy—Joseph's son from a previous marriage, probably James—leads the ass, in Giotto's early-fourteenth-century fresco of the *Flight into Egypt,* from the Arena Chapel in Padua, Italy. Roman Catholic tradition maintains the doctrine of the perpetual virginity of Mary by identifying the brothers of Jesus as "kin" or "cousins." In the Orthodox tradition that informed this painting, however, they are Joseph's sons by an earlier wife.

After traveling nearly 6,000 miles from Tel Aviv, suffering
serious cracks in transit, and then being successfully
restored, the ossuary of "James, son of Joseph, brother of
Jesus" had its first-ever public display at the Royal Ontario
Museum in Toronto in November and December 2002.

Brian Boyle, Royal Ontario Museum, Toronto

OH, MY GOD!

2,000-year-old relic linked to Jesus cracked on way to ROM
— Page 3

AFTER

BEFORE

— Royal Ontario Museum/Reuters

— Shanks' Biblical Archaeology Review/AP

A LIMESTONE box said to have contained the bones of Jesus' brother James was found to have cracks in it yesterday when the crate it was travelling in was opened by Royal Ontario Museum staff. The box, called an ossuary, arrived in Toronto after being shipped from Israel via New York. ROM said it will be repaired and ready for its international public debut Nov. 16.

The front page of the Canadian tabloid the *Toronto Sun* on Saturday, November 2, 2002, best captured the shock and dismay the public felt upon learning that the ossuary of James, the brother of Jesus, had been severely cracked during its trip from Tel Aviv to Toronto.

respects the Law by submitting to a vow of sorts. This ironically proves to be Paul's undoing, for while he is in the Temple precincts he is recognized and labeled as one who teaches Gentiles to break the Mosaic Law.

The story in Acts is told by Luke, who was probably present with Paul in Jerusalem when Paul had delivered the collection, a gift from the Gentile churches to the Jerusalem church for famine relief in about the year 58 (see Paul's descriptions of this endeavor in 1 Corinthians 16, 2 Corinthians 8–9, and Romans 15.25–27).

> When we arrived in Jerusalem, the brothers welcomed us warmly. The next day Paul went with us to visit James; and all the elders were present. After greeting them, he related one by one the things that God had done among the Gentiles through his ministry. When they heard it, they praised God. Then they said to him, "You see, brother, how many thousands of believers there are among the Jews, and they are all zealous for the Law. They have been told about you that you teach all the Jews living among the Gentiles to forsake Moses, and that you tell them not to circumcise their children or observe the customs. What then is to be done? They will certainly hear that you have come. So do what we tell you. We have four men who are under a vow. Join these men, go through the rite of purification with them, and pay for the shaving of their heads. Thus all will know that there is nothing in what they have been told about you, but that you yourself observe and guard the Law." (Acts 21.17–24)

Luke says that he and Paul were well received by the Jerusalem church, and this presumably means the collection was received as well, though it did not have the effect Paul wished of binding the Gentile churches to the mother church in Jerusalem.[7] On day two of their visit, they went to have an audience with James (v. 18), and all the elders were present as well. Paul gave a status report on his Gentile mission, which led to God's being praised by the Jerusalem leaders.

Then James and the elders made a request of Paul, though *request* may not be a strong enough term here. James was worried about the thousands of Jews who believed in Jesus but were also zealous for the Law. It seems they had heard a report that Paul was teaching Gentiles to turn away from Moses. To mollify these Christian Jews, Paul was being asked to join four men in their rites of purification and to pay their expenses (possibly out of the collection funds?). The intent was to show that Paul lived in obedience to the Law.

This request is not said to come specifically from James, but he at least agreed with it. Were they asking Paul to violate his principles? Was this an example of making a good show of things when the reality was otherwise? Would Paul have seen this as an opportunity to show he could be the Jew to the Jew? Perhaps Paul would have viewed it in such a light, but of course the most it could demonstrate was that he was sometimes observant of the Law and was happy to advertise on this occasion.

We see here that James was very much concerned about keeping intact the witness to observant Jews and to converts who were still observant Jews. He did not want this witness undermined, especially by Paul's failing to keep the Law while visiting Jerusalem. Since paying for others' purification rituals was not obligatory but optional under the Law, doing so would show Paul was an extremely pious Jew. The plan, however, backfired, as we know, and Paul spent the next two years under house arrest in Caesarea Maritima, where the proconsul lived.

Should we take seriously the suggestion that there were "thousands" of observant Jews among the early Christians in Jerusalem? Yes, I think we must, and they were apparently content with having James as their leader. He, too, was an observant Jew, and he believed other Jewish Christians should be as well. This can only mean that James would have had serious differences with Paul about the matter, since Paul saw such observance of the Law as optional once he became a follower of Jesus.

But would James undertake to critique Paul or the frequent misunderstandings of Paul (as in Acts 21.21) in print? In our next chapter we explore the letter of James and see what comes to light.

The story in Acts 21 also lets us know that James was still alive in the late 50s. In fact, Luke does not mention the death of James anywhere in his narrative. Luke and Paul left for Rome in about A.D. 60, which was before Festus left office and before the death of James during the interregnum between Festus and Albinus in 62. Luke probably did not know about the death of James since he left the vicinity of Jerusalem before this. This also means that James was still alive when Luke left the area in 60. In short, the evidence from Acts, Josephus, and the ossuary all point to the death of James after the year 60.

CONCLUSIONS

Sometimes those who are able to work out delicate compromises between people or groups with differing opinions are viewed as not principled enough, swayed by whichever direction the wind is currently blowing. This would be an unfair criticism of James. He was a Torah-true Jew who was committed to Jesus as the Jewish Messiah. He was the first great leader of the church who felt strongly about both the inclusion of Gentiles in this religious movement and the inclusion of Jews who would remain observant of the Mosaic Law. But how was this to be accomplished?

If James insisted, as did some hard-line Pharisaic Jewish Christians, that Gentiles had to be circumcised, even as adults, and keep all of the requirements of the Law, the possibility of including many Gentiles in the church would no doubt be stifled. On the other hand, if some compromise position were not crafted, both Jews and observant Jewish converts would be scandalized and might reject or abandon the Jesus movement. James chose to focus on the heart of the Law, indeed the heart of the Ten Commandments, which demands abstaining from idolatry and immorality.

James does not impose food laws from Leviticus or Genesis on Gentiles living in the Diaspora. Instead he says, in essence, what Paul urges in texts like 1 Thessalonians 1.9 ("You turned to God from idols, to serve a living and true God") and 1 Corinthians 8–10. Gentiles must stop going to pagan temples and engaging in the practices believed to be common in those venues—worshiping false gods, eating meat with blood in it in the presence of an idol as part of an act of worship, and engaging in sexual immorality at the idol feasts. In other words, he wants the Gentiles to make a clean break with the pagan religious practices of their past.

This was the minimum requirement James felt had to be met by Gentiles if Jewish and Gentile followers of Jesus had any hope of being able to associate with each other, worship together, even have table fellowship with one another. Perhaps he also thought that when Jews and Gentiles dined together the Gentiles would be sensitive enough not to scandalize the Jewish believers by imposing their own beliefs about nonkosher food and drink on the group fellowship (see Romans 14).

In all of this, James was remarkably similar to Paul. He differed from Paul, however, in believing that Jewish Christians needed to continue to observe the Mosaic Law. Had James's views prevailed in the Diaspora with Jewish Christians, both in their approach to their own practice and in their view and relationship with Gentiles, it is possible that more than a modicum of Jews might have continued to join the Jesus movement. As it was, Paul's views about the Mosaic Law and the fact that observance of it was optional prevailed, and the church became increasingly a Gentile enterprise.

Perhaps, in the end, James himself did not want the Diaspora Jewish Christians to focus on boundary-marking rituals like circumcision, sabbath observance, and food laws. Perhaps he saw something else as the heart of Jewish Christian piety. What might it be? In our next chapter we try to answer that question by examining James's letter to the Diaspora Jewish Christians.

1. See the discussion in Ben Witherington, *The Acts of the Apostles* (Grand Rapids, MI: Eerdmans, 1998), 539–44.

2. See Richard J. Bauckham, "James and the Gentiles (Acts 15.13–21)," in *History, Literature, and Society in the Book of Acts,* ed. Ben Witherington (Cambridge: Cambridge University Press, 1996), 154–84.

3. There is no evidence Luke knew Hebrew or Aramaic. He consistently omits Aramaic words and phrases in his two volumes, Luke and Acts, that are found in the earlier Gospel of Mark.

4. See Bauckham, "James and the Gentiles," 160–61.

5. The proof that this is what James is requiring here is that the term *idolothuton* is a technical term meaning meat sacrificed and eaten in the presence of an idol. It is not a term for meat found in a Gentile meat market somewhere. I have examined all 112 instances of this term, which occurs only in Christian sources and in two sources influenced by Christians. The term always carries the overtones of idol worship and refers literally to the pollution or stuff of idols. See Acts 15.20, which explains quite clearly that James is talking about food polluted by idols, something that was believed by some Jews to happen in temples when dining took place in the presence of the idol statues. Notice how Paul in 1 Cor. 10.20–21 says that it is a matter of dining with demons if you eat in the presence of idols. In other words, some Jews believed that while the pagan gods were not gods, they were nonetheless real spiritual beings, namely demons, which could negatively affect a believer and his or her food if one communed in their presence. Furthermore, the term *porneia* comes from the word *porne* (from which we get *pornography*) and has as its root meaning "prostitution," and in this case temple prostitution.

6. See Ben Witherington, *Conflict and Community in Corinth* (Grand Rapids, MI: Eerdmans, 1995), 186–232.

7. Paul may have viewed the collection in an eschatological light, as a fulfillment of the prophecies about Gentiles going up to Jerusalem and making offerings.

10

JAMES THE SAGE

The Gospels mention James only in passing. He seems to have come to prominence as leader of the Jewish Christian community and mother church in Jerusalem only after a life-changing encounter with his brother Jesus after the crucifixion. Paul mentions James only in his early correspondence, and only when there is a reason to do so. Luke, in writing about the early years of Christianity, naturally presents us with more detailed information about James since he had become such a crucial figure in the movement, but only in Acts 15 and 21 is he ever quoted and there only in summary form. If we are to hear the voice of James in any full way, our best chance is to pay close attention to the document that bears his name in the New Testament.

We have already seen James's ability to use the Hebrew Bible creatively—using the Greek translation over the Hebrew when it suited his interpretive needs. This suggests that James was probably bilingual. While his native tongue was Aramaic, as was Jesus', when he wrote to Jews or Jewish Christians in the Diaspora, he had to use Greek. To write in Greek he may have needed the assistance of a scribe (as Paul often used), or he may have been able to write Greek himself.

So did James write the New Testament book that bears his name?

DID JAMES WRITE JAMES?

Scholars are divided on the question of whether James wrote the letter that bears his name, but most think either that James wrote it or at the least that it contains his source material, even though a later editor may have arranged and polished the material.[1] The Greek of James is good *Koine* Greek (the common, spoken Greek of the New Testament era) with considerable rhetorical polish, which makes some scholars suspicious that a son of a carpenter could have achieved such sophistication.

This line of reasoning is questionable, however. Paul's letters are rhetorically sophisticated, and he probably spent time learning rhetoric, the art of persuasion, in a school in Jerusalem. Whether or not James also received such training, plenty of scribes in Jerusalem were so trained. A scribe was the ancient version of a secretary, and like modern secretaries they had a certain freedom to compose things for the one dictating the correspondence, depending on how much they were trusted. James could have hired such a scribe to compose a letter to Greek-speaking Jews or Jewish Christians in the Diaspora.

Several clues suggest that this letter ultimately derives from James. First, there is the self-effacing way the author identifies himself—as "a servant of God and of the Lord Jesus Christ" (1.1). The degree to which this letter echoes the teaching of Jesus supports the writer's identifying himself as a servant of the master teacher, Jesus (which we explore more fully below). Also, a later Christian writer likely would have called James the brother of Jesus, or James the Just of Jerusalem. The identification in James 1.1 is simple and believable. It assumes that the audience will know which James is speaking. Only one James is ever referred to in the New Testament without further qualification, and that is James the brother of Jesus.

Notice, for example, the respect shown to James and the authority he is assumed to have in Jude verse 1: "Jude, a servant of Jesus Christ and brother of James." As Richard Bauckham has shown at length, the brief letter of Jude was likely written by another of Jesus' brothers.[2] It is significant, then, that both of these brothers identify themselves as servants of Jesus. Notice also how Jude identifies himself in relationship to James as well, whereas James does not reciprocate in his letter.[3] This, too, suggests that the James in question does not have to establish his authority or further identify himself for his audience.

We can be fairly confident that we hear the authentic voice of James in the letter that bears his name, even if he had a scribe helping him or if there was some light editing of the letter after the fact by another Jewish Christian.

THE LETTER'S AUDIENCE

The letter of James is addressed to "the Twelve Tribes in the Diaspora." The term *Diaspora* means literally "dispersion" and refers to Jews living outside the Holy Land. While this phrase is a natural way to refer to Jews outside Israel, it is not a natural way to refer to the church. But remember, the earliest Jewish followers of Jesus, including James, did not see themselves as starting a new religion. It is clear enough from the content of James that the letter is addressed to those Jews who are followers of Jesus outside the Holy Land, but the author does not use any specifically Christian terms to identify the audience, such as those "in Christ" or the term *Christianoi* ("adherents of" or "belonging to Christ") from which we get the term *Christian*.

Again Bauckham can enlighten us: "Early Jewish Christians thought of themselves, not as a specific sect distinguished from other Jews, but as the nucleus of the Messianic renewal of the people of Israel, which was under way and would come to include all Israel. . . . What James addresses in practice to those Jews who already confess the Messiah Jesus, he addresses in principle to all Israel."[4]

This form of addressing the audience, however, tells us something else. It was written from Israel, not from somewhere in the Diaspora. And there was no place in Israel more appropriate for such a circular letter (circular in that it was meant to be copied and passed along) to originate than Jerusalem and the first Jewish Christian community.

The letter was written probably ten years prior to James's death or a bit later (around the year 52), after the Jerusalem Council and after the impact of Paul and his gospel had become well known in the Diaspora—since this is one of the issues he addresses. If this is correct, then there is an important connection between the letter of James and the letter to the Gentiles that resulted from the council cited in Acts 15. James, after he wrote to Gentile Christians in the Diaspora, then wrote to Jewish Christians in the Diaspora, explaining to them as well how they ought to live.

This letter was intended to help the audience not be misled or confused by some reports about Paul's message, as well as to confirm them in their commitment to various Jewish ways of viewing life and religious practice. The circular letter of James turns out to be a remarkable window into the mind of James and the way he thought about his fellow Jewish Christians.

JAMES AND THE JESUS TRADITION

The letter of James has many distinct features, one of which is that it uses many words (sixty, to be precise) that are not found anywhere else in the New Testament. James clearly has his own style and vocabulary. And yet he also reflects a profound indebtedness to the teachings of Jesus and other forms of early Jewish wisdom literature.

The material we find in James reflects the long and rich heritage of Jewish wisdom literature, which includes proverbs, aphorisms, riddles, parables, and various sorts of sage advice about topics having to do with everyday life. Such topics include what one does with one's money, prayer, how to handle an illness, curbing one's tongue, and the like. We find this sort of spiritual guidance in Proverbs, Ecclesiastes, Wisdom of Solomon, Sirach, and elsewhere. But most important, James is indebted to his brother's wisdom teaching found in the Sermon on the Mount (Matthew 5–7, with a shorter version recorded in Luke 6). A careful comparison of portions of Jesus' sermon, especially the form found in Matthew (which was more Jewish in flavor), and the letter of James tells us how closely the latter is indebted to his brother's teachings:[5]

On facing adversity with joy:

James 1.2: "My brothers and sisters, whenever you face trials of any kind, consider it nothing but joy."

Matthew 5.11–12: "Blessed are you when people revile you and persecute you and utter all kinds of evil against you falsely on my account. Rejoice and be glad, for your reward is great in heaven, for in the same way they persecuted the prophets who were before you."

Luke 6.22–23: "Blessed are you when people hate you, and when they exclude you, revile you, and defame you on account of the Son of Man. Rejoice in that day and leap for joy, for surely your reward is great in heaven; for that is what their ancestors did to the prophets."

James 1.4: "Let endurance have its full effect, so that you may be mature and complete, lacking in nothing."

Matthew 5.48: "Be perfect, therefore, as your heavenly Father is perfect."

On the Father's readiness to give:

James 1.5: "If any of you is lacking in wisdom, ask God, who gives to all generously and ungrudgingly, and it will be given you."

Matthew 7.7: "Ask, and it will be given you; search, and you will find; knock, and the door will be opened for you."

James 1.17: "Every generous act of giving, with every perfect gift, is from above, coming down from the Father of lights, with whom there is no variation or shadow due to change."

Matthew 7.11: "If you then, who are evil, know how to give good gifts to your children, how much more will your Father in heaven give good things to those who ask him!"

On the importance of living out one's faith:

James 1.22: "But be doers of the word, and not merely hearers who deceive themselves."

Matthew 7.24: "Everyone then who hears these words of mine and acts on them will be like a wise man who built his house on rock."

Luke 6.46–47: "Why do you call me 'Lord, Lord,' and do not do what I tell you? I will show you what someone is like who comes to me, hears my words, and acts on them."

James 1.23: "For if any are hearers of the word and not doers, they are like those who look at themselves in a mirror."

Matthew 7.26: "Everyone who hears these words of mine and does not act on them will be like a foolish man who built his house on sand."

Luke 6.49: "But the one who hears and does not act is like a man who built a house on the ground without a foundation. When the river burst against it, immediately it fell, and great was the ruin of that house."

On God's bias for the poor:

James 2.5: "Listen, my beloved brothers and sisters. Has not God chosen the poor in the world to be rich in faith and to be heirs of the kingdom that he has promised to those who love him?"

Matthew 5.3, 5: "Blessed are the poor in spirit, for theirs is the kingdom of heaven. . . . Blessed are the meek, for they will inherit the earth."

Luke 6.20: "Blessed are you who are poor, for yours is the kingdom of God."

On observing the commandments:

James 2.10: "For whoever keeps the whole law but fails in one point has become accountable for all of it."

Matthew 5.18–19: "For truly I tell you, until heaven and earth pass away, not one letter, not one stroke of a letter, will pass from the law until all is accomplished. Therefore, whoever breaks one of the least of these commandments, and teaches others to do the same, will be called least in the kingdom of heaven; but whoever does them and teaches them will be called great in the kingdom of heaven."

James 2.11: "For the one who said, 'You shall not commit adultery,' also said, 'You shall not murder.' Now if you do not commit adultery but if you murder, you have become a transgressor of the law."

Matthew 5.21–22: "You have heard that it was said to those of ancient times, 'You shall not murder'; and 'whoever murders shall be liable to judgment.' But I say to you that if you are angry with a brother or sister, you will be liable to judgment; and if you insult a brother or sister, you will be liable to the council; and if you say, 'You fool,' you will be liable to the hell of fire."

On the priority of mercy:

James 2.13: "For judgment will be without mercy to anyone who has shown no mercy; mercy triumphs over judgment."

Matthew 5.7: "Blessed are the merciful, for they will receive mercy."

Luke 6.36: "Be merciful, just as your Father is merciful."

On testing faith by what it produces:

James 3.12: "Can a fig tree, my brothers and sisters, yield olives, or a grapevine figs? No more can salt water yield fresh."

Matthew 7.16–18: "You will know them by their fruits. Are grapes gathered from thorns, or figs from thistles? In the same way, every good tree bears good fruit, but the bad tree bears bad fruit. A good tree cannot bear bad fruit, nor can a bad tree bear good fruit."

Luke 6.43–44: "No good tree bears bad fruit, nor again does a bad tree bear good fruit; for each tree is known by its own fruit. Figs are not gathered from thorns, nor are grapes picked from a bramble bush."

In praise of peacemakers:

James 3.18: "And a harvest of righteousness is sown in peace for those who make peace."

Matthew 5.9: "Blessed are the peacemakers, for they will be called children of God."

On the importance of asking God:

James 4.2–3: "You want something and do not have it; so you commit murder. And you covet something and cannot obtain it; so you engage in disputes and conflicts. You do not have, because you do not ask. You ask and do not receive, because you ask wrongly, in order to spend what you get on your pleasures."

Matthew 7.8: "Everyone who asks receives, and everyone who searches finds, and for everyone who knocks, the door will be opened."

Warnings against worldliness:

James 4.4: "Adulterers! Do you not know that friendship with the world is enmity with God? Therefore whoever wishes to be a friend of the world becomes an enemy of God."

Matthew 6.24: "No one can serve two masters; for a slave will either hate the one and love the other, or be devoted to the one and despise the other. You cannot serve God and wealth."

Luke 16.13: "No slave can serve two masters; for a slave will either hate the one and love the other, or be devoted to the one and despise the other. You cannot serve God and wealth."

On the relation between purity and intimacy with God:

James 4.8: "Draw near to God, and he will draw near to you. Cleanse your hands, you sinners, and purify your hearts, you double-minded."

Matthew 5.8: "Blessed are the pure in heart, for they will see God."

On the blessing of mourning:

James 4.9: "Lament and mourn and weep. Let your laughter be turned into mourning and your joy into dejection."

Matthew 5.4: "Blessed are those who mourn, for they will be comforted."

Luke 6.25: "Woe to you who are full now, for you will be hungry. Woe to you who are laughing now, for you will mourn and weep."

Warnings against judging others:

James 4.11: "Do not speak evil against one another, brothers and sisters. Whoever speaks evil against another or judges another, speaks evil against the law and judges the law; but if you judge the law, you are not a doer of the law but a judge."

Matthew 7.1–2: "Do not judge, so that you may not be judged. For with the judgment you make you will be judged, and the measure you give will be the measure you get."

Luke 6.37–38: "Do not judge, and you will not be judged; do not condemn, and you will not be condemned. Forgive, and you will be forgiven; give, and it will be given to you. A good measure, pressed down, shaken together, running over, will be put into your lap; for the measure you give will be the measure you get back."

Warnings on the snare of wealth:

James 5.2–3: "Your riches have rotted, and your clothes are moth-eaten. Your gold and silver have rusted, and their rust will be evidence against you, and it will eat your flesh like fire. You have laid up treasure for the last days."

Matthew 6.19–21: "Do not store up for yourselves treasures on earth, where moth and rust consume and where thieves break in and steal; but store up for yourselves treasures in heaven, where neither moth nor rust consumes and where thieves do not break in and steal. For where your treasure is, there your heart will be also."

Luke 12.33: "Sell your possessions, and give alms. Make purses for yourselves that do not wear out, an unfailing treasure in heaven, where no thief comes near and no moth destroys."

Warnings against swearing oaths:

James 5.12: "Above all, my beloved, do not swear, either by heaven or by earth or by any other oath, but let your 'Yes' be yes and your 'No' be no, so that you may not fall under condemnation."

Matthew 5.34–37: "But I say to you, Do not swear at all, either by heaven, for it is the throne of God, or by the earth, for it is his footstool, or by Jerusalem, for it is the city of the great King. And do not swear by your head, for you cannot make one hair white or black. Let your word be 'Yes, Yes' or 'No, No'; anything more than this comes from the evil one."[6]

These parallels between the teachings of Jesus and James clearly show that James knows a collection of Jesus' sayings in some form. The parallels by themselves rule out the theory that we should see the book of James as a sort of nonmessianic and non-Christian Jewish tract that has been slightly Christianized, as some have argued.[7] On the contrary, the letter of James is deeply indebted to his brother Jesus.

What is most striking about James's use of the Jesus tradition is that he rarely quotes it, nor does he attribute it to Jesus. Rather, he weaves various ideas, themes, and phrases from the Jesus tradition into his own convictions. Sometimes the parallels are obvious and striking, for instance, in the saying about perfection in James 1.4

and Matthew 5.48, and the saying on peacemaking in James 3.18 and Matthew 5.9 (the only two references to peacemakers in the New Testament). On the basis of the parallels between James and the form of Jesus' sayings found in Matthew, Patrick J. Hartin has convincingly concluded that the more Jewish form of Jesus' sayings found in Matthew are likely to be closer to the original form in which Jesus expressed them—as opposed to the more Hellenized (or even Gentilized) form of the sayings found in Luke.[8]

THE WISDOM OF JAMES

In the Jewish tradition, wisdom literature aims to convey practical wisdom for everyday life. But James also offers some distinctive advice, which again parallels his brother's teaching. Furthermore, the brief wisdom narratives found in James 1.23–24 (warning against being hearers and not doers of the Word), 2.2–4 (warning against making distinction among people based on social status), and 2.15–17 (warning against kind thoughts without kind actions) reflect a specific indebtedness to the Jesus tradition, since this form of wisdom material was not characteristic of Jewish wisdom literature before Jesus.

At the outset, James makes clear that we should seek "wisdom from above" to deal with life's trials and temptations. "If any of you is lacking in wisdom, ask God, who gives to all generously and ungrudgingly, and it will be given you" (1.5). The hearer[9] is not exhorted to learn the teachings of Jesus or the Law. Rather, the hearer is enjoined to pray for wisdom "from above" (James 3.13–18). James operates with the same theology as Jesus regarding the importance of fresh revelation to guide God's people through dark times. This approach is much like what we find in the intertestamental work the Wisdom of Solomon 7.7–8: "Therefore I prayed and understanding was given to me; I called on God, and the spirit of wisdom came to me." (The intertestamental period is the time between the writing of the last work of the Hebrew Bible—around the second century B.C.—and the writing of the New Testament.)[10] Unlike some of the sages from much earlier in Israel's history, such as those who contributed to

Proverbs, James does not exhort his audience to observe life or study nature in order to gain wisdom. Instead, wisdom is gained from God directly or is passed down to a person from a teacher.

A second feature of James's wisdom is that it is wisdom for the marginalized and oppressed minority. For example, what James says about riches and the rich in James 2.6 ("But you have dishonored the poor. Is it not the rich who oppress you? Is it not they who drag you into court?") and 5.1–5 (v. 3: "Your gold and silver have rusted") sounds a good deal like what Jesus says in Matthew 6.19 ("Do not store up for yourself treasures on earth"). Here again James stands with Jesus—and against traditional Jewish wisdom, which stressed that riches were a blessing from God. In the view of both James and Jesus, the brothers from the marginal town of Nazareth, riches were a dangerous temptation and a common trap for everyone.

In his letter James is not expressing his thoughts on all the subjects he thought important for Christians. James is specifically teaching a sort of community ethic, and so his comments emphasize how members of the community should relate to one another. For example, notice what he emphasizes in 4.11 ("Do not speak evil against *one another*") and 5.9 ("Beloved, do not grumble against *one another*"). He says things like "Not many of you should become teachers" (3.1). He does not say, "Go and make disciples of all nations" (Matthew 28.19). Yet it is clear from Galatians 2.8–9 that James was all for sharing the good news with both Jews and Gentiles, for Paul says James extended "the right hand of fellowship" to Paul and Barnabas and agreed they should go evangelize the Gentiles.

What sort of ethical concerns does James focus on? Here are a few of his emphases:

1. Christians should care for widows and orphans in the community (1.27). In fact, this is described as "pure and undefiled" religion.

2. Christians should keep themselves unstained by the world (1.27b). "Do you not know that friendship with the world is enmity with God?" (4.4)

3.   Christians should "fulfill the royal law according to the scripture, 'You shall love your neighbor as yourself'" (James 2.8–13). This entails following the Ten Commandments, among other things.[11]

4.   Christians should bridle their tongues ("No one can tame the tongue—a restless evil, full of deadly poison"; see 3.1–12) and their passions ("Those conflicts and disputes among you, where do they come from? Do they not come from your cravings that are at war within you?"; see 4.1–10).

5.   Christians should persevere in faith through trials and suffering (1.2–15; 5.10–11). "We call blessed those who showed endurance" (5.11).

6.   Christians should confess their sins to one another in the community (5.16).

7.   Christians should pray for the sick and suffering. "Are any among you suffering? They should pray. Are any cheerful? They should sing songs of praise. Are any among you sick? They should call for the elders of the church and have them pray over them, anointing them with oil in the name of the Lord. The prayer of faith will save the sick, and the Lord will raise them up; and anyone who has committed sins will be forgiven. Therefore confess your sins to one another, and pray for one another, so that you may be healed. The prayer of the righteous is powerful and effective" (5.13–17).

8.   Christians should retrieve the erring community member. "If anyone among you wanders from the truth and is brought back by another, you should know that whoever brings back a sinner from wandering will save the sinner's soul from death and will cover a multitude of sins" (5.19–20).

Again and again there are echoes of earlier Jewish wisdom literature, particularly from the intertestamental period, such as the

Wisdom of Solomon and Sirach. For example, compare James
1.27–2.9 on partiality to Sirach 35.15–16: "For the Lord is the
judge, and with him there is no partiality. He will not show partiality to the poor, but he will listen to the one who is wronged.
He will not ignore the supplication of the orphan or the widow
when she pours out her complaint." Or again, the same stress on
carefully controlled speech is expressed in Sirach 23.7–15 and
27.4–5 as we find in James 3.1–12, especially when it comes to
avoiding cursing and abusive speech.

But we can make too much of this similarity. All too often the
book of James has been viewed as nothing more than a rehashing
of conventional Jewish wisdom. Professor Bauckham, however, has
made clear that there is another side to the wisdom of James.[12] For
one thing, James treats ethics in an eschatological context much as
Jesus does. He is focused on God's final saving and judging activity
in his own day. James considers ethics in the shadow of the eschaton, with one eye on the horizon for the coming Judge who is also
the Redeemer. James 5.3 and 7 speak of the "last days" and the
"coming of the Lord." It is this coming that provides a sanction or
added seriousness to all of James's ethical teaching.

For example, James concentrates on the theme of wholeness
or perfection in this letter, a theme he derives from his brother
Jesus' Sermon on the Mount. This theme stresses wholehearted
loyalty to God, fulfilling the whole divine Law, acting in accord
with what one believes and says, and doing what brings wholeness
and peace to the community (see 3.14–4.1). The opposite is saying one thing and doing another, or being double-minded (1.8;
4.8). James follows Jesus in proclaiming that God demands more
under the new covenant than was demanded under the old one
because more grace and revelation have been given.

James speaks of community, just as Paul and other Christians
do, not by using words of hierarchy (such as by calling those he addresses "son" or "daughter"), but rather by addressing the audience as spiritual brothers and sisters. Honor or shame is
determined by speech and conduct, not by social considerations
such as gender, wealth, power, and the like. James does not want
his audience to fit easily into a fallen world. Rather, he wants them

to build a countercultural community that reflects its own values. This fits readily with the decree sent to the Gentiles (Acts 15) asking them not to conform to the dominant religious values of their world by attending feasts in pagan temples. In a similar fashion in his letter to Diaspora Jewish Christians, James expects his audience to live in the new revelatory wisdom that comes down from above and through Jesus, not just to return to an old source like Proverbs.

James was indeed a sage, but he was by no means simply reiterating material from Proverbs or the Wisdom of Solomon or following the teaching of Jesus ben Sira (as recorded in Sirach, or Ecclesiasticus). He had been too shaped by the radical wisdom of his own brother, especially when it came to issues of truth telling, impartiality, peacemaking, nonretaliation, perfection, and generosity.

The letter of James is intended to prevent the Christian community from losing its sense of identity. James does this by setting up carefully controlled boundaries affecting speech, behavior, and relationships. Remember that in Galatians 2, when men came from James complaining about Jewish Christians eating with Gentile Christians, the main concern was being a bad witness to other Jews. This focus on the big picture also explains James's behavior in Acts 21, where efforts are made to get Paul to present himself as an observant Jew in the Temple so the evangelism of Jews will not be harmed by Paul's mission to the Gentiles. Ensuring that the work of the church is not hindered is a high priority for James—as it was for Paul.

We have once more turned to the discussion of James and Paul. Two topics raised in James deserve some discussion: what James says about the Law, and what James says about faith and works.

JAMES AND PAUL REVISITED

Especially since Luther and the Protestant Reformation, Bible scholars have debated tensions between Paul and James over two matters: the role and purpose of the Mosaic Law in the church age, and the proper relationship between "faith" and "works" in salvation. But, as many scholars and church leaders have now concluded, in the end there isn't nearly as much difference between these two great leaders as we have been led to believe.

What is James referring to when he comments on the royal or perfect law (1.25; 2.8)? James is not simply referring to the Mosaic Law—though the Mosaic Law is certainly included. James stands in the tradition of Jesus ben Sira and other earlier Jewish sages (such as those who produced the Qumran documents found among the Dead Sea Scrolls), who drew both from the law and from other Jewish wisdom material for their teaching. They believed that all wisdom came from God and not all of it was found in the repository known as the Mosaic Law.[13]

There is no evidence in the New Testament that James sided with the radical Pharisaic Jewish Christians who demanded that Gentiles be circumcised and keep the food and sabbath laws. James did make demands on Gentiles, and clearly he also believed that Jewish Christians should remain observant Jews. This in part is what the letter of James is about. But notice that nowhere in the letter of James is there any discussion about food laws, strict sabbath keeping, circumcision, or any of the usual boundary-marker issues that Paul had to deal with when he was confronted by what he called Judaizers.[14]

The attempt to pit James against Paul (which found encouragement from German Reformer Martin Luther when he called the Epistle of James a "right strawy epistle") is wrong. While there are differences between the two writers, James was more of a mediating figure between the Judaizers and Paul than is usually realized. Paul was not averse to the realization that faith without good works is barren.[15] Indeed, Paul was prepared to talk about the *Law* of Christ (see Galatians 6 and 1 Corinthians 9). Paul was not anti-Law any more than James was a legalist.

What James says in his letter about obedience to God's Word and charity would have brooked no objection from Paul. For James the royal or perfect law of God includes

1. Mosaic provisions such as the Ten Commandments

2. The wisdom teachings of Jesus

3. Other early Jewish and perhaps even non-Jewish wisdom material

This hardly differs from Paul's approach to the Law of Christ. Galatians 6.1–2 ("Bear one another's burdens, and in this way you will fulfill the law of Christ") shows that the Law of Christ includes the teachings of Jesus. The Pauline ethical material (see Romans 12.9–15.6; 1 Corinthians 9.19–23) also includes various teachings from the Mosaic Law and other early Jewish material. Where James and Paul differed in these matters can be seen in Paul's words in 1 Corinthians 9.20–23:

> To the Jews I became as a Jew, in order to win Jews. To those under the law I became as one under the law (though I myself am not under the law) so that I might win those under the law. To those outside the law I became as one outside the law (though I am not free from God's law but am under Christ's law) so that I might win those outside the law. To the weak I became weak, so that I might win the weak. I have become all things to all people, that I might by all means save some. I do it all for the sake of the gospel, so that I may share in its blessings.

Paul believed that even for a Jew, such as himself, observing the Mosaic Law is a blessed option but not an obligation. James did not agree.

At the heart of the matter is a true difference of emphasis. James wanted to emphasize the continuity of the Jesus movement with biblical Judaism's approach to the Law. To him it was the fulfillment of the Mosaic Law and the reconstituting of God's Temple through Christ that create the people of God and allow the Gentiles to enter.

Paul, on the other hand, wanted to emphasize the new eschatological situation. Christ's death and resurrection had brought about a new era for the world. There had already begun a new creation, a new covenant, a new way of constituting the people of God. In Paul's view the Mosaic covenant, while glorious, had become a glorious anachronism (see Galatians 3.19–4.31). Christ himself (and so faith in Christ) had to be what circumscribed the boundaries of the community of Jesus—not the Mosaic Law and its covenant obligations.

James's anxiety over Paul's teaching expressed in Acts 21.21 ("They have been told about you that you teach all the Jews living among the Gentiles to forsake Moses, and that you tell them not to circumcise their children or observe the customs") was indeed prophetic. If Paul's approach to the Jesus movement prevailed, then it was likely that only a tiny minority of Jews would want to be involved in it, and the "church" would become a predominantly Gentile movement.

This was James's concern, and so he set out to preserve a form of Jewish Christianity in which there was less discontinuity with early Judaism than in the Pauline form of Christianity. This brings us to the famous discussion about faith and works in James 2.14–26:

What good is it, my brothers and sisters, if you say you have faith but do not have works? Can faith save you? If a brother or sister is naked and lacks daily food, and one of you says to them, "Go in peace; keep warm and eat your fill," and yet you do not supply their bodily needs, what is the good of that? So faith by itself, if it has no works, is dead. But someone will say, "You have faith and I have works." Show me your faith apart from your works, and I by my works will show you my faith. You believe that God is one; you do well. Even the demons believe—and shudder. Do you want to be shown, you senseless person, that faith apart from works is barren? Was not our ancestor Abraham justified by works when he offered his son Isaac on the altar? You see that faith was active along with his works, and faith was brought to completion by the works. Thus the scripture was fulfilled that says, "Abraham believed God, and it was reckoned to him as

righteousness," and he was called the friend of God. You
see that a person is justified by works and not by faith
alone. Likewise, was not Rahab the prostitute also justified by works when she welcomed the messengers and
sent them out by another road? For just as the body without the spirit is dead, so faith without works is also dead.

James is concerned to correct a misunderstanding of the
Pauline expression of the gospel. (See, for one example, Romans
3.28: "We hold that a person is justified by faith apart from works
prescribed by the law.") Paul was being misunderstood to say that
one is "justified" or saved or made whole before God by faith
alone and that righteous deeds or obedience to God's commands
once one believes are not required for salvation.

There are in fact several misunderstandings to be sorted out.
First, note that James is addressing those who are already Jewish
Christians (notice the reference to Christian brothers and sisters
in v. 15). James is not talking about how one becomes a believer
in Jesus; he is talking about the behavior of those who already are
believers in Jesus. James in verse 22 says that faith "was brought to
completion" by deeds. He does not say deeds are a prerequisite to
God accepting a person. Second, in James 2.24 James is speaking
about final justification or final right standing with God at the last
judgment. He is not referring to how one initially obtains right
standing with God in this life.

Yet at the same time, it is clear that James uses the Abraham
story in a much more traditional Jewish way to inculcate the idea
that good deeds flow out of faith, deeds such as Abraham's obedience to God in offering Isaac, and so he makes a very different
use of the Abraham story than does Paul in Galatians 3.6–9 and
Romans 4.1–15.[16] Paul uses the Abraham story to show how a person gains right standing with God: God reckons or credits a person's faith as righteousness.

The caricature that all early Judaism was grounded in legalism is simply false. Many oversimplify Jewish teaching in Jesus'
day as "works righteousness," lacking any emphasis on grace and
on how God's mercy takes precedence. The caricature that James

embodies such a "works righteousness" approach in James 2 is equally false. Good works are simply the natural and indeed expected outflow of saving faith for a believing person. You will know the tree by the fruit it bears. Neither Jesus nor Paul would have had a problem with that.

So we see two very different ways of using the Abraham story in Paul's letters and the letter of James. James uses the story to correct a misunderstanding about Paul's gospel, which suggested that obedience to God's "royal law" was optional once one was saved by faith. Paul uses the same story from Genesis 12, about God's call to Abraham to leave his home and go to Canaan, to correct the notion of the Judaizers that in order for Gentiles to have right standing with God at all they must be circumcised and keep the Mosaic Law. They are arguing against different misunderstandings of the implications of the crucial Abraham story in Genesis 12.

It is a historical mistake to pit James over against Paul in some radical way, as if Paul's message as he proclaimed it to Gentiles was being corrected by James. James is asking and answering the question, "How then shall believers, in this case Jewish Christians, live, as illustrated by the Abraham story?" Paul is asking and answering a different question: "How then shall believers, in this case mainly Gentile believers, be saved, as illustrated by the Abraham story?" The focus of each writer is different.

Richard J. Bauckham has this to say on the matter:

> That there are very considerable differences between James and Paul is not in doubt. But they should not be exaggerated at the expense of the notable similarities. . . . In a canonical conversation . . . between James and Paul there would be much nodding of heads and smiling agreement as well as some knitting of brows and some exclamations of surprise.[17]

It is quite true that the letter of James does not reflect the central Pauline message about salvation being grounded in the death and resurrection of Jesus, but then the letter of James should be compared to the more ethical sections of Paul's letters, such as we find in Romans 12–15, not the more theological sections. James, after all, is addressing those who are already Christians.

The faith James complains about is mere intellectual assent that does not affect behavior, whereas the works Paul complains about are the attempts to achieve right standing with God by merely human effort without faith.

The discovery of the ossuary of James provides an opportunity to reexamine much of what has been thought about James in the past, but it also invites us to correct caricatures of both James and Paul. The differences between them should be neither minimized nor exaggerated. This fresh historical evidence gives us an opportunity to correct false impressions about a form of early Christianity that came forth from James and the Jerusalem church, even though eventually it would largely die out.

CONCLUSIONS

The letter of James has not merely been neglected, it has been misunderstood. It has not merely been overlooked, it has been overburdened by the assumption that there is some anti-Pauline rhetoric in this document—as though Paul would be opposed to good works or obeying God's Word. But this is unfair to both James and to Paul. The legacy of Luther needs to be left behind when it comes to evaluating these two figures in early Christianity. With the finding of the ossuary of James we have a fresh opportunity to reevaluate the contributions of James to the Jesus movement.

James's letter embodies a concern for faithfully living out the essential teachings of the faith. It is not important whether James himself wrote this letter or dictated it to a scribe. What is important is the sum and substance of the letter, which calls Diaspora Jewish Christians to believe and behave in a way that is in accord with the wisdom of Jesus, a revelatory wisdom that came down, and comes down, from above. This wisdom echoes in various ways earlier Jewish wisdom, but it is filtered through the lens of the distinctive emphases and ideas of the wisdom of Jesus the sage.

James does not merely pass on a tradition, not even that

teaching of his brother Jesus. He reforms and refashions it to meet the needs of those he addresses while remaining faithful to the core values that underlie such teaching. James shows his creativity not only in the way he handles the sayings of Jesus but also in the way he responds to the misunderstanding of Paul's teaching. We noted how he could creatively use the story of Abraham and even the very same texts as Paul uses—for instance Genesis 12 and 15—to make very different points (compare James 2 to Romans 4 and Galatians 3). James does not merely pass along tradition. He creatively reshapes and applies tradition.

Unlike Jesus, James had a long ministry in the Holy Land—and in Jerusalem in particular. He had an extended opportunity to shape a growing, Jesus-centered community. His impact and legacy are evident in the accounts of his martyrdom and death, which show that even non-Christian Jews had great respect for James's spiritual and moral integrity, even if they differed with his belief in Jesus as Messiah and Lord. To these accounts of the death of James and to his legacy we turn in the next chapter.

1. See the discussions by Luke Timothy Johnson, *The Letter of James* (New York: Doubleday, 1995), and Ralph P. Martin, *James* (Waco, TX: Word, 1988).

2. See Richard J. Bauckham, *Jude, 2 Peter* (Waco, TX: Word, 1983).

3. It is interesting that this prescript to the letter of Jude bears a formal resemblance to the inscription on the James ossuary, in that Jude identifies himself in relationship to two relatives, and the last clause is "brother of James," just as the last clause on the ossuary is "brother of Jesus." The other similarity is that in both the prescript in Jude and on the ossuary, the identifications are in relationship to people to whom the writer is subordinate.

4. Richard J. Bauckham, *James* (London: Routledge, 1999), 16.

5. The form of the Sermon on the Mount found in Matthew is clearly more Jewish in flavor. For example, Matthew speaks of the kingdom of heaven as opposed to the kingdom of God, as in Luke; or again, Matthew has, "Blessed are the poor in spirit," as opposed to Luke, which simply has "Blessed are the poor."

6. See my discussion of this list in *Jesus the Sage* (Minneapolis: Fortress Press, 1994), 240–42.

7. See Johnson, *Letter of James,* 146–56, for the various theories on how Christian a book James actually is.

8. Patrick J. Hartin, *James and the "Q" Sayings of Jesus* (Sheffield, England: JSOT Press, 1991), 188–89.

9. As with other New Testament documents, the audience is primarily hearers rather than readers and so the text is written in a way appropriate for oral communication. For instance, the author uses wordplay (1.1–2; 1.13; 3.17), alliteration (3.5), and other poetic devices to enhance the impact of the words on the audience.

10. The Wisdom of Solomon, like the Wisdom of Jesus ben Sira (also called Ecclesiasticus), is an intertestamental Jewish text that focuses on giving sage advice. The earliest New Testament documents are probably Paul's letters, the first of which was composed about A.D. 49. It is more difficult to say when the latest Old Testament book was written, but it was probably before the Maccabean era, that is, before the second century B.C.

11. The emphasis here on the Ten Commandments, rather than on food laws, goes along well with the interpretation I suggested in the previous chapter for the source documents for the Jerusalem Decree.

12. In this section I am following the helpful treatment of Richard J. Bauckham, "James and Jesus," in *The Brother of Jesus* (Louisville: Westminster/John Knox Press, 2001), 126–29.

13. See Bauckham, *James,* 32.

14. Judaizers were Jewish Christians who tried to require Gentile Christians to be circumcised and to obey the entire Mosaic Law.

15. What Luther meant by calling James a "strawy epistle" is that it lacked substance; it lacked, in Luther's view, the gospel message about Jesus.

16. See the discussion in Ben Witherington, *Grace in Galatia* (Grand Rapids, MI: Eerdmans, 1998), 216–40.

17. Bauckham, *James,* 140.

II

THE DEATH OF JAMES

The decade of the 60s was a volatile and indeed violent one for residents of Judea under the rule of one bad procurator after another. Roman rulers during the empire seem to have regarded Judea as a minor and yet troublesome province. It was hardly a plum appointment for ambitious patrician Roman military leaders and politicians wishing to climb the ladder of success.

Rome generally tended to send its less-than-best procurators to govern this region in the 50s and 60s. Felix served under Claudius and then Nero as procurator of Judea from A.D. 52 until either 58 or 59. Felix had to deal with the fact that north of him in the Holy Land was Herod Agrippa II, who was given more and more land by Emperor Nero. Perhaps in an attempt to make peace with his subjects, the procurator Felix married a Jewish princess named Druscilla in the year 54. But since observant Jews saw this as an affront to Jewish marital customs, it seems not to have helped much.

For good reason, Felix was somewhat paranoid, and the account by the first-century Jewish historian Josephus of Felix's reign reads like the ghastly accounts of the reign of terror in the French Revolution. Felix was regularly executing one zealot or another (*Ant.* 20.161) and seems to have made it his personal mission to root out Jewish messianic troublemakers such as Eleazar the revolutionary (20.121). This only produced more violence among the Jews, leading to the rise of the so-called dagger-men (*sicarii*). These Jewish zealots went around executing Jews who were collaborating with Rome, such as Jonathan the high priest (20.163).

It was also during Felix's reign that the messianic pretender called "the Egyptian" rallied a group of Jewish followers and promised to bring down the walls of Jerusalem with a shout from the Mount of Olives (20.169–72). Felix sent out troops against this group, and the Egyptian escaped, which explains how Felix may have thought that Paul, when he was taken prisoner in the Temple precincts in Jerusalem, might have been this Egyptian (Acts 21.37–38).

In such politically troubled times, it is clear why the leaders of the Jewish Temple were concerned about maintaining the Temple and their roles in it. Once messianic figures or Jewish revolutionaries started executing temple priests, these priests would certainly be opposed to any sort of messianic movements—including the Jesus movement—that might arouse the suspicions of Rome and might lead to their own loss of political power. No doubt they kept a watchful eye on James and his fellow Jewish Christians in Jerusalem, seeing them as potential troublemakers who would endanger their fragile collaborative arrangement with the procurator.

In the years 52 to 68 there must have been increasing pressure on the church in Jerusalem to appear truly Jewish and truly loyal to the Temple and its hierarchy. This in part must have driven a request like that of James in Acts 21.21, asking Paul at least to appear as an observant Jew. It is fair to say that when Paul marched into Jerusalem with Gentiles and the collection in A.D. 58, he could hardly have picked a worse or more xenophobic time to visit. Jews, Jewish Christians, and especially Pharisaic Jewish Christians were more, not less, concerned about the non-Jewish direction of the Jesus movement. This is the backdrop not only to the arrest and detention of Paul in 58–60 but also to what would happen to James in A.D. 62.

The procurator after Felix, Festus, arrived in A.D. 60 with Judea on the verge of falling into pure chaos. Bandits and zealots plagued the land, and bad blood existed between Herod Agrippa II and the Temple hierarchy (*Ant.* 20.182–96). Festus was a capable man, and he was able to prevent all-out war from breaking out, but Judea was nonetheless a seething cauldron waiting to bubble over.

Festus, however, could not have known he was facing a divided Jewish leadership when he addressed the matter of Paul (Acts 25.1–5), and in any case he was off the scene rather quickly, for he died in office. This prevented a natural transition to the next procurator, Albinus. There was an interregnum, a gap between the rule of one procurator and the next, and so the high priest Ananus decided to seize the moment to strike at the heart of the Jewish Christian community.

Josephus provides a remarkably frank and direct report of what transpired in A.D. 62, a report that is critical of the Jewish Temple hierarchy.

JOSEPHUS ON THE DEATH OF JAMES

I will allow Josephus to speak for himself, for he provides us with the only early account of James's martyrdom, for the New Testament is silent on the matter.

> The younger Ananus, who as we have said, had been appointed to the high priesthood, was rash in his temper and unusually daring. He followed the school of the Sadducees, who are indeed more savage than any of the other Jews, as I have already explained, when they sit in judgment. Possessed of such a character, Ananus thought that he had a favorable opportunity because Festus was dead and Albinus was still on the way. And so he convened the judges of the Sanhedrin and brought before them a man named James, the brother of Jesus, who was called the Christ, and certain others. He accused them of having transgressed the Law and delivered them up to be stoned. Those of the inhabitants of the city who were considered to be the most fair-minded and who were strict in observance of the Law were offended at this. They therefore

secretly sent to King Agrippa urging him, for Ananus had
not even been correct in his first step [of convening the
Sanhedrin without Albinus' permission], to order him to
desist from any further such actions. Certain of them even
went to meet Albinus who was on his way from Alexandria,
and informed him that Ananus had no authority to con-
vene the Sanhedrin without his consent. Convinced by
these words, Albinus angrily wrote to Ananus threatening
to take vengeance upon him. King Agrippa, because of
Ananus' action, deposed him from the high priesthood
which he held for three months. (*Ant.* 20.199–203)

This account has struck the vast majority of scholars as frank
and unlikely to reflect later Christian padding or editing. It was
Christian copyists who in large measure preserved Josephus's
works through the centuries after the New Testament era, for
Jews often saw Josephus as an ambiguous figure who had collabo-
rated with Rome. When Josephus was captured by Vespasian
during the Jewish War, he not only prophesied (correctly) that
Vespasian would soon be emperor, but he also proclaimed that it
was God's will that Rome rule the region, and apparently he informed on other Zealots, too. The Christian copyists on occasion
edited his work, as is usually recognized, for instance, in the passage that speaks about Jesus (*Ant.* 18.63–64). Editing is not
thought to have taken place in this present passage.

Josephus, it is true, is a tendentious writer, and it is fair to say
that here his concern is not with James per se, whom he mentions
only in passing, but with chronicling how the Jewish and Roman
leadership acted. But it is often what one says in passing, which is
less likely to reflect the ax one is grinding, that is most historically
revealing.[1] So we need to consider the account carefully. Later we
will look at Christian accounts of the death of James, which do reflect later hagiographic and anti-Semitic tendencies,[2] but this passage does not do so.

The first thing to notice is that Josephus calls James "the
brother of Jesus," just as in the New Testament and also on the ossuary. The term used here is *adelphos,* not the Greek word for

cousin, and this independent testimony to the relationship of James to Jesus is both early and important. Josephus calls Jesus the so-called (*legoumenou*) Christ but does not call James the so-called brother of Jesus.[3] Thus, it was not just early Christian writers who called James the brother of Jesus. This early Jewish historian did so as well.

Second, the passage emphasizes that James was a Torah-true, faithfully observant Jew. Indeed, it is the basis of the complaint of injustice to Albinus, and it seems clear that Josephus definitely agrees an injustice was done to James. Furthermore, it was the strict Jews who complained about the injustice done to James. Presumably they recognized him to be a good and faithful Jew, perhaps in spite of his messianic beliefs about his brother. Indeed, the action against James was considered such an injustice that it led to Ananus being deposed.

Third, stoning was indeed a possible punishment for lawbreaking in the form of blasphemy, false teaching, or being a troublemaker and seducer of the Jewish faithful, and this is the punishment Josephus says James underwent.[4] The sentence is indeed more believable in this volatile and very Jewish setting than in the latter Christian accounts, which have James being pushed from the pinnacle of the Temple and then struck thereafter as well.[5] In short, James, like his brother, suffered a travesty of justice, at the hands of an unscrupulous high priest who was critiqued not only by Josephus but also by other fair-minded, Law-observant Jews of Jerusalem. There is nothing in this account that reflects later anti-Semitic or pro-Christian sentiments, and it deserves to be given its proper weight.

Clearly, then, James commanded respect not only within his own Jewish Christian constituency but also among other Jews in Jerusalem as well, including very strict ones. This could hardly have been the case if James had not been a pious and observant Jew himself.

It is then all the more remarkable that James was able to take a middle way between Judaizing Pharisaic Christians, on the one hand, and the Pauline line, on the other. The events also reveal what James was up against as he tried to forge a workable model

of Christian community that could include both uncircumcised
Gentiles and Jewish Christians, even strictly observant ones. James
was not only James the Just, faithful to the Law, he was James the
Mediator, whose broader perspective on the true essence of the
Law and of faith and grace shines through.

THE BURIAL OF JAMES

The discovery of the ossuary could fill in some of the missing
pieces in James's story. As we now know, with the discovery of the
ossuary, James appears to have been buried in Jerusalem and in a
thoroughly Jewish manner distinctive to the period of Jewish history between the rule of Herod the Great and the fall of the
Temple in A.D. 70. We know that the ossuary was found in an area
near or in the old City of David where there were Jewish tombs.
In other words, James was not likely buried in a graveyard specifically for Christians. He was buried with his fellow Jews.

Second, it is not likely that he was laid to rest in a family plot.
If James had been buried in a family cave where other ossuaries
were already in place, it is likely that, as in the case of the high
priest Caiaphas's ornate ossuary (discovered in 1990), the inscription would have been placed on the end of the box so his ossuary could be distinguished from the others, which would have
been placed lengthwise in niches in the walls of the cave. Instead,
we have an inscription on the side of the bone box, and not one
hastily scrawled on it for mere identification purposes, as in the
case of Caiaphas's and many other ossuaries. James's ossuary has
what can only be called an honorific inscription, and an odd one
at that, as we saw in part 1, for it mentions the name of not only
his father but also his brother.[6]

Also, James was not carried back to Nazareth and buried
there. His fellow Jewish Christians in Jerusalem were his primary
family and community at the time he died, and in all likelihood
they provided for his burial. And then, as we have already
learned, burial among Jerusalem Jews at that time was commonly
a two-stage process in which the body first was laid out and allowed to decay, and then the bones were taken and carefully put

in a ossuary. The skeleton was taken apart so it would fit within a rather narrow and often short container.[7]

As we learned in chapter 5, belief in a bodily resurrection was held in Judaism at the time of Jesus, at least among the Pharisees. Early Jewish Christians very much followed in the footsteps of the Pharisees in this matter. Remember that Jesus himself was laid out on a stone slab in anticipation of reburial. There was a precedent in the family for following this procedure for James. And since it was believed that Jesus had already been raised from the dead, James and other early Christians believed that they would also be raised. Notice how Paul in 1 Corinthians 15 calls Jesus' resurrection only the firstfruits, or beginning, of the resurrection of God's people. Early Jewish Christians believed their savior had been raised from the dead. They looked forward to a like destiny.

The Jewish Christians who buried James evidently wanted to honor him in death, and they apparently expected some would come and visit the burial spot and see the inscription written on the side of the box. The association with his brother is the most honorific part of the inscription. It also is the one means by which this James could be clearly identified by those who visited the tomb. This James had been known by Jews and Jewish Christians alike as "the brother of Jesus," the Christ or the Messiah, and hence the most notable and in some minds notorious first-century Jew. James's glory was in part a reflected glory, and he himself was perfectly comfortable with being known as a servant of Jesus. He was not one who sought honorific titles for himself.

THE IMMEDIATE AFTERMATH

What happened after James died? According to church tradition, he was replaced by another relative of Jesus named Symeon, son of Clopas, as head of the Jerusalem church.[8] Symeon is called a cousin of the Lord whom all deemed appropriate to be the next *episcopus*, literally "overseer" of the community, now translated as "bishop." This indicates that the connection with Jesus' family continued to be important to the Jerusalem church.[9]

The fourth-century church historian Eusebius also tells us that at the outset of the Jewish War, shortly after James's death, Jewish Christians in Jerusalem were warned by a prophecy to flee, and they did so to Pella, north of Jerusalem and Judea, east of the Jordan, and south of Galilee (*Hist. Eccl.* 3.11.1). Somewhere in the mid-60s, or at least by 67–68, Jewish Christians fled the deteriorating situation in Jerusalem, including the food shortages and infighting among Jews.

One reason to trust this tradition is that Pella is an odd choice of destination if one were making up an escape story. Damascus and Antioch, much farther north, were more likely to be chosen since they had clear and early connections with the Jerusalem church, as accounts in Acts confirm.

While it is not true that early Jewish Christianity died out because of the fall of Jerusalem and its Temple, it is true that it lost its central focus, for it was a Law-observant form of Christianity, and this included worship in the Temple. In quick succession, the Jewish Christian community lost its main leader, James, and then its main social context and religious focus when the Romans destroyed the Temple.

But did Jewish Christianity return to Jerusalem after the Jewish revolt against Rome in A.D. 70 and before the Bar Kochba revolt in the early second century?[10] Apparently some Jewish Christians did return, for Eusebius tells us that Symeon was not martyred until the time of the emperor Trajan in the early second century (*Hist. Eccl.* 3.32.1–6).

James had successfully established one form of the Jesus movement in Jerusalem, and it clung to its identity and location despite severe trauma and difficulties involving not one, but two Jewish revolts (including the Bar Kochba revolt). But we have already begun to discuss the James traditions in early Christian literature. It is time to do so in a more thorough manner. As we shall see, Christian literature provides a variety of traditions about James that postdate the material in the New Testament and Josephus; some of it helps us understand the historical James better, and some of it amounts to a series of legends about or involving James.

CONCLUSIONS

The death and burial of James are not recorded in the New Testament. This is in part because the one history book in the New Testament, the Acts of the Apostles, takes us only to the year 60, and James died after that. We must then rely on Josephus's account and to a lesser extent on the later Christian accounts of the event. Given the volatile and often violent situation that existed in Jerusalem in the decade of the 60s, James could have been martyred by Sadducean Jewish Temple officials. After all, the same priestly family seems to have been involved in some way in the crucifixion of James's brother Jesus.

Josephus's account of James's demise is credible, especially because the matter is simply used by Josephus as an illustration of the abuse of power by a renegade high priest. Josephus refers to James only in passing, and there is no reason to doubt he is correct in saying that James's martyrdom was seen as an abuse of power and an injustice by some fair-minded Jews who protested to the incoming procurator. What Josephus does not tell us is how and where James was buried. We must turn to the early Christian accounts for clues on this matter. Josephus does suggest that James was an observant Jew and that other such Jews took umbrage when he was unfairly executed.

Since stoning was a punishment reserved for particular crimes, it appears likely that James was accused of being either a blasphemer or a false teacher leading the faithful astray. In a detailed study, Bauckham concludes, "Our attempt to explain Josephus's account of the death of James has therefore left us with two plausible possibilities: that he was executed as a blasphemer or as a *maddiah* [one who leads astray the faithful] (of course it is possible that he was convicted of both crimes). Both possibilities have the advantage of coherence with the policies of the Temple authorities towards Jesus and the Jerusalem church at an earlier stage in its history."[11] This assumes that the action of the high priest was not purely malicious. Though Josephus portrays the priest in question as impetuous, this is simply his stock way of referring to young authority figures of whom he thinks poorly. It is more likely, since Josephus says the Sanhedrin was assembled, that a judicial verdict was passed on James, just as one was probably passed about thirty years earlier on his brother Jesus.

It is telling that this blow to the early Jewish Christian community did not immediately cause it to flee en masse. Rather, Jewish Christians seem to have stayed in the city long enough to allow the flesh of the deceased to desiccate and to rebury the bones. That would mean that the reburial likely took place in the year 63 or 64.[12] This also means that the now-famous inscription was written on the eve of the real outbreak of the Jewish revolt. Jewish Christians were not abandoning their city at this juncture. Rather, it seems that they were carefully and quietly honoring their dead leader and continuing in the tradition he had taught them, namely, practicing Jewish customs and speaking the language only Semites used in the region, Aramaic. The fact that Jude, another prominent brother of Jesus, Jesus' cousin Symeon, and perhaps a few other members of Jesus' family were at the center of the Jewish Christian community in Jerusalem, which had been their home base for a long time, may well have contributed to their loyalty to Jerusalem, even in increasingly dangerous circumstances.

In the next chapter we closely examine the early Christian traditions about the death and burial of James.

---

1. This was rightly emphasized in the helpful lecture given by Steve Mason, an expert in the interpretation of Josephus, at the Ossuary Panel Discussion at the Society for Biblical Literature (SBL) meeting, November 23, 2002, in Toronto, Ontario.

2. The term *hagiography* means writing that emphasizes someone's holiness or even turns someone into a saintly figure, polishing their halo a bit. Such writings then tend to pad the historical facts to increase the godly image. Anti-Semitism is a strong prejudice against things Jewish.

3. Louis Feldman pointed out at the SBL meeting in Toronto in November 2002 that the term *so-called* does not have to have a polemical edge. It can simply mean "the one who was named or known as" the Christ.

4. See the important essay by Richard J. Bauckham, "For What Offence Was James Put to Death?" in *James the Just and Christian Origins,* ed. Bruce Chilton and Craig A. Evans (Leiden: Brill, 1999), 199–231.

5. Nevertheless, there may be a historical memory behind the Christian account, for as Bauckham shows, it was the normal Jewish procedure for stoning to first push a person off a high place and then stone them (see Luke 4.29, where the practice was tried on Jesus). See Bauckham, "For What Offence," 202–4.

6. Greco-Roman inscriptions on sarcophagi could be quite extensive, in contrast to what we find on Jewish ossuaries, and they were often honorific. It was a regular feature of such inscriptions to tout one's accomplishments in life, as for example we find in the inscription mentioned in *New Documents Illustrating Early Christianity,* vol. 2, ed. G. H. R. Horsley (North Ryde, New South Wales: Ancient History Documentary Research Centre, Macquarie University, 1982), 84, which includes the line "and I having sailed around a great deal and served many magistrates. . . ." The James inscription is honorific only in the sense that it mentioned James's more famous brother, which confers honor back on James.

7. In James's case, the ossuary is just long enough to contain the longest bone as well as the smaller ones.

8. Eusebius is quoting Hegesippus in *Hist. Eccl.* 4.22.4.

9. As my doctoral student Laura Ice has suggested, this may have been because of the Jewish tradition about the priesthood being passed down within a family line. For example, one member or another of the family of Caiaphas was in power as high priest most of the first century until the destruction of the temple in A.D. 70. This conjecture becomes all the more plausible when we consider the fact that James was seen as one of the pillars of the new eschatological Temple God was building among his messianic people.

10. The so-called Second Jewish Revolt (really the third if you count the Maccabean wars) occurred in the early second century and was led by Simon bar Kochba. It was as ill fated as the revolt in the 60s. Thereafter the Romans imposed severe restrictions on Jews and especially on visits to Jerusalem.

11. Bauckham, "For What Offence," 228.

12. Sometimes in the hill country of Judea, with its more moderate climate, it could take a considerable period of time, even over a year, for a body laid in a cave to deteriorate until only the bones remained.

12

JAMES THE LEGEND

Legendary accounts relating to James are widespread throughout early Christian literature. Such accounts confirm James's importance as a principal founder of Christianity and, surely, as the leading brother of Jesus in the formative period of the faith. A legend is by definition a story or narrative that has some roots in history but has been expanded in nonhistorical ways. The remarkably large corpus of early Christian literature involving James comes from both some fringe Christian movements (such as Gnosticism) and from more mainstream groups.

Different motives drove the various works: (1) many early Christians were interested in trying to claim James for their own causes; (2) some wanted to fill in the gaps in the story of James in order to make better sense of the canonical record; (3) some sought to polish the halo over the head of someone who had been widely admired and recognized as a righteous person by Jews, Jewish Christians, and others. While some of these traditions cover aspects of James's life that we have covered previously, we deal with them together here because they are from a later period and are more historically doubtful. They reflect the veneration given to James as time went on.

JAMES IN THE NAG HAMMADI LIBRARY

The Nag Hammadi Library comprises papyri discovered in the sands of Egypt in 1945.[1] The texts in this collection generally have a Gnostic flavor. Gnostics believed that secret or esoteric revelation was needed to understand life and usually also that this insider knowledge could be derived only from seers or sages who had special connection with the divine. There tends to be a dualistic and ascetical bent to Gnosticism in which matter is seen as evil and spirit good, and Gnosticism was one stream of Christian tradition that was later suppressed.

The Gnostic movement, if we may call it that, seems to have been an offshoot of the developing Coptic Christian tradition in Egypt, which saw itself as descended from early Jewish Christianity. What is interesting about this Gnostic collection of documents is how many of them mention James or actually try to claim James in some way for their own causes. These include the Gospel of Thomas, the Apocryphon of James, and the First and Second Apocalypses of James.

These texts can be dated no earlier than 290–346, since they are connected with Father Pachomius, who established eleven monasteries in Egypt. We should not think of all these documents as being created at that time, especially not the Gospel of Thomas, which in its original form probably dates to the early second century. These documents were apparently hidden and buried on account of the pastoral letter of Athanasius in A.D. 367, which declared such Gnostic material heretical.[2] They nonetheless contain some interesting features that affect our estimation and understanding of James.

Pride of place among these documents should be given to the Gospel of Thomas. This Gospel venerates Didymos Judas Thomas, that is, Jude the brother of Jesus, believed to be Jesus' twin brother (hence the name *Didymos* and *Thomas*, which mean "twin" in Greek and Aramaic, respectively).[3] In the Gospel we find a surprising saying about James. Logion 12 (a logion is a saying) reads: "The disciples said to Jesus: 'We know that you will depart from us. Who is to be our leader?' Jesus said to them:

'Wherever you are, you are to go to James the Just, for whose sake heaven and earth came into being.'"

We find here the first reference to James as "the just" or "the righteous." Also, notice that it says the disciples are to "go to James." This likely refers to the fact that James was not itinerant. He was located in Jerusalem, and if one wanted contact with him, one had to go to him (just as we saw in Galatians 1–2, where Paul went up to Jerusalem to visit with James).

John Painter, whose book *Just James* contains the most thorough treatment of the James tradition, points out that the phrase about heaven and earth quoted above is a traditional Jewish one. Several early texts refer to the righteous and how God made creation especially for them. For instance, in 2 Baruch 14.19 we hear, "The world was created for the righteous" (see also 4 Esdras 6.55; 7.11 says it was created for Israel).

This suggests that this saying originated fairly early on in the Jewish Christian community and was adapted and adopted by both mainstream and more sectarian or fringe Christian groups. While it simply confirms what we know about James as a leader and a righteous person, it also tries to fill in a gap that the New Testament literature left out: how James became the leader of the Jerusalem church. The Thomas tradition suggests he was appointed directly by Jesus, while the Clement tradition (which we discuss below) suggests he was appointed much like the twelfth apostle in Acts 1.15–17.

The Apocryphon of James is another Gnostic text and claims to be a book of secret revelation written by James in the form of a letter. It, like the Gospel of Thomas, involves various sayings of Jesus, some of which have parallels not only in the synoptic Gospels, but also in the farewell discourses in John's Gospel. It was written well after those canonical Gospels and draws on them. Some scholars have suggested, since James is not specifically identified as Jesus' brother or as "the just," that another James, perhaps the son of Zebedee, is meant. This is unlikely, however, since it is James the Just that is referred to elsewhere in the Nag Hammadi documents.[4]

This book tries to further the reputation of James as an important early Christian leader by indicating that he, along with

Peter, received special, exclusive revelation not given to the Twelve. It is also interesting that at 1.9–10 of this document "James" says that he has composed his Apocryphon in the Hebrew alphabet. This probably reflects a memory that James did know the Old Testament, even knowing it in Hebrew.[5]

The Apocryphon also tries to make James a more crucial figure than Peter by having James utter the saying that the synoptic (or parallel) Gospels (Mark, Matthew, and Luke) attribute to Peter about leaving everything to follow Jesus (compare Mark 10.38 to Apocryphon 4.25–28). Here we see a tendency that I call "compensation." This document is written at a time when the legend and importance of Peter and other key early Christian figures is growing in some quarters, and there is apparently fear that James will be eclipsed. The response to this, whether in the Coptic Gospel of Thomas or in this Apocryphon, is to compensate by stressing James's importance, leadership, or closeness to Jesus or God.

More of the same sort of compensation can be found in the First and Second Apocalypses of James. The First Apocalypse is important because it names Addai as the successor of James, and Addai is clearly also named by Eusebius as a person who founded Christianity in Syria (*Hist. Eccl.* 1.13). This reminds us that these documents involving James, including Thomas and the First Apocalypse, seem to have originated in Syria, in the Jewish Christian community there. It is also valuable to note that Aramaic, the language of Jesus and his brothers, eventually evolved into Syriac, and there are those who believe that ancient Syriac versions of the Gospels preserve more of the Aramaic and hence more original forms of Jesus sayings from the Gospels than we know from their Greek versions. The James documents were taken to Egypt, put into Coptic (the Egyptian language of the time, which persists among the Egyptian Christian Copts until today), and were expanded according to the interests of Gnostics. For instance, in the First Apocalypse of James, the postresurrection dialogues of Jesus with disciples are set not on the Mount of Olives but on Mount Gaugela in Syria.

Several features of the First Apocalypse are of interest. First,

James is again called the Just in this document (31.30; 32.1–3; 43.19–23). Second, and surprisingly, his leaving Jerusalem and fleeing to Pella is mentioned (25.15). Third, James is clearly presented as the brother of Jesus (24.13–16).[6] Last, James is said to have authority over the Twelve as well as the early church (42.20–25). In this light, it seems clear that this document originated in a Jewish Christian community in Syria, even though later it was transformed into something of a Gnostic tract in Egypt. It provides more evidence that Jewish Christians were continuing to maintain the importance of James as an early Christian leader in the face of rival claimants such as Peter. There is very little in the Second Apocalypse of direct interest to us, except to say it attributes to James more secret revelations.

Painter is right in concluding that these documents seek to establish James as the proper successor of Jesus and the head of the early church. The authority of James seems to be partly rooted in the fact that he saw the risen Jesus, which becomes a basis for claiming he had revelations from the risen Jesus, as well as in his being the brother of Jesus.

JAMES IN EARLY CHRISTIAN SOURCES

Perhaps the most popular and influential apocryphal book connected with James is the Proto-Evangelium of James. This document names James as its author (25.1), though this can be deduced from the text itself, which says, "Now I, James, who wrote this history in Jerusalem, there having arisen a clamor when Herod died, withdrew myself into the desert until the tumult in Jerusalem ceased." It apparently was written in the second century[7] and was used by the Alexandrian church father Origen and was possibly known to Clement of Alexandria.

Because the fifth-century church father Jerome objected to the book's position that Jesus' brothers were children of Joseph by a prior marriage (rather than cousins), the book fell into disuse in the Western part of the church but remained popular in the East.[8] A measure of its popularity is shown by the fact that it was translated into Syriac, Ethiopic, Georgian, Sahidic, Armenian, Slavonic, and also Latin—languages from areas where various forms of the Orthodox Church would later develop.

Proto-Evangelium literally means the proto-Gospel or pre-Gospel and is sometimes called an infancy Gospel. The work is clearly dependent on the birth narratives found in Matthew and Luke, though it adds its own Jamesean twist to the tale. For example, at 17.2, James is said to be leading the donkey that the pregnant Mary is riding on with Joseph trailing along behind (see the painting by Giotto illustrating this scene in the color insert). What distinguishes this infancy or birth narrative from the ones in the canon is that the focus is on the virginity of Mary rather than on the birth of Jesus.[9] We saw in an earlier chapter that the presence of other brothers and sisters has caused concern among some with regard to Mary's purity. Underlying that concern is a sort of asceticism that sees sexual intercourse as in some way defiling.

The book sets out to narrate the miraculous birth of Mary first, but unlike in later Catholic traditions Mary's birth is here patterned on the birth of Old Testament figures such as Samuel. She, like Samuel, is dedicated as a child to God (7.1) and serves in the Temple. Her presence there, however, becomes a serious problem when she reaches puberty, because of the ritual impurity associated with menstruation in Jewish tradition.

Rather than offering a story of normal bethrothal, as we find in Matthew 1, the Proto-Evangelium of James sees Joseph being chosen to take Mary off the hands of the Temple hierarchy, with Joseph serving as a sort of guardian of the virgin (9.1). She conceives as a virgin, and in fact the story goes on to say that midwives inspect Mary after Jesus' birth. They discover Mary's virginity to be still intact (see 18.1–20.1). Already in this document we have the enhancement of the biblical story of Mary in two ways: her miraculous birth and her perpetual virginity are affirmed.

But in order to make the story plausible that Joseph had been married before and already had children, including James, it had to be posited that Joseph was considerably older than Mary, something Matthew and Luke nowhere suggest. Not only with regard to Mary, but also with regard to Joseph and the brothers of Jesus, this document would prove crucial for the formation of the Orthodox traditions about the Holy Family.

This book attributed to James asserts that in fact James and the other offspring of Joseph are not technically brothers or sisters of Jesus at all. Jesus is born of the virgin Mary without help from Joseph. James and the others are born of Joseph without help from Mary. There is no blood connection between James and Jesus in this tradition. For this reason, the ossuary inscription has implications for the Orthodox tradition as well, not because it asserts that James is the son of Joseph, but because it also asserts that he is the brother of Jesus.

Jewish tradition did allow adoption, and if Joseph accepted Jesus as his son, then Jesus could indeed be regularly called things like "the son (as was supposed) of Joseph" (Luke 3.23) or even the son of the carpenter (Matthew 13.55) without implying more than the adopted son, and he could even be included in Joseph's genealogy with a little finagling (see Matthew 1). But if the brothers of Jesus were cousins, they would simply have been called cousins, using the proper Aramaic and Greek terms.

Painter is direct in the way he assesses the historical evidence:

> There are no grounds for thinking that traditions asserting that Mary bore no other children after Jesus are historically reliable. Rather they are preoccupied with the preservation of the virginity of Mary. Once Mary's perpetual virginity had been accepted, it was necessary to find an alternative understanding of those who were spoken of as the brothers and sisters of Jesus.[10]

While there is perhaps a bit more room for debate than Painter allows about Mary's having children after Jesus, it must be said that the balance of the reliable and early evidence from the New Testament itself suggests that she did and that James was one of them.

It is a dubious process to start with the Proto-Evangelium of James as a basis for understanding Jesus' family relationships and then to read the earlier material in the canonical Gospels in its light. The dangers of anachronism in this procedure are considerable.

Another important document for our discussion is the so-called Gospel of the Hebrews, not to be confused with the New Testament document called the letter to the Hebrews. We do not actually have a manuscript that contains this document. It appears in brief citations in various church fathers' writings.

There is actually only one fragment related to James. It is known as fragment number 7 and is quoted by Jerome (*De vir inl.* 2). After the resurrection, we hear that Jesus immediately

> went to James and appeared to him. For James had sworn that he would not eat bread from the hour in which he had drunk the cup of the Lord until he should see him risen from among them that sleep. And shortly after this the Lord said: "Bring a table and bread!" And immediately it is added: He took the bread, blessed it and broke it and gave it to James the Just and said to him: "My brother, eat your bread, for the Son of Man is risen from among them that sleep."

Most scholars believe this Gospel dates to the second century. If this is correct, it reveals a tradition that differs from what we find in the Proto-Evangelium of James. Here, as we find only in the Second Apocalypse of James 50.13, Jesus calls James "my brother." James is also called James the Just in this passage, as we have seen in some other early Christian literature. This passage is unique in that it suggests James was present at the Last Supper before Jesus' arrest and, like Jesus, took an ascetic vow (Luke 22.18)—only James's vow has to do with his brother's resurrection appearance to him.

It is interesting that we find the phrase "risen from among those who sleep." This was the Jewish euphemism for death, used by Jews who believed that at least the righteous would return from death at the resurrection, refreshed and renewed. The point, then, is that death is no more permanent than sleep for those who rise from the dead.

Notice, too, the use of the title Son of Man for Jesus, which also suggests the Jewish Christian origin of this passage. The second-century Christian historian Hegesippus tells us that it was James's custom before he was martyred to call Jesus "the Son of Man" (Eusebius, *Hist. Eccl.* 2.23). "Son of Man" was a distinctively Jewish expression that Jesus himself regularly used and that meant a human being. But it also echoed the book of Daniel, where it designates the faithful representative of the people of God, and intertestamental literature, where it refers to an apocalyptic messianic figure.[11] The passage also suggests Jesus appeared to James first, and it concludes by Jesus' breaking James's fast for him and serving him bread.

There can be little doubt that this passage intends to promote James as the most important early church leader. Again, this community wants to prevent the legacy of James from slipping into obscurity and presumably, thereby, also to bolster the continued existence of some Jewish Christian community in the second century. Once again James is portrayed as a righteous and pious Jew whose connection with Jesus, including the risen Jesus, explains his place of leadership and importance in the early church.[12] That we find this importance of James argued for in a variety of ways suggests that rival traditions about Peter, and perhaps Paul, were eclipsing those about James, and various Jewish Christians sought to remedy the problem with these sorts of narratives.

There are two interesting and possibly related traditions about a debacle in the Temple involving James. The first is in Hegesippus (in Eusebius, *Hist. Eccl.* 2.23.4–18), and this tradition deserves to be cited at some length. It is probably indebted to Josephus's account of the death of James.

Control of the church passes together with the apostles, to the brother of the Lord, James, whom everyone from the Lord's time till our own has named the Just, for there were many Jameses, but this one was holy from his birth; he drank no wine or intoxicating liquor and ate no animal food; no razor came near his head; he did not smear himself with oil, and he took no baths. He alone was permitted to enter the Holy Place, for his garments were not of wool but of linen. He used to enter the Sanctuary alone, and was often found on his knees beseeching forgiveness for the people, so that his knees grew hard like a camel's from his continually bending them in worship of God and beseeching forgiveness for the people. Because of his unsurpassable righteousness he was called the Just and Oblias [in Greek "Bulwark of the people and Righteousness"] fulfilling the declarations of the prophets regarding him.

Representatives of the seven sects already described by me asked him what was meant by "the door of Jesus" and he replied that Jesus was the Savior. Some of them came to believe that Jesus was the Christ: the sects mentioned above did not believe either in a resurrection or in one who is coming to give every man what his deeds deserve, but those who did come to believe did so because of James. Since therefore many even of the ruling class believed, there was an uproar among the Jews and scribes and Pharisees, who said there was danger that the entire people would accept Jesus as the Christ. So they collected and said to James: "Be good enough to restrain the people, for they have gone astray after Jesus in the belief that he is the Christ. Be good enough to make the facts about Jesus clear to all who come for the Passover Day. We all accept what you say: we can vouch for it, and so can all the people, that you are a righteous man and take no one at his face value.[13] So make it clear to the crowd that they must not go astray as regards Jesus: the whole people and all of us accept what you say. So take your stand on the Temple parapet, so that from that height you may be easily seen, and your words audible to the whole people. For because of the Passover all the tribes have come together, and the Gentiles too."

So the scribes and Pharisees made James stand on the Sanctuary parapet and shouted to him: "Just one, whose word we are all obliged to accept, the people are going astray after Jesus who was crucified; so tell us what is meant by 'the door of Jesus.'" He replied as loudly as he could: "Why do you question me about the Son of Man? I tell you, he is sitting in heaven at the right hand of the great power, and he will come on the clouds of heaven." Many were convinced, and gloried in James's testimony, crying: "Hosanna to the Son of David!" Then again the scribes and Pharisees said to each other: "We made a bad mistake in affording such testimony to Jesus. We had better go up and throw him down, so that they will be frightened and not believe him." "Ho, ho!" they called out, "even the Just one has gone astray!"—fulfilling the prophecy of Isaiah: "'Let us remove the Just one, for he is unprofitable to us.' Therefore they shall eat the fruit of their works."

So they went up and threw down the Just one. Then they said to each other, "Let us stone James the Just," and began to stone him, as in spite of his fall he was still alive. But he turned and knelt, uttering the words: "I beseech Thee, Lord God and Father, forgive them; they do not know what they are doing." While they pelted him with stones, one of the descendants of Rechab the son of Rechabim—the priestly family to which Jeremiah the prophet bore witness—called out: "Stop! What are you doing? The Just one is praying for you." Then one of them, a fuller, took the club which he used to beat the clothes, and brought it down on the head of the Just one. Such was his martyrdom. He was buried on the spot, by the Sanctuary, and his inscribed stone is still there by the Sanctuary. He has proved a true witness to Jews and Gentiles alike that Jesus is the Christ.

This passage may be fruitfully compared with what we find in the Ascents of James, another early church document of which we only have fragments.[14] The Ascents of James relates a story about James ascending the steps of the Temple to enter into an ongoing debate about Jesus' messiahship. The debate was initiated by Peter and another early Christian named Clement (a leader in the church in Rome). In the midst of the debate, another figure called "an enemy" enters the scene and creates havoc, especially after he is refuted by James. This person turns out to be none other than Saul of Tarsus before his conversion. It is said that he throws James down from the top steps of the Temple and that James is left for dead. It should be clear from this passage that we are once again dealing with the rivalry issue and here James is seen to be superior not only to Saul of Tarsus but also to Peter and Clement, for James settles the debate.

The former and longer passage from Hegesippus is more substantive and shows how the legend of James could grow well beyond what the earlier New Testament or nonbiblical traditions said. Several points stand out. Notice at the end of the passage the mention that James was buried south of the Temple Mount near where he was first cast down and then stoned: "He was buried on the spot, by the Sanctuary, and his inscribed *stone* is still there by the Sanctuary." This tradition may be grounded in fact, for it claims the inscription is still visible in its own day. If this was true in the time of Hegesippus, the location of James's burial may indeed have been a place of pilgrimage. The location matches the region of the Silwan Valley, an ancient burial site, where the ossuary apparently was found.

The Greek word translated above as "stone" is *stele,* which is not a technical term for gravestone or headstone. It simply means an inscribed stone and could refer to an inscription on a stone box. The word *stele* is not found in the Greek New Testament or in the Septuagint. It is a term from extrabiblical Greek. Can it refer to an ossuary? As it turns out, it can. As far back as the time of Herodotus, and thus well before the New Testament and centuries before Hegesippus or Eusebius, this term was used to refer to a sarcophagus carved out of rock and inscribed (*Histories* 3.24). Thereafter, the term was used regularly in association with burial stones and, as we now know, sometimes with burial boxes.

Eusebius or his source could have chosen this term—rather than any of the terms used in the New Testament for stones used to close a tomb—to make clear he was talking about an inscribed ossuary. This would provide important confirmation that James was buried in such a box and that it was a place of pilgrimage some centuries after James's death. As we have said before, the inscription on James's ossuary is honorific and is meant to be read.

Notice, too, that this tradition from Hegesippus indicates that James was regularly called the Just. The fuller description of James's piety in this passage goes beyond a portrait of an early Jew and in fact tries to depict James as the prototype of a monk or desert father. He is also portrayed, in his forgiveness prayer, as being like his brother Jesus and like Stephen the first Christian martyr, each of whom prayed for divine forgiveness for those who were killing him (see Acts 7.54–60).

There may be anti-Semitic (anti-Jewish) overtones in the passage as well. It was not enough to push James off the Temple pinnacle. He had to be bludgeoned to death as well. This goes well beyond the common stoning mentioned in Josephus's account of James's death.

Notice also that James speaks of Jesus as the Son of Man, which, since this seems to be another Jewish Christian tradition, supports the supposition that that title was used by early Jewish followers of Jesus perhaps well into the second and third centuries.

We have already been dealing with some traditions found in Eusebius, but now we must turn to his chronicle directly to see what he tells us about James.

JAMES IN THE HISTORY OF EUSEBIUS

There is little dispute that after Luke, the author of the canonical book the Acts of the Apostles, Eusebius is not only the "father of church history" but also our most reliable source for that history. Eusebius follows the lead of earlier serious Hellenistic historians, like Luke, who carefully compared and even quoted from sources (see Luke 1.1–4).[15] Furthermore, Eusebius often tells us what his sources are, which sometimes allows us to check how reliably he quotes them. The end result is that though, like Josephus, Eusebius has some personal agendas to promote (and they are not hard to identify), he can be deemed a careful historian of that period.

Eusebius lived between A.D. 260 and 339, and he wrote his famous *History of the Church* (*Historia Ecclesiastica*) between 300 and 325 while living in Caesarea.[16] Eusebius was fortunate in that Caesarea was a center of Christian learning from before his time. There was the library of Pamphilus, an important early Christian teacher, to draw on, and it is evident the library included many earlier Christian sources, which Eusebius used liberally.

The very first reference to James in Eusebius is found in *Historia Ecclesiastica* 1.12.4–5 in his discussion of the individuals whom Jesus appeared to after the resurrection, and he quotes, with small modifications from 1 Corinthians 15. When he mentions Jesus appearing to James, he calls him "one of the alleged brothers of Jesus." He is thus well aware of an already existing controversy, because of the issue of Mary's perpetual virginity, about the exact relationship between James and Jesus. It is important that unlike some of the other traditions we have already discussed, Eusebius does not suggest there was any rivalry between James and Peter or between James and Paul. He mentions that Jesus appeared to all three of them in a special way. Eusebius, then, takes a less sectarian approach to the earlier material on James than do some Jewish Christian sources.

In his second mention of James, Eusebius, following Hegesippus, tells us that James was appointed bishop of Jerusalem after the death of Stephen (*Hist Eccl.* 2.1.2). This may simply be Eusebius's own deduction based largely on the account in Acts, since James does not really appear as a leader in Jerusalem before Acts 12, which is to say, after the account of Stephen's demise in Acts 7. Eusebius uses a source from Clement of Alexandria (2.1.3), which says that it was after Jesus' ascension into heaven that James became a leader in Jerusalem. This same passage includes the following:

> Then there was James, who was called the Lord's brother;
> for he too was named Joseph's son, and Joseph Christ's father, though in fact the Virgin was his betrothed, and be-

fore they came together. [He goes on to quote Matthew 1 here.] . . . This James, whom the people of old called the Just/Righteous because of his outstanding virtue, was the first, as the record tells us, to be elected to the episcopal throne of the Jerusalem church.

Eusebius then quotes directly from the late first-century Egyptian church father Clement to the effect that Peter, James, and John the disciples did not claim preeminence but rather chose James the Just as the first bishop of Jerusalem. Clement also refers to James and these others being entrusted with "higher knowledge," which was then distributed to other leaders such as the apostles and the Seventy.

This passage provides us with several crucial pieces of information:

1. Eusebius cites Clement from a now lost source saying James was Joseph's son, as was Jesus, but Eusebius qualifies this remark in two ways. He says James was "named" Joseph's son, and about Jesus he goes on to relate the tradition from Matthew 1.25 indicating that Jesus was born of a virgin. He notes as well that James is called the Lord's brother.

2. James is called the Just or Righteous for his virtue. Whether this virtue is tied to the fact that he faithfully complied with the Law or because he suffered martyrdom or both is not explained.[17] Notice, too, that we are told that James had long been called James the Just.

3. Eusebius, unlike his sources, speaks of the episcopal office James holds as the "throne," both here and at 7.19.1. It is hard to know where he got this idea, but perhaps it reflects the knowledge of the "seat of Moses" tradition from the synagogue, coupled with what is said about choice seats in James 2.3. But since Jesus is called both Lord and Christ in this passage, it is far more likely that the reference to the "throne" reflects the notion that James and

the other relatives who were leaders in Jerusalem were part of the royal family of King Jesus. This was a major reason they became leaders in Jerusalem.

4. Eusebius says that Clement of Alexandria mentions the tradition that James was thrown down from the pinnacle of the Temple and then beaten to death with a fuller's club.

5. There is a reference in this text to two well-known Jameses— the son of Zebedee and the son of Joseph. There is no confusion as to which James this text is speaking about, nor is there any reference to any other biblical James.

6. To judge from Babylonian Talmud San. 81b, which says that priests who defile the Temple in some way are to be taken out and clubbed, it is plausible that the tradition of James's being beaten comes from the notion that he was a priestly figure, ministering in some way in the Temple.[18]

In *Historia Ecclesiastica* 2.23.1–3 Eusebius provides his own summary of the death of James. In this passage Eusebius says James was elected to the throne of Jerusalem by the apostles rather than appointed (contrast 3.5.2–3). It is interesting that Eusebius stresses that the Jews respected James because of "the heights of philosophy and religion which he scaled in his life." This is more a Greco-Roman than a Semitic way of speaking of James's righteousness, which reflects the fact that Eusebius's audience was largely Gentile.

Eusebius is familiar with the accounts of Josephus, Hegesippus, and Clement regarding James's death. Eusebius believes that Hegesippus, whom he regards as having lived just after the apostolic age in the second century, gives the most careful account of James's death (2.23.3). In fact, however, the Josephus account is probably both earlier and more circumspect and deserves the nod as best reflecting the historical realities of the situation. While Eusebius is a careful historian by ancient standards, he does not always exercise the sort of critical judgment of his sources one might wish.

Our next passage of note in Eusebius (2.23.19) deserves to be quoted fully: "The account is given at length by Hegesippus, but in agreement with Clement. Thus it seems that James was indeed a remarkable man and famous among all for his righteousness, so the wise even among the Jews thought that this was the cause of the siege of Jerusalem immediately after his martyrdom, and that it happened for no other reason than the crime that they committed against him."

Not only here but in *Historia Ecclesiastica* 2.23.1–3 Eusebius links the martyrdom of James and the fall of Jerusalem as cause and effect. More specifically, he sees the fall of Jerusalem as God's judgment on the Jewish capital because of the injustice of killing James. Of course, this notion is absent from both the New Testament and Josephus[19] and reflects later anti-Semitic tendencies, as does the phrase "even among the Jews."

In Eusebius's day the Jews are clearly a community distinct from his own in a way that certainly was not the case in James's time. Neither would James have been pleased with Eusebius's attitude toward Jews. In a further passage, *Historia Ecclesiastica* 3.7.7–9, Eusebius suggests that the presence in Jerusalem of James the righteous one and other such Jewish Christians prevented judgment from falling on the city while they were there.

In more than one place, Eusebius discusses the succession of leadership in Jerusalem after James's martyrdom. The first of these two passages should be quoted:

After the martyrdom of James and the capture of Jerusalem which instantly followed, there is a firm tradition that those of the apostles and disciples of the Lord who were still alive assembled from all parts together with those whom, humanly speaking, were kinsmen of the Lord—for most of them were still living and they all took counsel together concerning whom they should judge worthy to succeed James and to the unanimous tested approval it was decided that Symeon son of Clopas, mentioned in the Gospel narrative, was worthy to occupy the throne of the Jerusalem see. He was, so it is said, a cousin of the savior, for Hegesippus relates that Clopas was the brother of Joseph. (*Hist. Eccl.* 4.5.1–4; see also 4.22.4)

Evidently Jewish Christians felt a strong need to keep the leadership in Jerusalem within the family of Jesus.[20] Eusebius knows that in his time there is dispute over the nature of the relationship of James to Jesus and Mary, and so he is cautious about how he speaks of members of the family. Here he states rather plainly that Symeon is a cousin of Jesus, being the son of Clopas (and his wife Mary). Nothing here suggests that Eusebius thinks James might also be a cousin of Jesus. We will have more to say on the early church controversy about that in the next chapter.

In his helpful summary of the evidence about James in Eusebius, Professor Painter concludes:

> James is portrayed as the brother of Jesus. Although Eusebius consistently qualifies the relationship as "so-called" or "supposed," that relationship is made a prominent reason for the leadership of James. The qualification is based on Eusebius' acceptance of the virginal conception of Jesus.[21] As part of the wider family of Jesus, James exercised leadership in the earliest church, and members of the family continued to exercise leadership at least until the reign of Trajan. Membership in the family was an important reason for their rise to leadership. The more important the family relationship is perceived to be in the early church, the less convincing are explanations that suggest only a remote relationship or indeed no "natural" relationship between Jesus and James at all. Acceptance of the virginal conception of Jesus means that James and Jesus could not have had a common father, although they had a common mother. This situation would have made them brothers, even if they were only half-brothers. Eusebius himself apparently accepted a close family relationship but was sensitive to the need to qualify it because James had been claimed as an exponent of tradition opposed to the "apostolic tradition."[22]

Painter is referring, in that last sentence, to the Gnostic traditions we discussed earlier in this chapter.

We have now surveyed the basic data from early Christianity about James, with one exception. We have reserved for the next chapter the discussion of the early church controversy over whether the brothers of Jesus were actually brothers or were more remote kin.

CONCLUSIONS

If one measure of a person's impact is the interest and verbiage stirred up after that person's death, then James was a towering figure in the early church. We have seen that many different texts and traditions about James circulated in the early church. Indeed, he was a figure of such importance that even a Jewish historian, Josephus, felt it important to mention his death, *and he mentions none of the Twelve or the apostles or later church leaders in this way.* To judge from Josephus, after Jesus himself, James was the most important person associated with the Jesus movement.

We noticed the tendency, as early as the Proto-Evangelium of James, to try to explain the exact relationship of James to Joseph, Mary, and Jesus. In the second century we first find the notion that James was the son of Joseph by an earlier marriage. It seems clear that the rising tide of asceticism in the church was beginning to dramatically affect how Christian writers evaluated the Holy Family, and that included how they saw James. As the tradition developed, James was portrayed in an increasingly ascetical manner, and in some strands of the tradition he was depicted as a priestly figure, found regularly in the Temple.

Perhaps most important, traditions about the death and burial of James indicate that James was killed below the Temple Mount and buried nearby. This fits with where we understand the ossuary of James was found. Even more intriguing is the evidence that Eusebius, quoting Hegesippus, may in fact refer to the inscribed ossuary of James still being visible in Jerusalem in the fourth century. The term *stele* can indeed refer to an inscribed stone ossuary.

Josephus notes that James was executed by stoning after a meeting of the Sanhedrin, and this suggests that his death was not just malicious but also was punishment for the crime either of blasphemy or of leading God's people astray or both. Unlike Jesus, James was not likely to have been accused of being a sorcerer or a magician, for we have no record of his performing miracles or exorcisms, such as Jesus is said to have done. Josephus sees James's execution as a miscarriage of justice, but his account nonetheless indicates that James was recognized as engaging in some controversial teaching, no doubt about Jesus, whom he called the Lord Jesus Christ in James 1.1.

In the next chapter we look at the debate between Jerome and Epiphanius and others about whether the brothers of Jesus were truly brothers. This debate had been simmering for a long time, at least since the early second century when the Proto-Evangelium of James was written, and those who were wise, like Eusebius, tried to sidestep the issue in the wake of the rising tide of asceticism and the monastic movement in the church. In the next chapter we will see what theological commitments to celibacy and asceticism did to the discussion of James and the Holy Family. That discussion was destined to shape both the Eastern and Western churches well into the modern era. It sparked a debate that James, the devout Jewish follower of Jesus, would surely have been surprised and shocked to hear about.

1. I am indebted to my friend Professor John Painter, whose thorough and critical study, *Just James* (Columbia: University of South Carolina Press, 1997), I am following at various points in this chapter.

2. See the discussion by Painter, *Just James*, 159–60.

3. This peculiar belief seems to have existed only among some Gnostic Christians in Egypt and perhaps in Syria.

4. See Painter, *Just James*, 164–65.

5. Which does not mean Hebrew was his spoken language, but it does mean that James, like his brother Jesus, as we see in Mark 6, could read and presumably write in Hebrew.

6. It is possible that this tradition reflects a remembrance that the bones of James were taken to Pella by the fleeing Christians as Jerusalem approached destruction in the late 60s.

7. We have Bodmer Papyrus V, which contains the book and dates to the third century.

8. See Painter, *Just James*, 198.

9. Rightly noted by Painter, *Just James*, 198.

10. Painter, *Just James*, 199.

11. It possible that "Son of Man" is the way James and other early Jewish followers of Jesus regularly referred to Jesus after Easter. However, we have no evidence of this in the letter of James, though Jesus is hardly referred to in that letter in any case. Perhaps this way of speaking of Jesus was a distinctive feature of the ongoing Jewish Christian community's Christology, as outside the Gospels we find it only once in Acts and in quotations from Daniel in Revelation. On the development of early Christian Christology, see Ben Witherington, *The Many Faces of the Christ* (New York: Crossroad, 1998).

12. Notice also that James's presence at the Last Supper, making him a disciple before the resurrection, stands at odds with the canonical tradition found in John 7.3–5. This story about James may be trying to correct a variety of earlier traditions, perhaps including the order of the witness list in 1 Cor. 15.

13. This is an interesting statement as it matches up with what James says about partiality in his letter.

14. This is yet another document that is extant only in other sources, in this case the Pseudo-Clementine document known as Recognitions. The passage in question is Recognitions 1.66–71.

15. Notice the judgment of Painter, *Just James*, 105: "Generally speaking, when we can check quotations against surviving works Eusebius proves to be a reliable scholar."

16. He was bishop of Caesarea from 313 on.

17. Painter, *Just James*, 112.

18. Painter, *Just James*, 116.

19. As we now have the text of Josephus. The earliest text of Josephus we have comes from the eleventh century and probably reflects at least some Christian editing. But Eusebius had access to much earlier manuscripts of Josephus's work, and it is possible he linked the fall of Jerusalem, not specifically to the death of James, but to a series of such injustices, which would have included the martyrdom of James. It seems clear that Josephus thought highly of James, as we saw in the previous chapter.

20. See Bauckham, *Jude, 2 Peter* (Waco, TX: Word, 1983), 5–133, for extensive discussion about the family of Jesus and the Jerusalem church succession.

21. Not his acceptance of the tradition about Mary's perpetual virginity.

22. Painter, *Just James*, 156.

13

BROTHER, COUSIN, OR KIN?

S ince the consensus of the best experts on Aramaic inscriptions and writing of the first century A.D. is that the ossuary of James is authentic, then it seems that the traditional teaching of the Catholic Church about Mary, Joseph, and the brothers and sisters of Jesus is wrong. The evidence—textual and now archaeological—shows that James was not a cousin but "son of Joseph, the brother of Jesus." But what is really at stake in this debate? How did the Catholic Church come to believe that Jesus could not have a brother?

We have already dealt with the biblical material in which James is called Jesus' brother (see chapter 7). But I have reserved the discussion of the later church controversy until now. The New Testament and Josephus bear no trace of such a controversy, and so I wanted to avoid the danger of reading things back into the original texts, which might happen if one starts with the later controversy.

BACK TO THE BIBLE

First we will explore a common argument used in the early church (and still today) to try to show that James was not a blood brother of Jesus. The earliest reference to Jesus' brothers comes in Mark 6.3 and Matthew 13.55, where the townspeople of

Nazareth list his siblings. Four brothers are named, and the sisters are simply referred to as a group. (Professor Bauckham is probably right that the naming of all four brothers reflects the fact that they were all well known in the early church.)[1]

The problem comes over the first two brothers listed, James and Joses. Some argue that these two men are the same as the James and Joses mentioned in Mark 15.40. The setting is the foot of the cross during Jesus' crucifixion: "There were also women looking on from a distance; among them were Mary Magdalene, and Mary the mother of James the younger and of Joses." Here we discover a Mary who is the mother of James the Little (or Younger) and Joses. Is this a way of identifying the mother of Jesus, only using his lesser-known siblings as a reference? Or is this Mary a different Mary and so, the argument goes, James and Joses could not be "brothers" of Jesus?

First, Mary the mother of James the Younger and Joses was probably not Mary the mother of Jesus. Let us compare the listing of women at the cross and at the tomb. In almost all of these listings of women, Mary Magdalene is mentioned first; then this other Mary, who is mother of James and Joses, is mentioned second or third (see Mark 15.40, 47; 16.1; Matthew 27.56, 61; 28.1; Luke 24.10; John 19.25). But let us focus on John 19.25: "Standing near the cross of Jesus were his mother, and his mother's sister, Mary the wife of Clopas, and Mary Magdalene." This suggests that this other Mary in Mark 15.40 is the wife of Clopas, not the mother of Jesus. In addition, it is hardly likely that Mary the mother of Jesus would be identified simply as Mary the mother of James the Little, especially while Jesus was still alive.

But does this mean that James and Joses are not the brothers of Jesus? There is little evidence to compel us to see the two brothers listed in Mark 6.3 as the same ones mentioned in 15.40. In the earlier portion of Mark's and Matthew's Gospels, the four brothers are almost always found in the company of Jesus' mother. Why would they go from being associated with Mary the mother of Jesus during Jesus' ministry to being associated with this other Mary at the foot of the cross? This solution muddies the picture more than it adds clarity.

Could James the Younger (or Little) be the same person as James the brother of Jesus? The argument linking these two figures does not hold up to close scrutiny. The most likely explanation for Mark's referring to this James as "the Little" is to distinguish him from the other Jameses introduced earlier in the narrative, such as James the son of Zebedee and James the son of Joseph and brother of Jesus. Nowhere else in the New Testament is the James we are discussing called "the Little" or "the Younger." Instead, he is regularly called the Lord's brother.

The most likely explanation is that there must have been another Mary who had another James and another Joses as her children. These were common enough names, and the women seem to have been close relatives with a shared ancestry of male figures to honor in naming their sons, and there is no good reason to identify any of these three people as members of the family of Jesus.

Let us assume, then, that Mary of Clopas is some sort of relative of Jesus' Mary. John calls them "sisters" (19.25). It is more likely that she is a sister-in-law than a sister, since it is hard to imagine parents naming two daughters by the same name. It is more likely that Clopas was a brother of Joseph. If Symeon, who takes over leadership of the Jerusalem church after James, is also this Clopas's son, and thereby a nephew of Joseph, it is understandable why he is called a cousin of Jesus by Eusebius.

Some have sought to identify this Clopas with the Alphaeus mentioned in the list of the Twelve as the father of another James (Mark 3.18; Matthew 10.3; Luke 6.15; Acts 1.13). They thereby wish to show that James the brother/cousin of the Lord was in fact one of Jesus' Twelve disciples! But grammatically this argument has hardly a leg to stand on. Why Mark or Matthew would identify the same person sometimes as James son of Alphaeus and sometimes as James the brother of the Lord and sometimes as James the son of Mary of Clopas is hard to imagine. And why they would portray James as one of the Twelve and then as someone who does not believe Jesus' claims before his crucifixion is simply nonsensical. This sort of reasoning is so convoluted, you can hardly tell the players without a detailed program.[2]

Identifying James the Little with James the brother of Jesus or with James son of Alphaeus is highly unlikely on the basis of the biblical evidence. But certain urgencies, such as protecting the idea of the perpetual virginity of Mary, were driving the discussion of such matters in the fourth century.

THE RISE OF THE COUSIN THEORY

All three ancient views of this matter are still alive today in the three main components of Christianity worldwide. Jerome, the fourth-century church father, taught that James and the other brothers were actually cousins of Jesus, sons of some woman and man other than the biblical Mary and Joseph. This is the most frequently enunciated position of the Roman Catholic Church. Helvidius, a contemporary of Jerome, maintained that James and the other brothers were in fact the children of Mary and Joseph, and so he denied the idea of the perpetual virginity of Mary. This is the usual Protestant view today. Epiphanius held that the brothers were sons of Joseph by a previous marriage. This is the Orthodox position today.

Jerome, on any showing, was a formidable figure. Born around A.D. 347, he was educated in Rome, Antioch, Syria, and elsewhere and was one of the leaders of the movement recommending chastity over the marital state for all Christians. His ascetical inclinations thus dovetailed with his advocacy of the perpetual virginity of Mary. But he was by no means popular, for he had a very confrontational approach to issues and was notably acerbic and polemical. Many in Rome were not happy about endorsing celibacy, not merely for priests, but for ordinary Christians, as a higher way to live. One of these was the layperson named Helvidius.

Helvidius argued against the perpetual virginity of Mary, and for the brothers of Jesus being her offspring, as follows: (1) Matthew 1.18, 25 implies that Joseph did "know" Mary (that is, have sexual relations with her) after the birth of Jesus because it says he did not know her until then. The reference to Mary being found with child "prior to when they came together" refers to prior to when they had a sexual relationship, not merely prior to when they lived in the same house. (2) The reference to Jesus as Mary's firstborn son (Luke 2.7) implies she had others later. (3) Various passages mention Jesus' brothers and sisters. (4) Tertullian agreed with his view, as did Victorinus of Pettau. (5) It was no dishonor that Mary was a real wife to Joseph, as the patriarchs all had wives.[3]

Jerome in his response in 383 basically resorted to ridicule and invective (he accused Helvidius of hardly knowing Greek) rather than cogent retort. He conceded that Tertullian supported Helvidius's case,[4] but then he argued that Tertullian became a heretic. Jerome resorted to misreading church fathers such as Ignatius of Antioch, who did not support the theory of Mary's perpetual virginity or the theory that the brothers were cousins (see *Ephes.* 19). All that Ignatius stressed was the virginal conception, which all the parties in this debate believed in.

Jerome had a weak case. He was right that the Greek word for brother, *adelphos,* can have the sense of spiritual brother, or fellow countryman, but the context would have to indicate this, as the term normally means blood brother. It could also occasionally refer to other close kinship relationships. But in regard to James the brother of Jesus and the other three brothers mentioned with him in the Gospels, no other kinship term is ever used in the New Testament. They are never called cousins, and there was indeed, as I have observed earlier, a perfectly good Greek word for cousin (*anepsios*). The question, then, is where is the evidence in the Gospels that these brothers were in fact cousins when they are not called such.

Jerome argued that James the Little was the same person as both James the brother of the Lord and James the son of Alphaeus. He also argued that Mary of Clopas was also Mary of Alphaeus, seeing Alphaeus and Clopas as two forms of the same name. There are variants to the basic argument of Jerome, but what they all have in common is the assertion, without good evidence, that James the Little is the same as James the brother of Jesus, which we have dealt with above.[5]

The nineteenth-century Bible scholar J. B. Lightfoot showed that up to the time of Jerome there was no notable support for the cousin theory. Jerome was the first notable advocate of this view.[6] Lightfoot is right that the identification of James the Little with the son of Alphaeus is necessary to Jerome's case, but alas, neither of these Jameses is likely to be the same as James the brother of Jesus. Jerome, as it turns out, was motivated to support not only the virginity of Mary but also the celibacy of Joseph.

In fact, Jerome varied some of his views later in his life so that he came closer to the Epiphanian view. For example, he later allowed that Mary of Clopas might have been a different person than the Mary who was the mother of James the Little, but this is fatal to his original argument for the cousin theory. As Painter says, it was Jerome's interest in the idea of celibacy and virginity as the supreme form of the Christian life that prompted him to argue as he did about Jesus, Mary, Joseph, and the other children and to insist upon the perpetual virginity of Mary and also of the celibacy of Joseph. In the setting of early Judaism, it is doubtful any Jew would have read these texts to suggest what either Jerome or Epiphanius argued.[7]

It is telling that John P. Meier, one of the leading Catholic New Testament scholars on the historical Jesus, has responded to the news about the James ossuary by saying that if indeed it is authentic, it is probably the last nail in the coffin of Jerome's view of the brothers of Jesus being cousins.

THE RISE OF THE HALF BROTHER THEORY

A far more probable view, and one held as early as the second century, is the Epiphanian view that Jesus' brothers originated from Joseph's prior marriage. It is found in the Proto-Evangelium of James (9.2; 17.1–2; 18.1), in the Gospel of Peter (as found in Origen, *In Matt.* 10.17), and in the Infancy Gospel of Thomas (16). It is a view that was accepted by Clement of Alexandria, Hippolytus, Origen, and subsequent church fathers. It is interesting that the three first-mentioned sources all have connections to or origins in the church in Syria and appear to go back to the beginning of the second century there. We know that the Syrian church emphasized certain kinds of ascetical piety that were at odds with early Jewish and Jewish Christian views that existed in Jerusalem in the first century.

The problem with the Epiphanian view, among other things, is that it does not pass the plausibility test when it comes to early Judaism. Early Jews were certainly not expecting the mother of the Messiah to be a perpetual virgin. Indeed, their views of human sexuality were not generally ascetical. Neither did they normally associate righteousness with abstention from sex. The burden of proof must be on those who want to argue otherwise in the case of Mary, especially when we realize that she was betrothed to be married before any divine intervention happened in her life.

We dealt with many of the arguments against the Epiphanian view in chapter 7: (1) There is no mention of the brothers of Jesus in the infancy narratives or in Luke 2.41–52. (2) Matthew 1.25 does not prohibit Mary and Joseph having sexual relationships after the birth of Jesus. (3) The absence of Joseph from accounts of Jesus' ministry does not mean he had to be older or that he was previously married. (4) The fact that the brothers of Jesus are often associated with Mary in all four Gospels suggests she is their mother. (5) Most important, there is nothing arising in the Gospel texts to push us in this interpretive direction. This scenario has to be brought from outside and imposed on the biblical texts.

Now the ossuary evidently raises a further problem with the Epiphanian view. The ossuary clearly seems to indicate that James is the brother of Jesus. But if James is the son of Joseph and Jesus is the son of Mary but James is not, then in fact James is not the blood brother of Jesus. The ossuary makes both Jerome's and Epiphanius's views on the matter seem doctrinally motivated. It remains the case that the view that best explains all the evidence with the least amount of special pleading is the Helvidian view.

The church father Origen in his *Commentary on Matthew*, which was written sometime before the year 250, comments at some length about "the brothers" in Matthew 13.54–56. Besides saying that the residents of Nazareth were ignorant of the virginal conception and so quite wrong about Joseph's being the actual father of Jesus, Origen also mentions the Epiphanian view and says that it is put forward by those who wish "to preserve the honor of Mary's virginity to the end." In other words, he admits that the Epiphanian view is not found in the canonical texts and is put forward for theological rather than historical reasons.[8]

Epiphanius has a passage from his work entitled *Panarion* (29.3.8–29.4.4), which dates from somewhere between 366 and 402. It may shed some light on our subject. The text reads: "James having been ordained at once the first bishop, he who is called brother of the Lord and apostle, Joseph's son by nature and spoken of as having the place of the brother of the Lord due to having been reared with him. For James was Joseph's son from Joseph's [first] wife, not from Mary, as we have said in many places and treated of more clearly." Epiphanius adds that James was dedicated as a Nazarite and exercised a priestly role, entering the Holy of Holies once a year, as a high priest would do. He goes on to say that James, like Jesus, was a virgin, never marrying (30.2.6)—a claim that seems to ignore 1 Corinthians 9.5, in which Paul asks, "Do we not have the right to be accompanied by a believing wife, as do the other apostles and the brothers of the Lord and Cephas?" (The claim reflects a certain ascetical Christian piety.)

What Epiphanius never comes to grips with, however, is that on his own showing Jesus and James could not be half brothers since they would share no common parent (James with Joseph and Jesus with Mary). To cover his tracks, Epiphanius then suggests that because James was reared with Jesus, he could be called his brother.

Epiphanius becomes censorious later in his tract, denouncing those who claim that Joseph and Mary had sexual relationships after the birth of Jesus (78.1.3). It becomes clear he is dependent on the Proto-Evangelium of James for his belief in and understanding of Mary's perpetual virginity (78.7.1–78.8.2). He asserts the theory that Joseph was only to be the guardian of a much younger Mary and that he sired James and the other brothers at forty but married a teenage Mary when he was over eighty! In other words, he is arguing that it was never intended to be a consummated marriage.

But Epiphanius has failed to do his math. By this reckoning James would have been seventy years old when Jesus died in A.D. 30 and well over a hundred when he himself died in 62.[9] Such an arrangement was almost completely implausible in early Judaism.

As we have noted, history is written by the winners. For example, Helvidius's tract has survived only by being quoted in Jerome. Jerome's influence proved enormous, not least because he translated the Bible into Latin. The net effect of Jerome's theory was equally enormous, according to Painter:

> It had the advantage of elevating the virginity of Mary and at the same time maintaining the virginity of Joseph. It resulted in the relegation of James, along with the other brothers and sisters of Jesus, to a secondary position. James the brother of Jesus ceased to be a point of focus or concern in any Western tradition.[10]

The discovery of James's ossuary should reopen the debate about James's relationship to Jesus and reassert the importance of James and of Jewish Christianity, and both Jews and Christians may recover a part of their Jewish heritage that has been neglected. That heritage involves seeing James as both the son of Joseph and the brother of Jesus and also as a good and observant Jew who followed his brother Jesus' example to the point of martyrdom. This James deserves to be given his due as the first leader of the Jerusalem church, which spawned all other churches.

CONCLUSIONS

The biblical data we have reconsidered in this chapter can be interpreted in more than one way. Yet not all possible historical explanations are equally probable. As we have seen, the most natural explanation taking into consideration the Jewish context out of which the Gospel stories arise, and taking into consideration the narrative logic of each of the Gospel accounts, is that Jesus had several siblings, four brothers and two sisters, and probably the oldest of these was James. These were probably children of Mary and Joseph born after Jesus was born.

We have reviewed the debate between Jerome, Epiphanius, and Helvidius and noted that Jerome's theory seems the weakest of the three explanations of the biblical data, but the theory of Epiphanius, which became dominant in the Orthodox tradition, is also problematic. It needs to be said that the inscription on the ossuary raises questions not only for Jerome's theory but also for that of Epiphanius. If James is truly the brother, or at least half brother, of Jesus, then they must have at least one parent in common. This is not the case with Epiphanius's view. The view with the fewest problems is that of the layman Helvidius, and it now seems to have received additional confirmation from the inscription on the ossuary.

If one wants to argue that *brother* simply means "kin" despite allowing that *son* literally means "son" on the ossuary inscription, then the burden of proof must be on those who want to make such distinctions. The ossuary inscription has no context that might encourage us not to read both *son* and *brother* literally. In the case of the one other ossuary inscription that mentions a son and a brother, there has never been any suggestion to regard them as anything other than literally that. The ossuary provides us with an opportunity to realize that Jesus' brother James played a crucial role in the origins of Christianity, as did other members of Jesus' family, including his mother (who also has an important and honored role after the crucifixion), likely his aunt, his other brothers, and his cousins. But it also provides a lot more. In the final chapter we consider some of the implications of this remarkable artifact for the study of early Judaism and early Christianity.

1. Bauckham, *Jude, 2 Peter* (Waco, TX: Word Books, 1983), 9.

2. This is one of the major flaws in Robert Eisenman's treatment of these issues in *James, the Brother of Jesus* (New York: Viking, 1996). By a midrashic sort of word or name association, Eisenman tries to identify one James with another and so only further confuses the issue.

3. Notice the defensiveness of the argument here. As my doctoral student Laura Ice has reminded me, in the Jewish environment in which Mary grew up, there might even have been a shaming issue involved with her marrying a man who was so old or so ascetic he would not or could not consummate the marriage. In Helvidius's Christian environment dominated by the ascetic piety of monastic figures like Jerome, Helvidius actually has to argue the opposite—that it would *not* be a disgrace for Joseph to have consummated the marriage. Two very different views of the goodness of human sexual intercourse are presupposed in these very different environments.

4. See *Adv. Marc.* 4.19; *De carne Christi* 7.

5. The critique by Bauckham, *Jude,* 20–25, and John Painter, *Just James* (Columbia: University of South Carolina Press, 1997), 200–223, of several of these variants, by J. McHugh and J. Blinzler, seems decisive.

6. J. B. Lightfoot, *St. Paul's Epistle to the Galatians* (London: Macmillan, 1874), 254–60.

7. Painter, *Just James,* 218, 220.

8. Painter, *Just James,* 201. I have dealt at length with the Epiphanian and with Jerome's views in my *Women in the Ministry of Jesus* (Cambridge: Cambridge University Press, 1984), and in *Women in the Earliest Churches* (Cambridge: Cambridge University Press, 1988).

9. See Painter, *Just James,* 211.

10. Painter, *Just James,* 211.

14

SON OF JOSEPH, BROTHER OF JESUS

What will be the impact of the James ossuary for under-standing first-century Judaism and the origins of Chris-tianity? Of course, it is too soon to know all that may result from this remarkable discovery. Yet some implications seem clear even at the outset, assuming that the authenticity of the ossuary and its inscription holds up, as we fully expect. As of now, the discovery has passed all the most rigorous physical and analytical tests, and the evidence in favor of its authenticity and significance has easily countered the rumors, misgivings, and critiques that have been expressed. So, like discoveries such as the Dead Sea Scrolls and the Gospel of Thomas, it promises to be a crucial link with the world of first-century Judaism and Christianity that will need to be taken account of from now on. Scholars are already revising their work in light of the discovery.

THE JEWISH CHRISTIAN MOVEMENT

In the third quest for the historical Jesus, which was launched in the 1980s and continues even today, there have been some pre-sentations of Jesus that hardly seemed Jewish at all: Jesus as a Cynic philosopher or an obscure peasant rather than a well-known and controversial Jewish teacher and preacher.[1] In this simple ossuary inscription, an inscription that unexpectedly mentions Jesus as the brother of the deceased, we are reminded that this Jesus was someone so important that linking James to him could instantly identify the James in question. In a social context lacking last names of the modern sort, this is a remarkable inscription.

But the inscription also reminds us that this James was someone so important that his community or family took the trouble to perform reburial and have an honorific inscription written in Aramaic on the side of his ossuary. Reburial was by no means a universal practice in the Judaism of the time. As we have seen, only some—perhaps especially those, such as the Pharisees, who believed in the resurrection of the dead—took the trouble to purchase an ossuary, have a name inscribed, gather the bones, and re-inter the deceased's remains. Someone or some group had to care a good deal about James. The use of an ossuary also shows that these Jewish Christians continued to follow the Jewish burial customs of that particular period.

The belief in resurrection was an important one in Judaism at the time of Jesus, even though one major sect, the Sadducees, rejected the belief. On the basis of Ezekiel 37, where the bones provide the basis for reconstituting a person, it seems to have been felt important to try to keep the bones of a deceased person together in one place. This would have been all the more the case with James, since early Christians believed that Jesus already rose from the dead and would return, perhaps even soon, to raise his followers. Thus, while ossuaries do not specifically indicate that the deceased believed in future resurrection, they do likely indicate some sort of strong belief in the afterlife, and in the case of James it surely does point to a belief in bodily resurrection.

Indeed, it would have been especially important in the case of James to keep his remains together, since the risen Jesus appeared especially and particularly to James (1 Corinthians 15). This was understood to be the basis or confirmation of his becoming a follower of Jesus. In other words, since Jesus rose from the dead, the early Jewish Christians expected a similar outcome for James and other righteous followers of Jesus. The righteous would be raised to life, and James was the paradigm of righteousness.[2] If the Jewish Christians who buried James had the same eschatological fervor as some early Christians, they perhaps believed that the onset of the Jewish revolt signaled that the end was indeed coming. This being the case, the founders of the Jesus movement were probably buried with particular care, and their grave sites visited with some regularity.[3]

The inscription is in Aramaic, not in Greek or Latin or Hebrew. It reminds us that James was an early Jew who spoke Aramaic, although he may also have known Hebrew and Greek. This also confirms the impression from the synoptic Gospels that Jesus spoke Aramaic. Why is this so significant? In the first place, ordinary Gentiles or Romans would not have been able to read this inscription. It was written by Jews for Jews.

Maurice Casey has translated portions of Mark's Gospel from Greek back into Aramaic on the assumption that at least parts of that Gospel were written in that language, originally by John Mark in Jerusalem in the 40s.[4] Some of the reviewers of this important work have simply scoffed at what Casey was attempting. This is unfortunate. Perhaps it takes something like the James ossuary to remind us that the earliest Jewish Christians were Aramaic speakers and that the sayings and stories of Jesus were first written down in Aramaic. This is not to say that the community could not have written some matters down in Greek as well, especially if writing to those who lived outside Israel, but when Jerusalem Jewish Christians spoke with each other, they surely spoke in Aramaic, as this inscription confirms.

The earliest Jewish Christians in Jerusalem, while not an exclusionary sect, focused their attention on Jews rather than on Gentiles as did Paul (see Acts 21.20). They did not intend to give up their Jewish customs or the language they and their fellow Jews spoke. They were prepared to be the Jew to the Jew. They were not prepared to be the Gentile to the Gentile because it meant giving up some their Jewishness or at least putting it on hold in some circumstances. The inscription was directed then to a specific audience—Jews, and in particular Jewish followers of Jesus.

As we have noted, the inscription is not simply an identification tag on the end of the box. It is an elegant honorific inscription written along one side of the box and not on its end, which
was customary if the inscription was intended merely to identify
the bones contained in the ossuary. The distinctive nature of this
inscription means it was expected to be seen with some regularity.
It is indeed possible that there were regular visitations to this ossuary. What can perhaps also be deduced is that the Jewish Christian community or at least a part of it intended to stay in
Jerusalem despite the difficulties of the 60s, and despite their
leader having been martyred. In other words, this ossuary would
thus represent an assertion of faith and hope in the future for
these Jewish Christians. We have suggested that James was probably not reburied until A.D. 63 or 64, for it would take some time
for the remains to be reduced to a skeleton. This reburial, then,
would be a significant assertion of faith in the face of turmoil.
The Jewish Christians wanted to remain in Jerusalem, the Holy
City, even if trouble came.

As we have said earlier in this book, James is a historical figure who deserves far more attention, as do the earliest Jewish
Christians. We have seen how not only in the first century but also
in subsequent centuries tensions and rivalries existed in the early
church, and a case was made for one or another Christian leader
being the most important founding figure. There was clearly a
struggle to try to prevent the importance of James from being
eclipsed, as we have seen in a variety of nonbiblical sources.

Clearly anti-Semitism was one of the factors that led to the
eclipse of James and what he stood for. An increasingly Gentile
church became uncomfortable with its strong Jewish heritage. A
modern revival of the study of James and a deeper examination
of the Jewish roots of the earliest Christians might further the discussion between Jews and Christians today of what they still share.
That commonality includes both the historical Jesus and the historical James.

James was an observant Jew who believed his brother was the
Messiah. He and the church he led felt that this was in no way
in conflict with their standing as religious Jews. And for a time,

at least, the religiously observant Jews of James's day seemed to see him as one of their own and so acted to redress the injustice done at his execution. James represents a religious identity that many no longer see as possible (there are "messianic" Jews who claim this same dual identity today, though more conventional Christians and Jews alike tend to find them controversial and problematic). Either one is a Jew or one is a Christian. James said yes to both, as did his brothers and family members, and the Jerusalem church, the mother church of early Christianity.

BEYOND THE JAMES AND PAUL FEUD

Further attention to the James of the New Testament, the brother of Jesus, should also help us get beyond talk of irreconcilable animosity or rivalry between Hebrews and Hellenists, between Jewish and Gentile Christians in early Christianity, and between James and Paul.[5] There is no good historical evidence that early on the Greek-speaking Jew Stephen represented some Hellenist Christian group that was at odds with James and Hebraic theology.

James was certainly an observant Jew throughout his life, and he never strayed from this orientation. He believed Jewish followers of Jesus should be obligated to faithfully observe the Law, whereas Paul regarded Jewish observance as a choice that Jewish Christians could make. James did not believe, as Paul did, that Christ came to liberate Jews from the demands of the Law. But unlike some Pharisaic Jewish Christians in Jerusalem, James also did not believe Gentiles had to assume the full burden of the Law. Indeed, he was prepared to allow them to focus on the heart of the Ten Commandments. The essence of the matter for including Gentiles was avoiding idolatry and immorality, not keeping the entire Jewish Law.

As Paul tells us in Galatians 1, James gave Paul the right hand of fellowship and endorsed his mission to Gentiles. There is no evidence that James and the more hard-line Judaizers held the same view on all matters, though it is likely he was concerned about Jews like Peter and Barnabas ceasing to be Law observant in Antioch. But that is a very different matter from imposing Mosaic ritual strictures about food, circumcision, and the sabbath on Gentile Christians.

From the point of view of understanding earliest Christianity, the revival of interest in James should prompt not only a reexamination of the spectrum of opinions in early Christianity, but also, and especially, a reexamination of claims that James and Paul were fundamentally at odds about including Gentiles in the new community or about the basis on which they were to be included. The evidence from Acts, the letter of James, and even from Galatians does not support this conclusion; neither should later controversies between Gnostic and anti-Gnostic forces in early Christianity, using James and Peter and Paul as a basis for such rivalries, be allowed to determine how we understand the historical James and the world of the first Christians.

CORROBORATING ACTS AND JOSEPHUS

The ossuary has been dated to within a rather precise range not only because of the fact that it is a Jewish ossuary and such ossuaries were used primarily in the first century until the destruction of the Temple in Jerusalem in A.D. 70, but also because of its composition and its inscription, which is in late Herodian Aramaic. We have seen how this fits with Josephus's account of the execution of James in the year 62. But it is also consistent with what we know from Acts 21–26, which indicates that Paul met James in Jerusalem in about 58 and that when he and Luke left Jerusalem in 60 James was still alive.

The latest event recorded in Acts 28 only takes us up to A.D. 62, with Paul in Rome.[6] This is why Luke would not record the death of James. James did not die before the latest event in his chronicle. James's death came shortly after or at about the time this chronicle was ended. In other words, both the positive evidence of James's being alive when Paul was on his last visit to Jerusalem (in 58–60) and the silence of Acts about the death of James support the idea that James died after 60–61. In short, the ossuary supports the accuracy of the accounts in the Bible and in

Josephus's history. It provides further support for what we already knew from these textual sources.

BEYOND PETER AND PAUL

The importance of the family of Jesus in the succession of leaders in Jerusalem has also been underappreciated. Not only James but also Symeon and other relatives of Jesus have been overshadowed by the emphasis on Paul or Peter and their influence. It is time to rectify this overemphasis. Catholics have stressed the Petrine heritage and Protestants the Pauline heritage, but with James and his successors we have a clearly and unashamedly Jewish form of early Christianity.

James was indeed the first head of the Jerusalem church, and he is the one who sorted out its earliest major crisis. The fact that we have a letter from his hand to Gentiles and a letter from his hand to Jewish Christians in the Diaspora confirms his power, authority, and importance.

It has been one of the notable and important trends of the last ten years that various Jewish scholars have made the New Testament and early Christianity their primary field of focus. Scholars such as Amy-Jill Levine, Paula Fredriksen, Daniel Boyarin, Mark Nanos, Alan Segal, Pamela Eisenbaum, and to a lesser degree Shaye Cohen and others have brought their knowledge of early Judaism, combined with an abiding interest in Jesus and his earliest Jewish followers, to the study of the New Testament. And they are following in the great tradition of an earlier generation of Jewish scholars, such as Geza Vermes and David Flusser, who pioneered the study of the literature and religious setting in which Jesus and early Christianity emerged. Their body of work has led to a rethinking of many of the supposedly well assured results of New Testament scholarship about the nascent days of the Nazarene sect in Jerusalem. Perhaps the anti-Semitic readings of the Paul-James controversy and of the tensions between Jewish and Gentile Christians can be overcome now with some prodding and rethinking. Perhaps James holds a key to understanding and exposing prejudices that distort reality.

Learning about James also provides an opportunity to update the stereotypes many Christians have of Pharisaic Judaism, seeing it as mere legalism with no appreciation of grace. This false impression is not surprising since the Gospels' condemnations of "the Jews" and especially of the Pharisees are so strident and common. Nonetheless, the fact is that in many ways, including in their belief in resurrection and a positive afterlife, Jesus and James were closer to the Pharisaic belief structure than to that of other Jewish sects of the time, such as the Sadducees. It is also not incidental that the most famous Christian convert, Saul of Tarsus, had also been a leading Pharisee.

The Pharisaic movement survived the fall of the Temple and became a Torah-centric movement coupled with an emphasis on oral tradition. Similarly, the Jesus movement also survived the fall of the Temple in A.D. 70 and became a Word-centered religious tradition, both in its oral and written forms. These two forms of early Judaism had more in common than is often thought. Since both modern Judaism and modern Christianity developed out of these two early Jewish movements, there is much more to be learned about our common roots. The ossuary of James prompts us to get on with the task.

WHAT OF MARY?

However controversial the discussion may become, the ossuary of James raises in a particular way the issue of James's relationship with Joseph's wife, Mary. In Protestant circles, Mary has all too often been neglected. In Catholic circles, later church traditions make it difficult to get back to the original historical realities, which are vital for understanding what authentic Christianity is.

If the historical evidence militates against the doctrine of Mary's perpetual virginity, how important is that belief? It is my understanding that the doctrine of the perpetual virginity doesn't have the authority or infallibility that an ex cathedra pronouncement has in the Catholic Church, though it does have the authority of a de fidei pronouncement, that is, a declaration intrinsic to the Catholic faith. Can the matter be revisited, as have so many beliefs and practices once considered sacrosanct in the Catholic tradition?

What should be the relationship between historical evidence and church dogma in the Catholic and Orthodox traditions? If new historical evidence calls into question traditions that are based on the Proto-Evangelium of James and not on the biblical and earliest texts, then these traditions need to weigh the matter of how strongly they should hold on to certain beliefs that may not be true or vital to Christian faith. The discovery of the ossuary provides a compelling opportunity for this kind of reassessment.

SUMMING UP

The ossuary should not be merely a vehicle for reopening old debates and even older wounds. With a sufficient amount of openness on the part of all, it could lead to a serious probing of what it means to call someone a Jew or a Christian in antiquity *and* today. In other words, especially for Christians, but also for Jews, the question is not so much, "Who was James?" Rather the salient question is, "If this devout Jew and brother and devout follower of Jesus was the revered leader of the original Christian community, then what does it mean to be Christian today?"

What might the implications of this ossuary be for the ordinary Jew or Christian?

First, the ossuary reminds us of the cultural distance that exists between us and those early Jews and Christians. Neither modern Jews nor modern Christians speak Aramaic or practice burial rituals the way James's community did. This cultural distance reminds us that we must be careful about what assumptions we bring to the study of an ancient artifact—and to our understanding of the Bible. The past is in many ways a foreign country. The people of biblical times and of the first centuries did indeed view and do things very differently than we do today.

Second, while the James ossuary may not convey any totally new information to believers, it does seem to provide further confirmation that the Bible often is speaking of real historical figures and real historical events, despite the skepticism about its historical truth that has emerged from many directions in our times. This historical confirmation of Gospel accounts is welcome news in a skeptical age that demands that you "show me" the evidence before I can believe. The ossuary evidently provides us with the earliest physical evidence that Jesus, James, and Joseph all existed, and not merely existed but lived as devout early Jews tied to the Holy Land, practicing Jewish burial customs and sharing the spoken language of Jews of that locale, Aramaic.

Third, in an age of visual and tactile learners, we now have a physical artifact, not just another text, to view and ponder. The effect of seeing the ossuary can be overwhelming. It was amazing to watch so many people file through the Toronto museum and stop and reflect on the significance of the ossuary. For many of them it was an unprecedented way to get in touch with their own roots and faith. The excitement about the discovery seems to lie largely in the fact that finally we can virtually touch Jesus through this name, Yeshua, on this inscription. For me the experience was like the first time I bought two first-century Jewish coins, a widow's mite and a Tyrian half shekel. It then occurred to me to wonder, Whose hands had this coin passed through? Could Jesus himself have handled these coins?

Physical objects provide a vital tactile connection with the past and with our ancestors, and this is especially so with a burial box that contained an ancient person's remains. There is, then, a certain mystery and wonder involved in coming into contact with ancient physical objects connected to important ancient people, especially those who have been formative for one's own faith.

Last, there is once more the matter of Jesus. To ask who was this James buried in this box is also to ask why he is called the brother of Jesus even on his ossuary. Why did Jesus continue to have such a celebrated presence three decades after he had died? Why was he mentioned on his brother's burial box so many years later? It is surely because the historical significance of Jesus did not decrease as the first century went on. Rather, it increased. Jesus was viewed not just as another famous Jewish teacher, but as the long-awaited Messiah by the earliest Jewish Christians and thus a more-than-human presence to be worshiped and followed as the way to reconciliation with God. The proof of this is clear enough from one of our earliest documents, Paul's first letter to the Corinthians.

In concluding his letter, Paul in 1 Corinthians 16.22 offers up a prayer in Aramaic, *"Maranatha,"* which means "Come, Lord." In other words, Jesus is already called Lord by Aramaic-speaking Jewish Christians, and he is prayed to. Now early Jews did not pray to people who were merely revered dead rabbis, teachers, or even prophets. They might well pray for a rabbi to be raised on the last day, but they would not pray *to* him and implore him to come.

Yet that is what Paul is doing here, and he is probably echoing a prayer he heard offered in the Jerusalem church, where such prayers were spoken in Aramaic. The dramatic importance of such a prayer should not be underestimated. Jews were forbidden to pray to someone other than God. This prayer strongly suggests that Jesus was included within the earliest Aramaic-speaking Jewish Christians' understanding of God. In other words, Jesus was already viewed very early on as divine by his earliest Jewish followers, and this included James. The notion that seeing Jesus as a divine figure was added only late in the first century and was done so only by Gentiles is simply not true.

Notice how James begins his letter to his fellow Jewish Christians in the Diaspora by mentioning that Jesus is the Lord and the Christ or Messiah (1.1). Indeed, this way of viewing and talking about the historical Jesus is found all over the New Testament, and, with the exception of Luke and Acts, the whole New Testament was written by Jews!

We must allow the significance of this radical faith in Jesus as divine to sink in. It was not Gentiles or second- or third-generation believers who, as some scholars have alleged, first placed the robes of divinity on the historical Jesus. No indeed, Jesus was recognized as divine Lord after and as a result of the appearances of Jesus to a large number of early Jews, as the earliest witness list in 1 Corinthians 15.5–8 shows. One of these people was James himself. It was those who knew Jesus before his death who first confessed him and prayed to him in exalted terms.

The earliest confession of the followers of Jesus seems to have been "Jesus is [the risen] Lord" (see Romans 10.9; Philippians 2.5–11), and one of the earliest Aramaic prayers of Jesus' followers was "Come, Lord." These practices arose out of the earliest community of Jesus' followers, the Jewish ones in Jerusalem.

We must assume, then, that James was instrumental in championing this understanding and experience of Jesus, since he was Jesus' brother and in a real sense Jesus' successor in leading the messianic Jesus movement in Jerusalem and beyond. And we see in Josephus's account of James's death that James had to pay the ultimate price for his faith in Jesus as Lord. We are told that James was stoned, probably because he was accused of blasphemy (calling someone other than Yahweh "Lord" or "God"). In other words, James, like other early Jewish followers of Jesus, saw it as a logical extension of his Jewish faith to think of Jesus in divine terms and pray to him. These followers continued to think of the Father as God, but they spoke of Jesus as divine Lord as well (see 1 Corinthians 8.6).

While there may have been some Jews before Jesus' day who expected and believed in a divine Messiah, it is clear that once Jesus came, their numbers increased. There must be a reasonable historical explanation for this remarkable phenomenon. The answer surely lies in the life, teaching, ministry, and death of Jesus and in what his earliest followers were convinced happened to Jesus only two days after he was laid out in a tomb in preparation for reburial a year or so later in an ossuary. The answer must also lie in part in the connection between the life, practice, and faith of James and the life of his brother Jesus. This is why Paul went up to Jerusalem to talk to him and to Peter after Paul's dramatic conversion on the Damascus road (Galatians 1.18–19).

Thus, at the heart of the mystery of James is also the mystery of Jesus, his brother. To explore and learn more about the former may unlock our understanding of the latter. Perhaps now at the beginning of a new millennium as well as a new century the ossuary of James will finally prompt us to take the full measure of the significance of these early Jews, James, and Jesus. Perhaps in

James's life, death, and burial, as freshly revealed by the discovery of his ossuary, we can discover anew the true origins and nature of our faith and heritage. If so, it is fair to say that both Jews and Christians can benefit greatly from learning a good deal more about their roots and thereby about who they are. It is, as Shakespeare once wrote, "a consummation devoutly to be wished."

1. For a review of the many Jesuses on offer, see Ben Witherington, *The Jesus Quest* (Downers Grove, IL: InterVarsity Press, 1995).

2. One form that the belief in resurrection took in early Judaism was a belief that not all would be raised but only the righteous, those who had done good (see John 5.28–29).

3. Notice how in Mark 16.1–8 the women go to pay their respects at Jesus' tomb, even though they know he is already properly buried. (We know that the tomb had already been closed because the women wonder who will pull away the stone.)

4. Maurice Casey, *Aramaic Sources of Mark's Gospel* (Cambridge: Cambridge University Press, 1998).

5. The important study of Craig C. Hill, *Hellenists and Hebrews* (Minneapolis: Fortress Press, 1992), dismantles the case of F. C. Bauer, which has had such influence in the twentieth century.

6. Luke indicates that Paul stayed under house arrest in Rome for two years, and he arrived there in 60.

Part III

IS IT A FAKE?

WHERE MATTERS STAND

15

SUMMARY REPORT OF THE EXAMINING COMMITTEES FOR THE JAMES OSSUARY AND YEHOASH INSCRIPTION

June 20, 2003 [released July 16, 2003]
To: Shuka Dorfman, Director-General,
Israel Antiquities Authority

THE COMMITTEES' ESTABLISHMENT AND SELECTION OF MEMBERS

Word of the almost simultaneous discovery of the bone box known as the James ossuary and the Yehoash inscription, from an unknown source (not from a methodical excavation), together with the emotions raised by the finds and extensive public interest amongst Jews and Christians, obliged the Israel Antiquities Authority (IAA), the body responsible for all archaeological activities in Israel, to take action, to examine the finds and formulate a position on the subject. The IAA agreed to a short exhibit of the ossuary in Canada.

Numerous articles, all appearing within a short period of time, either confirm or deny the authenticity of the items. If the pieces are authentic (particularly the Yehoash inscription), then they are of great scientific value. The IAA was thus bound to do everything possible to arrive at the truth and present its conclusions.

After consulting with senior IAA advisers, IAA director-general Mr. Shuka Dorfman resolved to make every possible effort to examine the genuineness of the two finds. He then consulted scholars from various disciplines at the IAA and other [institutions] and set up two expert committees to examine the items from a scientific aspect and reach a conclusion regarding their authenticity. One committee was designated as the Writing and Content Committee and would use its knowledge of epigraphy and paleography to investigate whether the material content and language used are compatible with the Hebrew and Aramaic of the designated period. The second committee, the Materials and Patina Committee, was to examine the substance of the materials, composition of the patina, and additional materials present and to perform any and every possible examination, including a morphological study of the items.

The Writing and Content Committee was comprised of two subcommittees, whose members were authorities on the First Temple period—archaeologists, linguists, historians, paleographers, and epigraphers who would study the Yehoash inscription. The second subcommittee consist[ed] of archaeologists [and] Second Temple period linguistics scholars who would study the ossuary. The Writing and Content Committee would consult, if needed, with Professor Y. Naveh, an authority on ancient Hebrew writing of international repute, and with Dr. L. Y. Rahmani, an authority on ossuaries who had collected and published a vast amount of information on the subject.

The Materials Committee consisted of a geologist expert appointed by Dr. Amos Bein, director of the Geological Survey of Israel, who guaranteed his institute's backing and scientific assistance (in spite of the conclusion reached earlier by two of the Geological Survey's geologists), a petrograph expert, C14 researcher, and antiquities conservators with experience in ancient patina.

A great deal of attention was devoted to the choice of committee members. One consideration was the degree of involvement of each scholar in earlier research on the two items. Director-General Dorfman decided on a mix of committee members. The most suitable experts were chosen even if, in the past, they had expressed an opinion on the subject, as well as top scholars who had never been involved with the authenticity question.

The committee members were given specific guidelines: to arrive at the truth based on pure research only—without taking into account any other related factors regarding the collector, current gossip, rumors, or prejudices. Each scholar would work in his or her own discipline. The Writing and Content Committee members would work alone during the early stages [and] would later meet jointly. The Materials Committee members together photographed and took samples of the material so that the exact location and size of the sample would be precisely documented.

At the opening committee meeting, each member was given a file containing most of the published research and professional material gleaned from the Internet, plus a large amount of information from the collector.

Following are the names and institutional affiliations of the committee members:

THE WRITING COMMITTEE

Dr. Gideon Avni, Director of the Excavations and Survey Department, Israel Antiquities Authority, committee chairman

Prof. Shmuel Ahituv, Ben Gurion University, expert on Ancient Hebrew inscriptions

Dr. Tal Ilan, Bar Ilan University, historian, expert on the Hebrew and Aramaic names in the Second Temple period

Dr. Esther Eshel, Bar Ilan University, expert on the history and development of Hebrew script

Prof. Avigdor Hurowitz, Ben Gurion University, world-renowned expert on ancient Middle Eastern languages

Dr. Hagai Misgav, Hebrew University, expert on ancient Hebrew script and inscriptions

Prof. Amos Kloner, Bar Ilan University, archaeologist, expert on burials and burial customs during Jerusalem of the Second Temple period

Prof. Roni Reich, Haifa University, archaeologist, expert on First and Second Temple periods

THE MATERIALS COMMITTEE

Dr. Uzi Dahari, deputy director, Israel Antiquities Authority, committee chairman

Prof. Yuval Goren, Tel Aviv University, archaeologist and expert on petrography and identification of materials and sources

Dr. Avner Ayalon, Geological Survey of Israel, geologist, expert on identification of materials through the study of isotopes in rock

Dr. Elisabetta Boaretto, Weizmann Institute of Science, C14 expert

Ms. Orna Cohen, expert conservator, specialist in identification and restoration of ancient patina

Mr. Jacques Neguer, Israel Antiquities Authority, expert on antiquities conservation and restoration

Each committee member received an official appointment from the IAA director-general (Appendix 1). [Editor's note: Appendixes were not released with this report.]

Dr. Avner Ayalon received an additional appointment from Dr. Amos Bein, director of the Geological Survey of Israel, as the authority for the instruments to be used in the examinations, based on his experience in geochemical applications and petrography identification and classification of materials (Appendix 2).

All the committee members participated on a completely voluntary basis.

THE COMMITTEES' WORK

At the first meeting of the two committees, on Wednesday, March 26, 2003, Mr. Dorfman presented the members with their aims—"to determine the authenticity of the two items. These determinations will be of dramatic significance both from an ideological and financial aspect" (Appendix 3, minutes of the meeting). The committee chairmen then met with their members and formulated work rules and a time schedule (Appendix 4, letter sent by Dr. Avni to the Writing Committee; Appendix 5, protocol from materials committee's first meeting, setting forth directions for research).

A room in the IAA offices was specially prepared to house the two items. Extremely powerful lighting, ultraviolet light, an illuminated magnifying lens, microscope, and binoculars were provided. The room was available to committee members at any time. They received digital close-ups of the two inscriptions. Members of the Materials Committee naturally visited more than the others, [to] take samples and close-ups. Moreover, the members sampled patina from other ossuaries and inscriptions in the IAA storerooms for comparison.

Each committee member was given up to three months to submit a final report summarizing his or her opinion and reasons for the conclusions drawn.

The Materials Committee met for two additional meetings to exchange ideas and discuss research directions.

Three committee members were asked to prepare, in addition to their written report, a visual presentation for the minister of education, the IAA director-general, and the other committee members. Jacques Neguer prepared a visual presentation of the objects' morphology; Yuval Goren a presentation of the petrographic composition of the materials and patina; Avner Ayalon a presentation of his geological research.

The research was conducted at the regular workplace of each member, and on his or her own time.

ABSTRACTS OF FINDINGS

The Yehoash Inscription Committee

Prof. Shmuel Ahituv (Appendix 6A):

The inscription was written by a speaker of modern Hebrew who borrowed segments from the original sources and composed a text that seemed biblical to him or her but failed. Therefore, the text is a forgery.

Prof. Avigdor Horowitz (Appendix 6B):

The Yehoash inscription appears to be a combination of elements collected from various sources and pasted together. . . . Each element attests to a lack of understanding of ninth century B.C. Hebrew. All the elements together clearly prove that the text is a forgery.

Dr. Hagai Misgav (Appendix 6C):

From the paleographic aspect, it appears that the inscription was written by someone not living in the First Temple times, but who wrote according to samples from that period. In other words, the inscription does not appear authentic.

Prof. Roni Reich (Appendix 6D and 6D1):

It appeared to me at first that the inscription was authentic, as I wrote in my report. For one reason, it was difficult for me to believe that a forger (or group of forgers) could be found that would be expert in all aspects of the inscription . . . and could produce such an object. But I was convinced, in the end, that it is a forgery after being shown the committee's data and material.

The Ossuary Inscription Committee

Prof. Amos Kloner (Appendix 6E):

It is clear that the engraving on the bone box dates from a different period than its original installation. The inscription appears new. The writer tried giving the letters an ancient appearance by using samples from contemporaneous inscriptions.

Dr. Tal Ilan (Appendix 6F):

Even if the ossuary is authentic, there is no reason to assume that the deceased was actually the brother of Jesus. But I am of the opinion that the inscription is a forgery.

Prof. Roni Reich (Appendix 6D and 6D1):

The inscription does not exhibit a combination of configurational or substantial effects that would imply forgery. But I was convinced that the inscription is a forgery when presented with the findings by the Materials Committee.

Dr. Esther Eshel (Appendix 6G):

From my examination of the inscription and the data I received, it appears to me quite clear that the inscription is not authentic and was added at a much later date (possibly in two stages).

THE MATERIALS COMMITTEE

Jacques Neguer (Appendix 6I):

The ossuary is authentic. Its inscription is a forgery. All the various scratches on the ossuary are coated in the original patina, and only the inscription and its immediate surroundings are coated with an artificial patinalike material of round crystalline granules. The inscription cuts through the original patina and appears to have been written by two different writers using different tools.

Ms. Orna Cohen:

Ossuary: The first part of the inscription is new, cuts through the original patina, and is coated with a granular patina that appears to have been produced from chalk dust mixed with water and spread on the inscription. The end of the inscription "brother of Jesus" appears authentic; in some places there seems to be remains of old patina, but in order to produce a uniform effect, this too was spread with the same granular substance.

Inscription: The "patina" on the inscription side was dissolved in water and therefore looks like earth rather than patina. When the letters were cleaned, the manner of inscription was exposed. The technique appears new and does not match the original wear on the stone. The manner in which the letters were scratched does not resemble any form of ancient stone inscription.

In summary, both inscriptions are false.

Prof. Yuval Goren (Appendix 6J):

Ossuary: The ossuary itself is authentic based on the accumulation of patina and varnish (varnish = patina from a biological source).

The inscription was inscribed or cleaned in a modern period. Its coating is not a result of nature and was probably accomplished by crumbling and dissolving chalk (or perhaps the powder falling from the engraving process) in hot water and spilling the suspension on the inscription and surrounding area in order to blur the freshly carved inscription.

Inscription: The stone is greywake, an exotic stone for Israel, originating in north Syria or western Cyprus.

The original silicate patina exists on the reverse side of the tablet, hard and firmly attached to the stone. The engraved letters did not appear to have undergone any corrosive process, as would be expected from an ancient inscription.

The inscription coating has a different composition from that of the patina on the back of the stone and appears to be an artificial mixture of clay, crumbled chalk, carbon, and microscopic granules of inert metal. It appears that this mixture was dissolved in hot water before being spread on the inscribed side, after which the stone was heated to a temperature of no higher than $4000°C$ in order to harden the new coating and give it the appearance of patina.

Method: The "patinization" is similar in both cases, but on the ossuary, chalk powder only was used, and on the Yehoash inscription a mixture of clay or red soil, chalk powder, carbon, and metal granules.

Conclusions: The inscriptions on both items are forged and date to modern times.

COMPOSITION OF ISOTOPES IN OXYGEN IN THE OSSUARY AND THE
YEHOASH INSCRIPTION

Letters patina
Yehoash inscription
surface patina
sea chalk

Dr. Avner Ayalon (Appendix 6K):

Oxygen possesses three isotopes: oxygen 16, 17, 18. When atmospheric conditions (moisture and temperature) vary, the relationship between these isotopes changes, especially between oxygen 16 and 18 (the amount of oxygen 17 decreases greatly and is difficult to measure). I sampled the patina of the Yehoash inscription and the original patina in various places on the ossuary distant from the inscription, and for comparison took samples from the surface and inside the letters inscribed on other ossuaries. The result is clear: Patina samples from the other ossuaries and from the James ossuary away from the letters fall within the acceptable isotope range for patina accumulation in the Jerusalem area within the last three thousand years. Patina samples from the letters of the James ossuary and the patina of the Yehoash inscription fall out of this range, showing that the letters' patina could not have formed within the Jerusalem area's climatic conditions.

"Patina" of such an isotope composition was probably created from a mixture of materials and water heated to a temperature that does not [naturally] exist in our area.

Therefore, I conclude that "patina" in the Yehoash [inscription and] the ossuary letters is forged (details of the stages of the Materials Committee's work in the presentation in Appendix 10).

Dr. Elisabetta Boaretto (Appendix 6L):

The ossuary patina does not contain material that can be sampled for C14 and is thus irrelevant for dating by this method.

The inscription patina contains very small but adequate quantities of carbonates that can be tested in an accelerator. Such a sample was taken by the Israel Museum and sent to Florida for examination. Due to the small quantity of material, carbon was collected from several places on the inscription stone so that the sample is not a representative one but rather an average of the material sources. The resulting date received (after calibration) is 390–200 B.C. I didn't collect any material for further analysis because I don't believe such an analysis to be significant toward determining authenticity, for the following reasons: (a) the test for dating the carbon is irrelevant since ancient carbon can be added to the falsified material; (b) the objects, since their discovery, have passed through many different places without any documentation. Exposure of the objects to modern pollutants can affect results of dating analyses.

Based on the above, I conclude that no relevance can be placed on a date received from C14 dating of the Yehoash inscription.

SUMMARY

On June 15, 2003, the committees met, first separately and then jointly, in order to arrive at a collective conclusion. I presented the results of the Writing Committee to the Materials Committee and [the] results of the Materials Committee to the Writing Committee.

The two committees then joined in the director-general's office (Appendix 7, Protocol of Concluding Session), where a discussion took place to which the collector, Mr. Oded Golan, was invited (in response to the request of Mr. Golan's lawyer) to present his argument and position on the matter of the two items. At the conclusion of his presentation, Mr. Golan was asked a number of questions by the committee members.

At the conclusion of deliberations, the committee members summarized the results of their research and wrote an abstract of their findings (Appendixes 8 and 9), as follows: "We, members of the committee for examination of the content and script in the Yehoash inscription and the James ossuary ("James son of Joseph brother of Jesus") conclude that to the best of our scientific judgment:

A. The Yehoash inscription is a forgery.

B. The James ossuary inscription is a forgery.

We, the committee members for examination of the materials of the Yehoash inscription and the James ossuary, conclude that the patina on both items is forged and significantly varies from the original patina on the items.

Respectfully,
Dr. Uzi Dahari
Deputy Director and Chairman of the
Materials Committee and Committees Coordinator

16

DON'T CLOSE THE BOX YET: THE JESUS INSCRIPTION MIGHT BE REAL

Hershel Shanks
Reprinted from the *Jerusalem Post* Opinion Section,
Friday, August 15, 2003

I don't know for sure whether the bone box, or ossuary, inscribed "James, son of Joseph, brother of Jesus" is authentic or a modern forgery. And I don't know for sure whether the ossuary's owner, Oded Golan, is a forger or not. But I do know one thing for sure: the Israeli authorities are handling the situation very badly—at least from this side of the Atlantic.

Let's start with the investigation of Golan. Instead of collecting evidence and, if justified, charging Golan with a crime, the Israel Antiquities Authority (IAA) and the police are trying to pressure him into confessing. After being interrogated at home, he was called to the police station for further questioning. There they fingerprinted him, mugged him, and handcuffed him.

There was no reason to put him in handcuffs; this was not a fugitive who might flee. Why did they handcuff him? I asked IAA chief investigator Amir Ganor. "To pressure him," was the response.

Next they sent a team of six people to his home one night at eight in the evening and team-interrogated him for almost thirty hours—yes, through the night and into the following night. Then, with still no confession, they arrested him—but without charging him! (The newspapers, at least in America, didn't report the fact that he had been arrested only for questioning.) The police came to pick him up in the middle of the night.

This was not a man they suspected of being violent or of fleeing. Why pick him up in the middle of the night? And why arrest him if they weren't prepared to charge him?

After four days in jail in the Russian Compound, Golan was released—again without being charged with any offense. Even after this, stories in the United States reported his arrest without reporting that he had been released and never charged. Everyone here quickly concluded he was guilty.

Several weeks before, the IAA leaked to a newspaper that they had found half-forged seals in Golan's workroom. The story spread like wildfire from one newspaper to another. The *Jerusalem Post* recently reported that "an elaborate antiquities forgery lab was found in his home."

If true, the half-forged seals and the forgery lab would be powerful evidence against Golan. So why haven't they released pictures of these half-forged seals and forgery equipment? In the United States prosecutors might say they didn't release pictures of this evidence because they didn't want to prejudice the jury against the defendant.

But in Israel there are no juries. So if they have the evidence, why haven't they charged Golan with a crime? All they have done is smear him in the newspapers. This is no way to process a serious criminal case.

The IAA proclamation that the James ossuary inscription is a forgery is just as vulnerable to criticism. On June 18, the IAA held a press conference and pronounced the inscription a forgery— no qualifications, no maybes, all 100 percent clear. This conclusion was immediately suspicious because no report was released at the press conference.

Nearly a month later a summary report in English was released. It told little but indicated that there were a number of appendixes, which supposedly contained more detailed information. When these appendixes were finally released, they turned out to be individual statements by members of the committee concerning their own expertise, most of which had nothing to do with whether or not the inscription was a forgery.

In short, there is no final report, no document explaining the committee's conclusion and signed by the committee members. Moreover, only two of the individual statements are relevant to the scientific finding that the ossuary is a forgery. These statements—by Dr. Avner Ayalon of the Israel Geological Survey and Professor Yuval Goren of Tel Aviv University—are themselves deficient in that they explicitly state they are not final reports.

They contain no details of the studies performed on the ossuary. Each of the two statements says that at some time in the indefinite future a scientific report will be published in a professional journal.

Hence, at this point other scientists all over the world who are keenly interested in the result of the IAA committee cannot review it. This is no way to assure the world of the integrity of the IAA's conclusion.

But that is not the worst of it. The separate statements of Ayalon and Goren do not even use the word *fake* or *forgery*. Quite amazingly, that is, these two critical statements do not say the inscription is a forgery.

What they say is that they found a "grayish coating easily removed with a toothpick" on the inscription area (Goren) and that this "could not have formed naturally in conditions of temperature and typical water composition in the Judean Hills in the last two thousand years" (Ayalon).

This conclusion is supposedly based on the ratio of oxygen isotopes of different weights found in the coating.

What could account for this coating? Goren tells us, "The inscription was engraved (*or at least, completely cleaned*) in modern times" (my emphasis). In the summary of the report earlier released, Goren says the same thing: "The inscription was inscribed or cleaned in a modern period."

In other words, the coating could be the result of an attempt to hide the forgery or the result of a cleaning.

A recorded interview with Amos Bien, the head of Israel's Geological Survey, makes clear the distinction between calling the inscription a forgery and saying that the coating in the inscription might be the result of a cleaning.

As head of the Geological Survey, Dr. Bien appointed Ayalon to the committee, and Bien sticks by Ayalon's findings: there is a coating on the inscription that was not created by the natural processes by which patina is created on limestone that rests in a cave for thousands of years.

Yet Bien still thinks the ossuary inscription is authentic!

"We didn't decide the inscription is fake," he said. "If somebody would like to preserve the inscription, or would like to improve its appearance, and he would like to clean it, and thereafter to make it shine better, and he made [a] procedure of cleaning, and thereafter adding warm water and so on, he may have created some carbonate particles which may provide this isotopic composition."

And all agree that the inscription was indeed cleaned in modern times!

According to Golan, his mother cleaned it, perhaps many times, while it was sitting on their porch decades ago. The dealer who sold it to Golan may have cleaned it to emphasize the inscription for prospective purchasers. The scientists on the IAA committee themselves noted that it had been cleaned, and so did the scientific team at the Royal Ontario Museum (ROM) in Toronto that studied the inscription after it was displayed there last November and December.

So there is no question that the ossuary has been cleaned. According to the ROM study, it was cleaned not only with an unknown solvent, but with a sharp instrument so that some of the letters were actually enhanced.

What is interesting, however, is that only the first part of the inscription seems to have been cleaned. Again, the IAA committee and the ROM team are in agreement on this. But the IAA committee makes no connection with another significant fact that it discovered. In the incisions in the last two words of the inscription, "brother of Jesus," the IAA committee found original ancient patina. The IAA committee made no connection between this fact and the fact that the latter part of the inscription had not been cleaned.

The conclusion the IAA committee drew from the fact that ancient patina was found in the last two words of the inscription displays its bias. The committee wanted very much to find—or imply—that the inscription was a forgery. So it concluded that the last two words of the inscription—"the brother of Jesus"—"may be" authentic.

This implies something like a fifty-fifty chance, but it is nothing of the sort. What the committee should have concluded was that that there is no reason to question the authenticity of the last two words of the inscription.

If the IAA committee put it this way, however, it would have been faced with the somewhat daunting task of proving that the first part of the inscription is a modern forgery despite the fact that the last two words are authentic.

It can be done, but it's not easy. That is, it's possible but highly unlikely.

Moreover, the IAA committee did not even extend the courtesy to the Royal Ontario Museum and the earlier team from Israel's own Geological Survey, both of which had previously studied the inscription and found it authentic, of addressing their studies and explaining how they had erred.

The IAA's conclusion may be correct, but it is not hard to understand why the world cannot have confidence in it, especially in light of the fact that so many experts (in Israel and abroad) continue to maintain the inscription is authentic, despite the IAA committee's conclusion.

And many scientists I have talked to say they can express no opinion without a scientific report on the tests performed, although they are skeptical, to say the least.

I don't think the IAA realizes how significant this ossuary is for the Christian community worldwide, especially in the United States. How else to explain the absence from its committee of any New Testament scholar? Of any Christian? Of any non-Israeli? All were readily available in Jerusalem but were ignored.

To preempt what is likely to be a growing call for an independent, international team of experts to restudy the ossuary inscription, the IAA should itself propose this. Such a team, perhaps appointed by ASMOSIA (the Association for the Study of Marble and Other Stones in Antiquity), would clear the air and give the billions of concerned people all over the world confidence in the conclusion.

17

ISRAEL ANTIQUITIES AUTHORITY'S REPORT ON THE JAMES OSSUARY IS DEEPLY FLAWED

André Lemaire
(Reprinted from *Biblical Archaeology Review,*
November/December 2003)

The Israel Antiquities Authority (IAA) recently formed a committee to decide whether the James ossuary inscription and the Yehoash (or Jehoash) inscription are authentic or forgeries. I readily acknowledge the difficulty of the committee's task. I also acknowledge the quality of the research and publications by my colleagues, some of whom I have known for decades. I therefore hesitate to comment on the work of the IAA committee, but its conclusions, announced at a widely publicized press conference, are at variance with my own conclusions regarding the inscription on the James ossuary. (I shall not address the question of the Yehoash inscription.) If I kept silent, people would think that I was convinced by the IAA committee or that I simply do not want to take into account their position—which is not the case. [Editor's note: The inscription was first published in André Lemaire, "Burial Box of James the Brother of Jesus," *Biblical Archaeology Review,* November/December 2002.]

Therefore I have no choice but to critically assess the committee's work. After all, that is what the committee members presumably did with my own research into the ossuary inscription—although there is not a single mention of my findings by any of the committee members.

The final committee report—really only statements of the individual committee members; there is no final report of the committee as a whole—begins by setting forth the convening authority's guidelines for the committee members. These are indeed laudable, for they stipulate that committee members are "to arrive at the truth based on *pure research only—without taking into account any other related factors regarding the collector, current gossip, rumors, or prejudices*" (italics supplied). Furthermore, "Each scholar is to work in *his[/her] own discipline*" (italics supplied).

It was also anticipated that "*the exact location and size of the sample would be precisely documented*" (italics supplied).

Finally, "Each committee member was given up to three months to submit a *final report* summarizing his/her opinion and *reasons* for their conclusions" (italics supplied).

How closely did the committee members follow these instructions?

Before considering this question, I will make a few remarks about the choice of committee members. One can always complain that this or that person was chosen or not chosen. For me, the selection is not very important if, but only if, the persons chosen provide a detailed scientific report that can be reviewed by colleagues.

I can also understand the convening authority's decision to appoint certain members "even if [as the introduction to the "Final Report" states] they had, in the past, expressed an opinion on the subject." What is disturbing, however, is that apparently only people who expressed their opinion *against* the authenticity of the inscriptions were chosen and that no mention was made of the previous materials examinations by the Geological Survey of Israel (Jerusalem) researchers and the Royal Ontario Museum (Toronto) curators.

The IAA committee consisted of two different committees—

the Writing and Content Committee and the Materials Committee. The content committee was divided into two subcommittees—one for each of the inscriptions. Strangely enough, the subcommittee on the ossuary inscription did not include any paleographer or epigrapher. In contrast, the Yehoash subcommittee included "authorities on the First Temple period—archaeologists, linguists, historians, paleographers, epigraphers who would study the Yehoash inscription." But the subcommittee on the ossuary inscription "consist[ed] of archaeologists, [and] Second Temple period linguistic scholars who would study the inscription." Is the omission of paleographers and epigraphers (specialists in analyzing and dating scripts) from this latter subcommittee accidental? Or is there simply a printing error in the report?

Two other preliminary oddities (and then I will get to substance):

The introduction to the report notes that "If the pieces are authentic (*particularly the Yehoash inscription*), then they are of great scientific value" (italics supplied). Is the James ossuary inscription—"James, the son of Joseph, the brother of Jesus"—not of such great scientific value as compared with the Yehoash inscription? What are we supposed to infer from this?

Second, there is also a danger in having a single materials committee deal with both the ossuary inscription and the Yehoash inscription. (This is in contrast to the content committee, which included two separate subcommittees.) The danger is that a factor that applies to only one of the inscriptions will affect the judgment of the committee regarding the other. For example, the report refers to the "almost simultaneous discovery" of the two objects. The fact is that they were not "almost simultaneously discover[ed]"; they were almost simultaneously *published*—the ossuary inscription in *Biblical Archaeology Review* (*BAR*) late in 2002 and the Yehoash inscription in early 2003. [Editor's note: See Lemaire, "Burial Box"; and Shimon Ilani, Amnon Rosenfeld, and Michael Dvorachek, "Archaeometry of a Stone Tablet with Hebrew Inscription Referring to Repair of the House," *GSI Current Research* 13 (2002): 109–16.] Their discoveries were decades apart.

Now let me turn to the individual statements—which constitute the final report—submitted by the members of the content
subcommittee for the ossuary inscription and by the materials
committee.

There were four members of the ossuary Writing and Content subcommittee.

Professor Amos Kloner is identified as an "archaeologist, [an]
expert on burials and burial customs during the Second Temple
period [in] Jerusalem." He states that, to him, "the inscription
looks new." This is enough for him to conclude that it is a forgery.
He also states that the forger worked "using contemporary examples." He simply jumps to this negative conclusion without explanation or argument.

Actually, the fact that an inscription looks new is not really a
problem for an experienced epigrapher who sees many inscriptions, some in bad—very bad—condition and some in good—
even very good—condition. For example, take the famous Tel
Dan inscription, excavated by Israeli archaeologist Avraham
Biran. It is in excellent condition and has great historical value (it
contains an extrabiblical mention of David). Using Professor
Kloner's criterion, we would have to declare it a forgery. (So
much for the "it's too good to be true" argument.) Indeed, Professor Giovanni Garbini has declared the Tel Dan inscription a
forgery,[1] as have members of the so-called Scandinavian school of
biblical studies.[2] Does Professor Kloner agree with their judgment?

Professor Kloner also makes a surprising historical assertion.
He says that "the family of Jesus and James had no burial cave in
first-century Jerusalem." This was probably true when Jesus died
in about A.D. 30, but we do not know what the situation was thirty
years later, in A.D. 62, when James died. From the New Testament
(which is our main source), it seems that Jesus' family did not return to Nazareth but instead stayed in Jerusalem after the crucifixion. This is quite clear regarding James himself and seems
probable for Jesus' mother, Mary, and his other brothers (Acts
1:14). After Jesus' death, leaders of the Christian community
seem to have consorted with Jesus' family.[3] Later tradition located

Mary's tomb in Jerusalem. So there is really no basis for Professor Kloner's assertion; indeed, it might reveal a certain failure to appreciate the history of early Christianity.

Of course this entire discussion in Professor Kloner's statement is gratuitous because it has no bearing on whether the inscription is authentic. That problem remains the same whether James was buried in a family tomb or in another tomb.

Dr. Tal Ilan is identified as a "historian, expert on the Hebrew and Aramaic names in the Second Temple period." But she is not an epigrapher or paleographer. She specifically states this, acknowledging immediately that she is not "an expert on . . . carved inscriptions, or paleography." Therefore, she says, on the question of the authenticity of the inscription, she will rely on what "experts have determined." She does not identify these experts, however. (From the opinion she espouses, one can only guess that she relies on the "expertise" of one Rochelle Altman, who is not a serious scholar of Second Temple period paleography but who early on in this controversy gained momentary fame by declaring the inscription to have been forged by two different hands.)

Although the committee's guidelines instructed Dr. Ilan to work "in her own discipline" and although she admits she is not a paleographer, she nevertheless opined on matters of epigraphy. "The second part [of the inscription] seems scratched out in more cursive script. . . . [This] may suggest that the reference to the brother could have been added later." Oddly, this would contradict colleagues on the committee who say that the last part of the inscription may be authentic and that the forger added only the first part—as she herself proposed later on (see below).

Dr. Ilan also tells us, "In the summer of 2002, before *BAR* published its ossuary sensation, I had the opportunity to observe and photograph the [ossuary] inscription. The letters were clear and their context did not raise in me any special interest. The names were plausible." From this brief mention, it appears that at that time the inscription looked authentic to her.

Quite inappropriately, Dr. Ilan reproaches Christian scholars in general—incidentally, the committee included not a single

Christian and no New Testament scholar of any faith. Dr. Ilan re-marks: "Christian scholars will always be interested in artifacts from the period of early Christianity, using these finds to blow out of all proportion their Christian religious relevance in an attempt to prove (or disprove) the truth of that religion." This would seem to reveal a prejudice that contravenes the committee's guidelines calling for members to base their conclusions on "pure research only—without taking into account any . . . preju-dices." (On this subject, see also the "joke" Dr. Ilan makes about Jesus' words, discussed below.)

Apparently assuming that Christian scholars have overblown the significance of the inscription, even if it is authentic, Dr. Ilan tells us that "even if the ossuary [inscription] is authentic, there is no reason to assume that the deceased is actually the brother of Jesus (the first Christian)."

Dr. Ilan notes that Professor Camil Fuchs, head of the statis-tics department at Tel Aviv University, made a statistical study based on the appearance of the three names in the inscription—James, Joseph, and Jesus, in their specific relationship—assessing the likelihood that the reference would be to the people men-tioned in the New Testament. In general, Dr. Ilan approves of Fuchs's study. But while Professor Fuchs found that probably 1.71 people named James in first-century Jerusalem might be de-scribed as son of Joseph and brother of Jesus, Dr. Ilan raises the figure to ten. But it is not clear on what basis she does this.[4] She gives no explanation or calculation to support her new figure. This is hardly scientific and in fact reveals her prejudice.

Moreover, in her criticism of the identification of the ossuary as that of the New Testament James, Dr. Ilan fails to consider the second step in the identification. It is not merely the statistics, but the fact that the deceased's *brother* is named *on the ossuary*. A brother is mentioned on only one other known ossuary inscrip-tion.[5] This important datum is totally missing from Dr. Ilan's anal-ysis.

Turning to the area of her own expertise—ancient Hebrew and Aramaic names—Dr. Ilan detects a forgery in the mis-spellings she sees in the names on the ossuary. Both Joseph and

James, she says, are misspelled. In the inscription Joseph is spelled *YWSP.* Dr. Ilan claims that "during the Second Temple period the name Joseph was *always* written as Jehoseph [YHWSP]" (italics supplied).

In her own book, however, she expresses herself differently: "During the Second Temple period the name YWSP was *almost* universally spelt YHWSP" (italics supplied).[6]

But even this is expressed too strongly. In more than 10 percent of other inscriptions, the James ossuary's spelling YWSP occurs.[7] For Dr. Ilan, however, the spelling of Joseph on the ossuary is "very rare and raises doubt about its authenticity." This conclusion is not justified by the facts. We cannot say that a phenomenon is "very rare" when it occurs in more than 10 percent of cases. If Dr. Ilan's argument were applied to all other inscriptions, more than 10 percent would be declared forgeries—or at least be considered suspicious.

She errs just as badly, or worse, with the name James. It is spelled *Y'QWB* in the ossuary inscription. Dr. Ilan claims that "the spelling *Y'QWB,* with *vav,* was found on two ostraca at Masada but never on any papyrus or ossuary of the period." But this is an error, one that is repeated in her book.[8] If she had simply looked at the concordance in L. Y. Rahmani's catalogue of ossuary inscriptions,[9] she would have seen that, out of the five occurrences of this name on ossuaries, three, a majority, are spelled *Y'QWB,* as on the James ossuary.[10] The situation is precisely the opposite of what Dr. Ilan wrote in her committee statement (and published in her book). The spelling on the James ossuary appears more frequently on ossuaries than the alternative spelling.

Dr. Ilan presents an interesting reconstruction of what the alleged forger did. Based on what two other committee members (Dr. Orna Cohen and Dr. Avner Ayalon) wrote—that original ancient patina was found in the second half of the inscription (Cohen) and in the last letter of the inscription (Ayalon)—Dr. Ilan "suggest[s] that the forger came into possession of an ossuary bearing an authentic inscription 'brother of Jesus.'. . . Such an ossuary could easily fire the imagination of a forger, who added the name of the brother of Jesus Christ to the ossuary to raise its value." This suggestion is based on Dr. Ilan's notation that "*All the epigraphists* have already concluded that the hand which inscribed the words 'James son of Joseph' is not the same one as that which inscribed the words 'brother of Jesus'" (italics supplied). Without specifying who "all the epigraphists" are, we can only guess that Dr. Ilan is referring to the opinion of Rochelle Altman, already mentioned. For Dr. Ilan, I obviously do not count as an epigraphist, nor do Professor Frank Cross of Harvard, Father Joseph Fitzmyer, formerly of the Catholic University of America, Dr. Ada Yardeni (author of *The Book of Hebrew Script*), and Joseph Milik, a prominent Dead Sea Scrolls epigrapher—all of whom see only one hand in this inscription. So much for "all the epigraphists."

In the last paragraph of her statement, Dr. Ilan tells us she "would like to end with a joke." Readers may need some background information to understand this joke, so here it is: For the brother of the deceased to be mentioned on an ossuary is highly unusual. One possible explanation would be that the brother was responsible for the burial. Of course, this explanation cannot apply in James's case, because Jesus was already dead when James was killed—unless the resurrected Jesus buried his brother.

This is what Dr. Ilan makes a joke of. What if (she says) the resurrected Jesus really was responsible for the burial? Jesus, Dr. Ilan "jokes," would thereby be proving his own words in Matthew 8:22: "Let the dead bury the dead." In this way, Dr. Ilan concludes, we would be "allowing Jesus to live up to his own principles." Some joke!

Professor Ronny Reich is designated in the report as an "archaeologist, expert on [the] First and Second Temple periods." Professor Reich examined the inscription "with naked eyes" and did not find any difference in the hands of the inscription (in contrast to Dr. Ilan). He noticed that the engraver carved the letters with the aid of a ruler and carved them "from the ruler downward . . . [the] same method as Second Temple period scribes." Whoever wrote the inscription, he says, was a speaker of Aramaic. Insightfully, Professor Reich noted that "if the inscription had read 'Yosef [Joseph] son of Ya'acov [James] brother of Yeshua

[Jesus],' no one would have raised an eyebrow, and the inscription would have quietly entered the statistical lists without a further thought." Professor Reich is almost certainly right on this point. All this attention—and suspicion—is attributable to the fact that New Testament figures may be mentioned.

As to the authenticity of the inscription, Reich concludes: "It appears that each of the characteristics of the inscription, as detailed above, and all of them together, with no exception, indicate an authentic late Second Temple period (mainly first century C.E.) inscription." Nevertheless, he decided the inscription is a forgery because of the findings of the Materials Committee, whose scientific examination concluded that the coating or patina on the inscription was "produced and placed inside the letters in an artificial manner and could not have been produced in nature in ancient times. . . . As a result, I am forced to change my opinion on the matter." He does not use the word *fake* or *forgery*. Neither does he discuss the possibility that this particular patina could have been the result of modern cleaning of the ossuary. More on this later.

Professor Reich finds that the inscription is not very important "if we overlook the religious feelings (that could arise among Christians today) evoked by this inscription." Apart from these, however, he continues, "Its significance for the study of Jewish society at the close of the Second Temple period is slight. The inscription does not add any new onomastic or prosopographic data."

Does the inscription have historic significance, or is its significance slight? True, Jesus and James are already well known from the New Testament and from Josephus, as well as from early Christian tradition. But still, if the inscription is authentic and the identification is accepted, this is the first clear case of a Christian Jew (or, more correctly, a Nazarene; see Acts 24:5) being buried according to common Jewish custom. It is also archaeological confirmation that Aramaic was used by this group, and it is the earliest epigraphical attestation of Jesus of Nazareth.

Most Jewish scholars seem to treat James as if he were not Jewish. But Nazarenes (Christian Jews) were still considered Jews at least as late as A.D. 70, when the Romans destroyed Jerusalem and the Temple. To consider the Nazarenes as non-Jews before the Roman destruction is an anachronism. It would be like saying that the Essenes, who were responsible for the sectarian documents among the Dead Sea Scrolls, were also not Jews. But no scholar takes that position.

The inscription also has significance in reflecting the diversity of Judaism at the close of the Second Temple period and in revealing the Jewish roots of Christianity.

Professor Reich considered three possible reasons for naming the brother in this ossuary inscription. He did not consider a fourth—namely, that "brother of Jesus" was a kind of nickname used of James during his lifetime. This is a distinct possibility attested by the literary tradition (Josephus and New Testament).

Dr. Esther Eshel, an "expert on the history and development of Hebrew script," gives a brief report—of less than a page. She states her opinion that "the inscription is not authentic, and was added later to the original ossuary (possibly in two stages)." She offers several reasons for this conclusion.

Dr. Eshel says she is not aware of any ossuary "where the letters are so deeply engraved and the decoration on the same ossuary [three rosettes faintly visible on the opposite side of the ossuary] . . . so worn as in the ossuary before us." For this, she cites Rahmani's catalogue. But this catalogue is not complete. And some of the ossuaries in the catalogue are not illustrated. Most important, in several cases cited by Rahmani, the inscription clearly appears to have been incised more deeply than the decoration.[11] Moreover, the James ossuary inscription is certainly not the only case where the erosion and encrustation on the side with an inscription seems different from that on the other side.[12] Sometimes there is even a difference on the same side of the ossuary.[13] For an ossuary in which the decoration is worn and the inscription on the other side is clear and deep, see no. 62, plate 10, in Rahmani's catalogue. Should we therefore declare this a forgery?

That the James ossuary may have been reused after the rosette decoration had faded is a possibility, but this suggestion seems unnecessary to explain the contrast between the rosettes on one side and the inscription on the other.

Dr. Eshel also finds that the inscription was made by "two different chisels"—so, she says, "I have been told" by committee members who gave the inscription "a very precise examination." Not only is this contradicted by Professors Kloner and Reich, who hold a different opinion, but the experts on whom she relies are not identified. Here again is a case where, contrary to the IAA guidelines, one "expert" improperly adopts others' arguments, thereby contravening the guideline that each committee member is to write "in his [or her] own discipline."

Actually, the "variations in handwriting, thickness and depth of the incised letters," which Dr. Eshel finds suspicious, are exactly what can be expected on an inscription that was not incised mechanically or according to a printed model. If "variations in handwriting, thickness and depth" were the criteria, we would have to declare numerous inscriptions in Rahmani's catalogue to be forgeries. For example, in no. 12, plate 2, the two *alefs* are different; in no. 26, the *shins* are different. In no. 35, the depth of the letters seems different.

If there were no variations in the shapes of the letters and their thickness and depth, if all the letters were exactly the same shape and the same height and the same depth, then it *would* probably be a fake! This would mean that the inscription had been made mechanically or with a printed or computerized model.

Dr. Eshel also makes a paleographic argument: "There is a significant difference between handwritings in the first and second parts of the inscription. The first part is written in the formal style of a scribe and the second part is cursive." In a footnote, I discuss each letter in the twenty-letter inscription, as to whether it is formal or cursive.[14] This examination shows that formal and cursive are all mixed together—as is not uncommon in ossuary inscriptions. Using *F* for "formal" and *C* for "cursive," this is how the letters of the inscription break down: CFFCFFFCCFFCFCCC-CFCF.

In short, we have a mixture of formal and cursive shapes in this inscription. It is incorrect to say that one part is formal script and the other is cursive script. Moreover, the mixture of formal and cursive letters is a well-known fact, underlined several times by expert commentators. In a footnote I quote a number of experts on this common phenomenon.[15]

Dr. Eshel's final argument is that the forger copied the word *brother of* (*'HWY D*) from the only other appearance of this word on an ossuary. She observes, "When comparing the words 'brother of Jesus' on this ossuary to ossuary no. 570 [in Rahmani's catalogue] . . . a surprising resemblance can be seen. The letters [in *achui,* 'brother'] *het, vav,* and *yud* are quite similar, and the most exceptional letter *dalet* is identical. In both inscriptions, only the descending line [of the *dalet*] survived. It thus seems that the writer copied the inscriptions from this [other] ossuary."

I invite readers to make this comparison for themselves [see the illustrations in chapters 2 and 4 of this book]. Look carefully and you will see that on ossuary no. 570, the second, third, and fourth letters of *brother* (reading right to left, *het, vav,* and *yod*) slope down on the right, while in the James ossuary inscription, they are clearly vertical.

The fifth letter (*dalet*) appears as a descending line on the other ossuary, as well as on recent pictures of the James ossuary. This shape of the *dalet* is anomalous, and that such a close duplicate is found on the James ossuary would ordinarily arouse suspicion. However, this problem exists only if you use a picture of the James ossuary taken *after* it had cracked on the trip from Israel to Toronto for exhibition at the Royal Ontario Museum. One of the cracks went right through the inscription—indeed, through this *dalet.* When the ossuary was restored, part of the *dalet* disappeared, namely the top left stroke of the letter. This stroke is clearly visible, however, *in the pictures taken before the crack.*

So the argument that the alleged forger "copied the inscriptions from this [other] ossuary," as Dr. Eshel contends, is baseless.

In short, the James ossuary inscription does not raise any paleographic, linguistic, or orthographic (spelling) problems, and there is no reason on these grounds to cast doubt on its authenticity. This is underlined by Dr. Reich's initial conclusion: All signs point to a Second Temple period date. Clearly that was also the reaction of Dr. Ilan when she first saw the inscription; she raised no question as to its authenticity until I suggested the identity of the deceased (James) in my *BAR* article. Clearly it is not the inscription itself that raises problems but the identification of the deceased with a historical personage mentioned in Christian tradition. The easiest and simplest way to reject this interpretation is to cast doubt on the authenticity of the inscription.

The tendency to cast doubt on Northwest Semitic inscriptions is not new. The same thing was done with the Mesha Stele, discovered in 1868, which contained the first mention of the God of Israel and of an Israelite king, Omri. Several articles were published in scholarly reviews that cast doubt on its authenticity, the last one as late as the 1940s.[16] In 1993, the discovery of the Tel Dan inscription with its reference to *BYT DWD*, "House of David," was followed by several articles in scholarly journals, some of which doubted David's existence and proposed a different interpretation of these letters. Professor Giovanni Garbini questioned the authenticity of the inscription because it seemed "too good to be true." Russell Gmirkin continues the debate in a journal published in Sweden.[17]

Let us now turn to the work of the materials committee. I am not myself an expert in the fields of geology and isotopes of oxygen, so I cannot comment from the viewpoint of a scientist who knows these fields. But apparently even an expert would not be able to comment because, as the two scientists who wrote relevant statements on these aspects of the ossuary inscription admit, their report is not final, as I previously noted. They say they will write a final report sometime in the future and publish it in a professional journal. Until that time, however, scientific comment is well nigh impossible. My own comments, however, are based on common sense. Do the statements filed by the committee members make sense? You be the judge.

Two of the five committee members filed very short statements. Dr. Elisabetta Boaretto is an expert in carbon-14 dating, a test that can be applied only to organic materials. Since there are none on the ossuary, her expertise is not particularly relevant, as she recognizes. The statement of Jacques Neguer, an expert in antiquities conservation and restoration, is only eleven lines long. He makes no argument that is not presented in the other statements, which I treat elsewhere.

Dr. Orna Cohen is a conservator, "specializing in identification and restoration of ancient patina." She describes three factors that lead her to conclude that the inscription only "*suggests* forgery" (italics supplied). This seems to mean that she is not sure the inscription is a forgery.

The first factor she cites is that "the patina in the letters is grainy . . . not similar to natural patina." How did this patina get there? According to Dr. Cohen, "It appears that ground chalk mixed with water was used to coat the letters." She then jumps on an evil motive without considering whether other, less nefarious, reasons may explain this grainy patina—perhaps it was the accidental result of a cleaning.

Why is this grainy patina here? Dr. Cohen guesses, "*Probably* to camouflage the intervention of the inscription" (italics supplied). Again, she is not sure. But she assumes the worst (to camouflage a forgery), without considering other, more benign, possibilities.

Then she drops a bomb. She finds that the same yellowish patina that is on the *side* of the ossuary is also in the incisions of the letters of "brother of Jesus." Her exact words are: "A microscopic examination revealed the same yellowish patina as on the ossuary surface inside the letters 'brother of Jesus.'" If I understand this correctly, it means that she finds the last two words of the inscription to be authentic! And if the last two words are authentic, then, based on the paleographic, linguistic, and orthographic considerations outlined above, the entire inscription is very probably authentic. Paleographical analysis shows that the entire inscription was engraved as a continuum. And linguistically it would be difficult to explain an ossuary that was inscribed only "brother of Jesus," with nothing else, but waiting to be completed by a forger.

Dr. Cohen does not reach this conclusion, however. Instead, she finds that "even though part of the inscription *may be original,* the inscription *in its entirety* is a fake" (italics supplied). This sentence is completely illogical and reveals her prejudices. How can one say, "Even though *part* of the inscription may be original, the inscription *in its entirety* is a fake"? In the same sentence, we have two statements that contradict each other!

This brings us to the two geological statements, which really form the basis for the IAA committee's conclusion. Dr. Avner Ayalon, of the Israel Geological Survey, a geologist and an "expert on identification of materials through the study of isotopes in rock," appears to have performed the tests, which were then analyzed by Professor Yuval Goren, an archaeologist who is also an "expert on petrography and identification of materials and sources."

Both men specifically declare that their statements do not constitute a final report. Dr. Ayalon emphasizes at the outset that "this document does not constitute a scientific article or report." Professor Goren states, "The following detailed summary is not a scientific article." Therefore, unfortunately, it is impossible for other experts to review their work. It must be taken on faith, which apparently is what the other members of the committee did.

Dr. Ayalon took seven patina samples and tested them for the ratio of isotopes of oxygen of different weights. He finds that the patina in the last letter of the inscription seems old. But instead of concluding that there is no reason to doubt the authenticity of this letter, he tries to explain it as a testing mistake.

Moreover—a harbinger of things to come—Dr. Ayalon suggests in the next to last paragraph of his statement that the variations in the isotope ratio could be caused by water "at temperatures of 40–50 degrees centigrade." Water boils at 100 degrees centigrade. Would it not be possible that an energetic cleaning with warm water (40–50 degrees centigrade), perhaps with soap or soap powder, could have created a patina with the isotope ratio he found? Dr. Ayalon does not explore this possibility.

This brings us to the Final Interpreter, Professor Goren. He lets the cat out of the bag, so to speak. He concedes that "the inscription was engraved (*or* at least, completely cleaned) in modern times" (italics supplied). Why does he put the alternative in parentheses?

Elsewhere Goren explains that the person who created the coating applied it "in order to blur the freshly engraved signs."

How can he tell? Is there not another possible explanation—a rigorous cleaning with a brush and warm water?

Interestingly, in the first quotation above (with the *or*), Goren puts the possibility of cleaning in parentheses; in the later quotation (the coating was applied "in order to blur the freshly engraved sign"), the explanation of cleaning disappears altogether. The same phenomenon appears in his "Abstracts of Findings," where he wrote first, "The inscription was inscribed or cleaned in a modern period," but, later on, the alternative explanation of a cleaning is no longer considered.

In fact, we know that the ossuary was cleaned. Not only did the owner tell us of this possibility, but the GSI's first examination also recognized this, as did the Royal Ontario Museum (ROM) team, which found that it was cleaned with a sharp instrument to such an extent that some of the letters of the inscription were "enhanced." Yet the ROM team found no reason to question the authenticity of the inscription. Most significant, however, only the first part of the inscription was thoroughly cleaned. This may well explain why the ancient patina remains in the letters in the second half of the inscription.

Let us look at what is probable—aside from the conjecture that the suspicious coating was a forger's effort to conceal his dirty work.

The owner says that he bought the ossuary several decades ago from a Jerusalem antiquities dealer in the Old City. On the market, the price of an ossuary depends on the quality of its decoration and/or its inscription. An uninscribed, undecorated ossuary has very little value. Obviously, the seller wants to show off his goods to advantage, emphasizing the quality of the decoration and the clarity of the inscription. In this case, the decoration was so faint he may not even have noticed it. Even if he did, he could not argue that this significantly increased the ossuary's value. The inscription, however, was a different matter. He very probably tried to clean it. How? With a brush, warm water, and perhaps a nail to get inside the letters. In this way, the letters would look sharper. Admittedly, this is conjectural, but at least it is a plausible scenario.

Later, according to the owner, the ossuary was placed on the balcony of his parents' apartment. The balcony was partially open, and from time to time rain would come in, and standard heating was sometimes used during the winter. Later on, the ossuary was on a balcony and in a small back room of his apartment and from time to time cleaned by maids.

Still later, the owner put the ossuary in storage, where it was when he first showed me a photograph of it. In the Tel Aviv area, it would have been in a much wetter atmosphere than in a Jerusalem cave—and also in a much warmer climate, with more variation in temperature.

The possibilities are better stated by Dr. Amos Bein, the director of the Israel Geological Survey, who told Canadian filmmaker Simcha Jacobovici quite specifically that the work Dr. Ayalon did for the survey did not show that the inscription was a forgery. In Dr. Bein's words: "We didn't decide the inscription is fake," he said. "If somebody would like to preserve the inscription, or would like to improve its appearance, and he would like to clean it, and thereafter to make it shine better, and he made [a] procedure of cleaning, thereafter adding warm water and so on, he may have created some carbonate particles which may provide this isotopic composition."

As between the two explanations—forgery or cleaning—the latter is consistent with the paleography and the linguistics, both of which indicate that the inscription is one continuum.

Surely, the explanation for the patina as a result of a modern cleaning (or cleanings) is at least plausible. In fact, this explanation has been espoused by two previous materials examinations, one by the Israel Geological Survey and the other by the ROM. Their studies, however, were not mentioned by the IAA committee.

For all these reasons, I'm afraid little confidence can be placed in the IAA's conclusion on the ossuary.

A more detailed version of this paper was published in the Polish Journal of Biblical Research *5 (December 2003).*

1. Giovanni Garbini, "L'iscrizione aramaica de Tel Dan," in *Atti della accademia dei Lincei, Scienze morali, storiche filologiche, rendiconte* (Rome, 1994), 9.5.3, pp. 461–71.
2. "Face to Face: Biblical Minimalists Meet Their Challengers," *Biblical Archaeology Review*, July/August 1997, 26–42, 66, esp. 36–37.
3. See Eusebius of Caesarea, *Ecclesiastical History* 3.11; 4.22,4.
4. She gives as her reason: "The reservoir of names from which parents could have chosen their children's names was small and therefore the chance of choosing these names was higher, and increased as other names were already taken in the family."
    I am not sure I understand what she is saying. In fact, Professor Fuchs did take this problem into account. He specifically stated: "It is important to note that, since we assume that no two brothers in the family bore the same name, the probability of a child being given a certain name depends on the name given to the previous born male offspring in the family."
5. No. 570 in L. Y. Rahmani, *A Catalogue of Jewish Ossuaries in the Collections of the State of Israel* (Jerusalem: IAA, 1999).
6. Tal Ilan, *Jewish Lexicon of Jewish Names in Late Antiquity I, Palestine 330 B.C.E.–200 C.E.* (Tübingen, Germany: Mohr Siebeck, 2002), 17.
7. As she herself notes in her book, out of thirty-two attestations on ossuaries, two ossuaries (and three attestations) use the spelling YWSP (Rahmani, *Catalogue*, no. 573, with two attestations, and Emile Puech, "Ossuaires inscrit d'une tombe du mont des Oliviers," *Liber Annuus* 32 [1982]: 355–72, esp. 358), i.e., about 10 percent of cases. She also rightly mentions the Beney Hazir inscription (CIJ 1394) with two attestations (D. Barag, "The 2000–2001 Exploration of the Tombs of Benei Hezir and Zachariah," *Israel Exploration Journal* 53 [1993]: 98–110, esp. 92), as well as papyrus Murabba'at nos. 28 and 31, Yadin papyrus no. 7 (three different personages, about ten attestations) and Yadin papyrus no. 44 (probably a mistake for Yadin papyrus no. 9.5), which makes at least seven instances (and more attestations) of this spelling, "compared to nearly 50 instances of 'Yehoseph'": This would come to over 10 percent!
8. Ilan, *Jewish Lexicon*, 172.
9. Rahmani, *Catalogue*, 293.
10. Two are written Y'QB (Rahmani, *Catalogue*, nos. 290, 865) and three Y'QWB (Rahmani, *Catalogue*, nos. 104, 396, 678; this spelling is confirmed by the drawings).
11. Rahmani, *Catalogue*, no. 573, pl. 82; see also nos. 332, 552, 572.
12. See also Rahmani, *Catalogue*, no. 446, pl. 62, where the lid presents erosion and encrustation while the other side looks brand new.
13. See Rahmani, *Catalogue*, no. 796, pl. 116.
14. *Yod* (letter nos. 1, 8, 15, 17) is written as a simple, short, approximately vertical stroke without a small crook, hook, or loop at the top; this shape is cursive.
    'ayin (nos. 2 and 20) can be considered formal even if it appears sometimes in cursive script.
    kuf (no. 3) is formal.

vav (nos. 4, 9, 14, 19) is a simple vertical stroke, longer than the *yod* but also without a small crook, hook, or loop at the top; this shape is cursive.

bet (nos. 5, 6) is formal.

resh (no. 7) is formal.

samek (no. 10) can be considered formal even if it appears sometimes in cursive script.

final pe (no. 11) can be considered as formal even if it appears sometimes in cursive.

alef (no. 12) is cursive.

het (no. 13) is formal.

dalet (no. 16) is cursive.

shin (no. 18) is formal.

15. J. T. Milik, "L'epigrafia offre un bell'esempio di scrittura mista: BNH è calligrafico ed il resto è cursivo," in P. B. Bagatti and Milik, *Gli scavi del "Dominus Flevit," parte I: La necropoli del periodo romano* (Jerusalem, 1958), 79, and *passim*. Rachel Hachlili, in "The Goliath Family in Jericho: Funerary Inscriptions from a First Century A.D. Jewish Monumental Tomb," *Bulletin of the American Schools of Oriental Research* 235 (1979): 31–66, esp. 60, writes, "The ossuary script in the Jericho inscriptions combines cursive and formal elements, resulting in different forms of the same letter, often appears [*sic*] together in a single inscription."

This phenomenon is also attested in the Greek ossuary inscriptions: "An interesting paleographic feature occurs in this inscription: the use of cursive letters side by side with lapidary forms; the *alpha* at the end of the word *Kyria* is cursive. The more common lapidary *alpha* also appears in this inscription—in the word *kai* . . ."; see Tal Ilan, "The Ossuary and Sarcophagus Inscriptions," in *The Akeldama Tombs: Three Burial Caves in the Kidron Valley, Jerusalem,* ed. Gideon Avni and Zvi Greenhut, IAA Report no. 1 (Jerusalem, 1996): 57–72, esp. 57.

16. A. S. Yahuda, "The Story of a Forgery and the Mesha Inscription," *Jewish Quarterly Review (JQR)* 35 (1944): 139–63. W. F. Albright's prompt answer, "Is the Mesha Inscription a Forgery?" *JQR* 35 (1945): 247–50, seems to have closed the debate.

17. See Russell Gmirkin, "Tools, Slippage, and the Tel Dan Inscription," *Scandinavian Journal of the Old Testament* 16, no. 2 (2002): 293–302. The same charge was made earlier by Niels Peter Lemche in "Face to Face: Biblical Minimalists Meet Their Challengers," *Biblical Archaeology Review,* July/August 1997, 36–37.

18

BONES OF
CONTENTION

*Why I Still Think the James Bone Box
Inscription Is Likely to Be Authentic*

Ben Witherington III
(Reprinted from *Christianity Today* 47, no. 10, October 2003)

The press conference of the Israeli Antiquities Authority was announced with much fanfare, and headlines went out around the world—JAMES OSSUARY DECLARED HOAX, INSCRIPTION SAID TO BE CERTAINLY A MODERN FORGERY. Of course, it was not possible in June to critique this finding since the scientific reports that were said to be the basis of it were not released. Two months later, as I am writing this, only a summary of the findings has been released (though it is called a "final report"). One must wonder why the IAA is holding back the data, when the commission finished its work nearly three months ago.

As it is, the summary of findings of the various committees reveals major problems. If the scientific reports that are the basis of these summaries are not more substantial than the summaries, then certainly the headlines were not merely premature but probably inaccurate as well.

CURIOSITIES

Let us start with a few facts. First, only a few weeks after the IAA's much ballyhooed press conference, careful scholars from

Toronto published more of their findings. They concluded that the inscription on the James ossuary is certainly not a modern forgery. Toronto Museum curator Ed Keall could hardly have been clearer in his article, which appeared in the July/August *Biblical Archaeology Review*. Thus, at a minimum, we have a divided scholarly house in regard to this ossuary, and the attempt by the IAA to close the case on the James ossuary files has failed.

Second, Simcha Jacobovici, the producer of the Discovery Channel's special on the James ossuary, also held a news conference near the end of June. In it he pointed out various of the problems underlying the IAA's report and the way IAA proceeded with its examination. For example, the head of the Israeli Geological Survey initially silenced his two associates who first authenticated the patina on the ossuary, in effect overruling them. He then stated publicly that if French epigrapher André Lemaire still thinks the inscription is authentic, it probably is. Then he retracted this statement. In fact, Lemaire does still believe the inscription is authentic. His detailed refutation of the IAA's findings and his devastating critique of the process will be published this fall in *Biblical Archaeology Review*. [It is reprinted as chapter 17 of this book.] Something is rotten in Jerusalem, and this whole investigation begins to look more and more political.

Third, at a July panel discussion in Jerusalem after the showing of the Discovery Channel special *The Brother of Jesus,* Ada Yardeni, a leading Israeli authority on Hebrew and Aramaic script, continued to maintain that the inscription was authentic and that nothing the IAA's report had revealed disproved this conclusion.

Fourth, two independent examinations of the IAA's report indicate that it is far from conclusive. A team of scholars at the University of Kentucky has compared the IAA's summaries with the reports from Toronto. This team consists of Dr. Sue Rimmer (an organic petrographer) and Drs. Ana Carmo and Harry Rowe (both isotope geochemists). Their preliminary findings note the "many inconsistencies in the information we have looked at both in terms of data/observations and interpretations" and state that "the issue of whether the inscription cuts the ossuary's primary patina is unresolved" (despite the claims of some in the IAA that its report resolves the matter). The team also asks, "Is it true that only three additional ossuaries were sampled for comparison with the oxygen isotope data? On what basis were these selected?" Obviously a larger sampling is needed before one can draw sweeping conclusions.

In addition, Dr. John Eiler of the California Institute of Technology makes the important point that by its own report, the IAA admits that the film found in the ossuary letters is *not* identical to the patina on the Yehoash inscription—the other artifact the IAA was accusing collector Oded Golan of faking. This means that these two artifacts should not be treated as part of a coordinated effort at forgery. Rather, each must be evaluated individually. Eiler insists that we need a double-blind test done by scientists who have no stake in the authenticity of the ossuary.

Fifth, only a few people have noticed that there were no New Testament scholars or New Testament archaeologists on the IAA committee that studied the James ossuary. This is a glaring omission. One would have hoped for at least one specialist who could relate the ossuary and its relevance to the New Testament.

Curiouser and curiouser this becomes: No internationally known scholars on this commission were from anywhere outside Israel. Nor were there any Christian scholars on this commission, even though some outstanding ones live in Jerusalem. Christian participation would have assured us that theological agendas were not at play. The conclusions of the study would have been far more convincing had there been a balanced and internationally represented team of experts on the IAA commission. A scientific inquiry wants to guard against predispositions and biases. There are serious problems with a self-chosen body like the IAA commission, especially when several of the members on the commission spoke publicly against the authenticity of the ossuary inscription *before* they conducted scientific tests on it.

The IAA, long before the James ossuary came to light, has repeatedly made clear that it has an agenda—to stop looters and forgers—and in the bargain to oppose collectors, who in its view aid and abet looters and forgers. These are basically admirable aims (though I do not think it is necessary to tar all collectors with the same brush), but James and his ossuary should not have been made the poster child of this crusade. It is such a high-profile artifact that it needed to be studied dispassionately. The environment of extreme suspicion that surrounded this investigation, and the attempt to proceed by a process I can only call "justification by doubt" (a process in which one shows one's scholarly acumen by discrediting something), leaves me worried that the conclusions must surely be dubious at best. It is clear that the ossuary must undergo further tests in the wake of this report.

PROBLEM FINDINGS

What specific things need to be said about the published summary of findings? To begin with, no one disputes the presence of some sort of modern substance or film on some of the letters on the James box. Oded Golan told us long ago that his mother tried to clean the first part of the inscription. The fact that a modern chalky substance and evidence of modern tap water has been found on the inscription is no surprise. What the IAA calls fake patina, placed on the letters, is probably no more than modern cleanser and water. Perhaps the antiquities dealer also attempted to clean the ossuary inscription to make it easier to sell. Remember that neither the dealer nor Golan (when he bought the ossuary in the seventies) had any idea of its potential significance until Lemaire pointed it out last year.

It is especially disturbing that the oxygen isotope test was allowed to be the determining factor in concluding that the inscription was a forgery when (1) such a test apparently has not been tried on ossuaries before (that is, there was no controlled study or data to compare these results against); (2) this test can only prove there is evidence of modern water in the inscription, not that there is no ancient substance or patina in the inscription; and (3) the verdicts of the epigraphers on the IAA team were mixed, as their report shows, *until* the isotope test results were presented. In other words, one type of test with no track record was used as a trump card to rule out any questions raised by other sorts of studies. This is not good scientific procedure.

The real question is this: Is there evidence of any ancient patina or other substances in some of the letters? The answer is yes. Not only did the Israeli Geological Survey verify this more than a year ago, but if one reads the summary report carefully, it is clear the IAA cannot rule this out. For example, the report says that the word *Jesus* on the box may be genuine. This is especially remarkable because it goes directly against the earlier conclusions of those who wanted to argue that the first part of the inscription was genuine but the second part (*brother of Jesus*) was not.

The IAA notes that there is evidence in some of the letters of modern enhancement, particularly at the beginning of the inscription. No one denies this. But enhancement is not creation, and it is simply mind-boggling that the IAA can be so confident that the inscription cuts through the patina on the ossuary, when the Toronto team (which also examined the letters carefully under electron microscope) says it does not.

SCIENTIFIC SINS OF OMISSION

There are some glaring omissions in the summary report. First, as the Toronto team pointed out, some surface marks (or scratches on the ossuary) appear to be ancient, and these scratches go *through the letters* at several points. If the inscription was modern but the scratches were ancient, we would expect those scratches to stop at the top of the letters and restart below them. They do not do so.

Second, there is the ultraviolet light test done on the ossuary in Toronto. This seems to me to be a far more exacting scientific test than the oxygen isotope test when it comes to determining the authenticity of the inscription itself, and not the presence of a modern substance on the inscription. If there was evidence of modern tampering or modern forging of letters on an ancient ossuary, then this should have shown up under ultraviolet light. But nothing showed up under ultraviolet light. The inscription blended right into the surface of the box, which suggests it is as ancient as the ossuary itself. This test was presented on the Discovery Channel special for all to see. Why has the IAA ignored the data presented by other scholars?

Third, there is the issue of fissures found in the inscription side of the ossuary. These were created over a very long period of time, as the deposits in them suggest, and they go through various of the letters. This is not the same thing as the cracks caused by Golan's shipping the ossuary from Jerusalem to Toronto in the fall of 2002.

TIME FOR SOME RETHINKING

One final matter needs attention: What about the fact that the inscription appears less weathered than the rosettes, which are only faintly visible on the back of the ossuary? This fact seems to have been decisive in helping Professor Frank Cross of Harvard to conclude the inscription is probably a forgery. But there are a whole series of problems with this conclusion.

First, notice the differences between the rosettes on the Caiaphas ossuary and those on the James ossuary. Those on the Caiaphas ossuary, which dates to the same era, look like they were carved last week. The ones on the James box look very faint and weathered. Wouldn't they have both aged at the same rate, since they are both made of Jerusalem limestone and both from the same era and both were put in caves in Jerusalem to start with? Here is one answer: We know that construction work on and around the Temple and the Temple Mount had ground to a halt by the time James died in A.D. 62. This left a lot of stonemasons with too much time and limestone on their hands. How did they continue to make a living? One thing many of them did was carve ossuaries, which were apparently becoming increasingly popular in the period between Jesus' burial (A.D. 30) and that of James (A.D. 63). Of course, stonemasons carved ossuaries well before they were sold. Some ossuaries were not sold for a very long time. Undoubtedly some were left out in the quarry or yard where the stone was being kept, especially modest ones, such as the James ossuary.

More elaborately carved ossuaries made of higher quality stone, such as the Caiaphas ossuary, would not be left to the elements.

Jerusalem can have severe weather. Limestone, especially poor porous limestone, such as the James box is made of, is subject to weathering. It is my theory that (1) the James box was carved long before it was bought and inscribed, and (2) once inscribed it went into the tomb, thus protecting the inscription from the same weathering the box's rosettes endured. Hence the inscription looks much less faded than the rosettes. Add to this the modern attempts to clean the letters but not the rosettes, and we come up with a perfectly reasonable explanation for the difference in apparent wear. Professor Lemaire will cover other possible explanations in his forthcoming *BAR* article [reprinted as chapter 17].

In late July the Israeli police arrested Oded Golan, the owner of the ossuary, on suspicion of forgery. They released him soon afterward and have yet to press formal charges. Clearly if he is a forger, they should prosecute him. But André Lemaire says Golan does not have the knowledge or skill to be a forger. If the James ossuary is a forgery, then as Frank Moore Cross said in the Discovery Channel special, the forger is a genius, so skillful that he fooled the world's leading experts in various fields (paleographers, archaeologists, biblical scholars, and others). Furthermore, there is no evidence that Golan has made any money or attempted to make any money on the James ossuary or the Jehoash inscription (another artifact he brought to light, but one that is certainly not authentic). Yet making money is what forgery is all about.

This soap opera will continue to run for some time. Whatever happens with Golan, the authenticity of the James ossuary inscription does not stand or fall with him. That must be determined by the experts.

But until all the experts gain access to the IAA's data, I can affirm that André Lemaire and the Toronto scholars and I have not yet found any smoking gun in the IAA's report. I am still convinced the inscription is likely to be genuine and will be vindicated as even further study and testing is done. In the meantime, let the scholarly debate continue, and let no one think that the IAA report is anything like the definitive word on this issue. Only God has the last word.

The ossuary still cries out to us, as Jesus once said the stones of Jerusalem would do—and what it says is James, and what it says is Joseph, and best of all what it says is Jesus. The ossuary is just possibly the Word made visible.

THE TOP TEN NEW TESTAMENT ARCHAEOLOGICAL FINDS OF THE PAST 150 YEARS

How Do Shrouds, Boats, Inscriptions, and Other Artifacts Help Us Better Understand the Christ of the Ages?

Ben Witherington III
(Reprinted from *ChristianityToday.com*, posted online September 23, 2003)

Mention archaeology to most people, and they think of dramatic finds of artifacts that confirm or confute some cherished belief about antiquity or ancient history.

The truth about archaeological explorations, however, is somewhat less dramatic and much more mundane most of the time. Rarely does one find something that relates to a specific person or event. Most of the time one must be content with helping fill out the picture of the social world or context of some part of the ancient world—evidence of how people lived, what burial customs they followed, what sort of houses they built, what sort of artisanship they showed. This is why some have said that archaeology is the study of durable rubbish.

But occasionally something comes to light that is certainly more significant than rubbish and even relates directly to a figure in the Bible. Such an event occurred recently when the James ossuary came to light. To appreciate the significance and rarity of that find, it will be useful to first review the top finds of the last 150 years insofar as they are relevant to the study of the New Testament, and more particularly of Jesus and his context.

DIGGING INTO NEW TESTAMENT ARCHAEOLOGY

Archaeology is both an art and a science, and as applied to the study of the New Testament it is a recent phenomenon. Furthermore, the truth is that New Testament archaeology has lagged significantly behind Ancient Near East and Old Testament archaeology, not least because those early Christians left few remains or artifacts behind. They were not kings or emperors or pharaohs, and most of them did not live in mansions or villas for the well-to-do. They have left us some texts, but with rare exception there is little else by way of a direct trace of the first-century figures spoken of in the New Testament.

Most scholars would say that the age of modern archaeology began sometime in the latter portion of the nineteenth century and only really accelerated into prominence as a discipline in the twentieth century. It is an ever-changing science in the wake of the ever-increasing technological breakthroughs and advances in modern scientific methods of scrutinizing and testing ancient items. And I would say that a certain scientific breakthrough forms a good starting point for discussing New Testament archaeology.

The breakthrough I have in mind is the invention of photography. In the nineteenth century, and not long after the popularization of flash photography, a man named Segundo Pia was given the privilege of taking pictures of the *Shroud of Turin,* alleged to be the burial shroud of Jesus.

He could not have anticipated what he would find when he went into his darkroom. Before he printed up the positive images of the shroud, he examined the negatives in the dim light of the darkroom. What he saw astounded him. It was the positive image of a badly beaten or crucified man. But the positive image was found on the negative! This caused something of a sensation at the time and led to over a century of study and examination (at various points) of the shroud. Could it really be the image of Jesus? Do we finally have a clue what he looked like? This possibility seemed to have been ruled out when the shroud was allowed to be carbon dated in the late eighties, and the date that came to light from the testing was from the early Middle Ages. But wait. We know the shroud was scorched in a fire in the early Middle Ages, and it appears that the carbon-14 testing may have been skewed because a scorched part of the cloth was tested, and also because the microbiotic coating on the shroud was not cleaned off before testing. Even careful scientific testing does not always produce indisputable results. Naturally, an image of Jesus would be the biggest find of any sort relating to the New Testament. But the jury is still out on the shroud.

During the twentieth century, and accelerating after World War II, there were a plethora of important finds for understanding the Gospels and the rest of the New Testament. For example, we now have five thousand manuscripts or portions of manuscripts of the New Testament. Many, indeed most, of these have been discovered in the last hundred or so years. The earliest piece of the New Testament we have is *a small portion of John 18* copied on a piece of papyrus and dating to about A.D. 125. Of course we know that the New Testament books were written in the first century. But we don't have any of the original manuscripts. What we do have are copies of copies of copies. It can be said, however, that today, as a result of careful critical textual study and lots of hard work, we are closer to the original form of the Greek text of the New Testament than at any time since at least the third or fourth century.

If we are talking about artifacts other than texts, the following is important. The now famous *House of Peter* in Capernaum, which was found in 1906 but was properly excavated only between 1968 and 1998, has provided us certainly with very early evidence of a house church in which Christians met after the time of Christ, and it is not impossible it was a house where one of the original Twelve may have lived, at least for a time.

Of course mention must be made of the *Qumran scrolls,* which began to come to light in 1946–47, but despite some occasional exaggerated claims, these scrolls do not contain any portions of the New Testament or any Christian documents. They provide evidence of how a particular sect of early Jews lived near the Dead Sea and what they kept in their library (mostly books from the Hebrew Scriptures we call the Old Testament). Indirectly, these scrolls shed light on the time of Jesus, on some early Jewish beliefs, and on their messianic hopes, but we find no direct evidence of Jesus or his family or his movement here (despite the eccentric and widely rejected claims of one scholar that the Teacher of Righteousness might in fact have been James, the brother of Jesus).

Of more direct relevance is the finding of the *Pontius Pilate inscription* at Caesarea Maritima in 1962. This provided inscriptional confirmation of the existence of Pilate and the role he played in Judea for over a decade (he is called a prefect in the inscription). Here we actually have confirmation of one or more biblical claims about a historical figure. Of a more grisly nature was the find in 1968 of the ossified foot complete with spike of a crucified Jewish man called Yehohanan. This provided some confirmation about the process of crucifixion, though interestingly the Gospels do not directly mention the nailing of Jesus to the cross in the crucifixion accounts (only afterward is this suggested in John 20:25).

The various excavations at *Herodian sites* (Masada, the Herodium, the Temple Mount) have certainly confirmed the image of Herod as a builder with dreams of grandeur and have helped us reconstruct what the Temple and Temple Mount must have looked like in Jesus' day. It gives us a feel for a Temple-centered religion and helps us to imagine what Jesus saw and what he must have found objectionable. It only confirms the megalomaniac that Herod is depicted to be in the New Testament and in Josephus's writings.

From the 1970s to the present there have been excavations at

Scythopolis (also known as Beth Shean), the Greco-Roman city that was part of the Decapolis, the only city in the Decapolis east of the Jordan. It reminds us that Jesus lived in a milieu not far removed from the Greco-Roman world. The same can be said, and even more so, about the significant excavations done at Sepphoris, Herod Antipas's own building project just outside of Nazareth. It is possible, though we have no direct evidence of this, that Jesus or members of his family, since they were woodworkers or carpenters, may have worked in this city and been exposed to a very Hellenized way of life. We cannot be sure, however, of this conjecture.

There was much ado about the finding of the *Jesus boat* in the 1980s, a first-century fishing boat found in the mud flats of the northwest corner of the Sea of Galilee when the lake was low. It does provide us with an image of the sort of boat, made of handhewn beams, that Peter and Andrew, or the Zebedee brothers, may have practiced their trade in. There was not, however, an inscription in the boat saying, "Jesus slept here."

THOSE BONES OF CONTENTION

We now come to the finding of ossuaries, two of which call for special mention. In the early 1990s the finding of the *burial box of the high priest Caiaphas* caused a great deal of stir. This highly ornate limestone burial box reminded one and all that Jews between 20 B.C. and A.D. 70 practiced reburial. It is probably not an accident that the rise of this practice paralleled the rise of the Pharisaic movement. Pharisees, as we know, had as one of their chief beliefs a conviction about the bodily resurrection of the dead, in particular of the righteous. Reburial was practiced because of this strong form of a belief in the afterlife.

Ezekiel's prophecy had said that God could put flesh back on "those dry bones." Thus it was deemed more than wise, it was deemed a religious duty, to keep the bones together, in sure and certain hope of the resurrection.

Last, and perhaps most important, there is the *James ossuary*, which Hershel Shanks and I dealt with in some detail in the first

part of this book. It is my belief that this ossuary, having passed
several batteries of scientific tests, is indeed the burial box of
James the brother of Jesus. As such it is the oldest physical evidence of any kind that Jesus and his family existed. Remember
that the manuscripts we have of the New Testament date no earlier than the second century. Here finally we have an artifact that
is directly connected to various central figures of the New Testament dating to within thirty or so years of Jesus' death (in A.D.
30). Here we have what I like to call the Word made visible.

What really is the significance of this find? First, it reminds us
that James and Jesus and the holy family were all Jews, indeed
thoroughly Jewish.

Second, it underscores that they spoke Aramaic, the language
Jews spoke to each other in the Holy Land. This was not the language of the Jews of the Greco-Roman world west of Jerusalem.
The inscription is not in Hebrew, the sacred language of the Old
Testament; not in Greek, the lingua franca of the Greco-Roman
world; not in Latin, the language of the Romans. No, the inscription shows Jews talking to Jews.

Third, the ossuary itself reminds us that early Christians like
James believed in resurrection. James is in the box because of a
belief in the resurrection. But there is more to be said. The inscription on the box is unusual, almost unique. Most ossuaries do
not have inscriptions on them, and of the two hundred fifty or so
that do have inscriptions, only one other mentions a brother. We
can say with some assurance that when someone adds something
to the ossuary inscription beyond the usual "X, son or daughter
of Y," it is honorific in character. In the one other ossuary that
mentions a brother, it appears he is mentioned because he is
more famous than the deceased, and the deceased will be identi-
fiable through mention of the name of the brother. The same
seems to apply to the James ossuary.

But let us think about this for a minute. James lived in an
honor and shame culture, and crucifixion was the most shameful
way to die in that culture.

If crucifixion had been the final event in Jesus' earthly life,
then it is hard to believe that thirty years later someone would be

bragging on an ossuary about being related to him. The last part of the inscription reads, almost emphatically, "His brother [is] Jesus!" or "He's the brother of Jesus!" What had happened that redeemed the honor of the crucified Jesus? It was his resurrection. So, I like to say, James is in the box, and Jesus is on the box, because of the resurrection. And perhaps, if we are able to test the bone fragments of the box soon and compare the DNA evidence to the evidence produced in the 1980s about the gene string and DNA derived from the blood samples on the Shroud of Turin, we may just have a double confirmation of the artifacts I have discussed at the beginning and end of this essay. Stay tuned.

For now I will say this. We live in a Jesus-haunted culture, yet it is also one that is largely biblically illiterate. Furthermore, we live in a culture of increasingly visual learners who nonetheless are largely skeptical about biblical faith. They demand, "Show me." Well, perhaps in the fullness of time and at the cusp of a new millennium God has seen fit to make the Word visible once more in the form of an ossuary.

You will remember the story of Jesus entering Jerusalem on a donkey. The disciples and crowd were singing, "Hosanna, blessed is the One who comes in the name of the Lord." A critic demanded that Jesus silence such acclamations. Jesus replied, "I tell you that if these are silent the very stones would cry out!" While most archaeological stones are mute, this one called the James ossuary is indeed crying out. And it is saying James, and it is saying Joseph, and it is saying Jesus. Here finally we can see what an impact archaeological work and study can have on the study of the New Testament, and indeed on the search for the historical Jesus and his family. The James box is not durable rubbish; it is an enduring legacy, the Word made visible.

As such it provides some confirmation and gives us one more reason for the hope that is within us.

20
———

A CURATOR'S
PERSPECTIVE

Edward J. Keall
Senior Curator, Near Eastern and Asian Civilizations
Department, Royal Ontario Museum
Curator for the James Ossuary Exhibition,
November 2002–January 2003

Over the years as a museum curator specializing in Middle Eastern archaeology, I have had to deal with telephone inquiries from
the public about strange objects and have sometimes listened to
weird interpretations of what is written in ancient texts. Fashions
for what appeals to people tend to change over time. Reports of
sightings of Noah's Ark on Mount Ararat were common in the
1960s; today, Noah's name is more likely to be tied to our new
knowledge of the dramatically changing sea level in the Black Sea
in ancient times and the idea of a monstrous flood that drowned
entire settlements. The medium of contact too has changed. I receive e-mail inquiries forwarded to me from the Royal Ontario
Museum's Web site operators and today far fewer telephone calls.

THE JAMES OSSUARY

On October 10, 2003, I picked up the phone at my desk in the
museum to answer what I immediately took to be an old-fashioned
crank call. The speaker explained that a professor at the University of Toronto had suggested he contact me with his overture. I
still have the yellow scratch-pad sheet that I wrote on that day. In

large letters across the page, with lines doubled in places as I
doodled while listening to the pitch, I wrote "James son of Joseph
brother of Jesus." At the top of the page in smaller letters was the
name "André Lemaire," and over to the right, in the corner
"anon. Jo, bought 15 years ago." In squares I wrote "Suwan" (*sic*,
an alternative spelling for the Silwan valley) and "Olives" (meaning Mount of). Finally, I added at the bottom the name of the
caller, "Hershel Shanks," and a telephone number. The item in
question was an ossuary said to be from a cemetery in the Silwan
Valley near to the Mount of Olives, on the east side of Jerusalem.
It had been purchased some years before by an anonymous collector and had recently been brought to light by a reputable
scholar at the Sorbonne who was the first to recognize the significance of the inscription carried on one side of the ossuary. The
inscription was interpreted as saying that it once contained the
bones of James, the brother of Jesus of Nazareth.

As it turns out, I was being approached with the idea that the
Royal Ontario Museum (ROM) might be interested in presenting
a special exhibit of the James ossuary in November—to coincide
with city of Toronto's hosting of three large biblical and archaeological society conventions whose annual meetings were to be
held here that year, namely the Society for Biblical Literature, the
Biblical Archaeology Society, and the American School for Oriental Research. There was a sense of urgency imparted by Mr.
Shanks, for he told me that a press release would be made on October 21 announcing the public heralding of the ossuary in the
forthcoming (November/December) issue of *Biblical Archaeology
Review* (*BAR*), of which Shanks is the editor. I was warned that
other prestigious institutions in the United States would be interested in displaying the ossuary if the ROM did not make its decision quickly. To the credit of the ROM's senior management, the
idea was an attractive one, and a positive decision was made. Our
preliminary inquiries had shown that the item in question could
be legally exported from Israel, and we felt that we could meet
the excessively short deadline to put the ossuary on display by
November 14. I was cautious about being swept along with the
hype about the ossuary being "the earliest archaeological evi-

dence for the existence of Jesus" and intended to try to present as balanced a picture as I could when the exhibition development team at the ROM hastily started its work. At that time, since I hadn't seen the ossuary itself, my only real source of knowledge was Lemaire's article, which by then had appeared in print in the most recent issue of *BAR*. My first sight of the ossuary was in its fractured state, as it had arrived at the ROM's shipping dock. The headline of "OH, MY GOD!" on November 2 in the *Toronto Sun* best sums up the media frenzy that followed the announcement that the ossuary had been inadequately packed and fractured in transit.

OSSUARIES

As has been indicated earlier, an ossuary (a term derived from Latin meaning literally "bone box") is a secondary burial casket, often made of stone, used to collect the disarticulated bones of a deceased person after the flesh of the corpse has disintegrated. In a museum collection context, the period most celebrated for ossuary use is that of the late Second Temple period in Jerusalem, from 20 B.C. to A.D. 70. The practice was likely motivated in part by the need to comply with the rule of same-day burial and the scarcity of burial grounds for the Jewish community in the area of rocky Jerusalem.

Ossuary use has actually been documented in several other widely scattered cultures in the Middle East, dating back thousands of years. In ancient Palestine, pottery ossuaries have been documented from the fifth to fourth millennia B.C. It is thought that these Chalcolithic-period ossuaries were meant to represent houses, suitable abodes for the dead. But the Chalcolithic (Ghassulian) culture represented here disappeared without a trace, so we have no observable link with this past. Secondary burials are reasonably well known in the same region for the subsequent Early Bronze Age periods. It is often suggested that the practice might have been the result of nomadic pastoralists transporting a person's bones to a final sanctified burial place. But secondary burials also involved use of a communal charnel pit inside a shaft tomb, not an individual grave. Later, more conventional graves were constructed to house fully articulated bodies. So, again, we have no discernible connection between the Jerusalem ossuaries and the past. At first glance, we might imagine a link to the past through an ossuary lid bearing the name of Uzziah, a king of Judah in the eighth century B.C. He died as a leper, and the warning "do not open" is very appropriate. But the paleography of the inscription reveals that it was a secondary burial of the first century B.C. We have no tangible evidence of the practice during the Exile period. Since the Second Temple period ossuaries actually look like stone versions of wooden household chests, and even the chiseling techniques seem similar to that of woodcarving, it is conceivable that some earlier ossuaries were made of wood. But there is absolutely no archaeological evidence for this that we can see. At best we may envisage some wooden caskets used for shipping bones from abroad for burial in Jerusalem.

The growing habit of stone ossuary use in the later first century is said to have been fostered by the idea of the expected resurrection of the body, as advanced by the Pharisees. It was important, therefore, to keep an individual's bones together while allowing the flesh to decay. Absence of the flesh from the skeleton meant the detachment of a person from his or her sins. We gain a fascinating insight into the practice through a rabbinical commentary in the Mishnah portion of the Talmud, compiled in the third century A.D. but referring to the first century. The text deals with how to treat the disarticulated bones. One rabbi is reported to have said "sprinkle them with wine and oil." Another suggested "oil but not wine, because wine will cause the bones to decay." This was countered by the advice that wine and oil would encourage worms. The commentary then offers Rabbi Eleazar bar Zadok's explanation of how his father had instructed him to perform the ritual. "Son, bury me first in a trench [possibly meaning niche]. In the course of time, collect my bones and put them in an ossuary; but do not gather them with your own hands." When it was time, Eleazar entered (presumably the cave) and rent his clothes over the bones and placed dry herbs on them. The explanation he gave—"as he did to his father, so I did to him"—indicates that we can attest to this practice for at least three generations.

Stone ossuaries were quarried from the soft limestone or chalk of the Menuha Formation that are common in the Jerusalem area. An image recently posted on the Internet of an exposed swath cut through bedrock for road-building purposes gives us the perfect sense of the kind of chalk formation in the Jerusalem area that was used for ossuary quarrying. Horizontal bands of flint nodules, which separate the otherwise uniform calcium carbonate into layers, would have provided ideal seams for quarrying the stone for ossuary use. Conceivably, individual blocks could have been quarried using a wire saw and a grit abrasive. Alternatively, using a hammer and cold chisel to strike sharp blows along a line would have easily fractured the rock and allowed a block to be levered out. The size of the block was designed to produce a big enough casket to accommodate the long bones intact. From the inventory of other ossuaries known in collections, we may conclude that the individual in the James ossuary was small in physical stature, with a thighbone (femur) of around 20 inches or 50 centimeters in length. Of the other ossuaries, some are smaller, some larger. We assume that the smallest ones were for children.

Ossuaries for those who could afford it were placed in family cave-tombs. Again, from the Talmud, we can draw clues about the physical conditions appropriate for a family crypt. Ideally there would be a circulation space for the pallbearers, a shelf for preparation of the corpse, and a niche for housing the body until the dried bones could be transferred to an ossuary and moved to one side, in order to accommodate the laying out of a more recently deceased person. Known use of ossuaries, as attested archaeologically, is mainly concentrated in a very narrow window of time between about 20 B.C. and A.D. 70. Some ossuaries have been found to contain lamps and flasks for oil, and since these are topologically known they give us circumstantial evidence for the date of the ossuary.

It is a fact that hundreds of ossuaries are known in both public and private collections, and many more can be suspected to have been discarded in illicit antiquities' operations because they carry no decoration or inscription. Plain stone boxes do not have much market appeal. So, although many are known in collections, a high proportion have not come from professionally controlled excavations, and we have lost in the process a lot of potentially priceless information about the contents of the caskets. The practice of stone ossuary inhumation was largely disrupted in Jerusalem after A.D. 70, when the Temple was destroyed and the Jewish population dispersed. Clay ossuaries found outside Jerusalem may be associated with the dispersed population. A remnant of the community may have remained in Jerusalem, but the numbers of those who had the resources to have the stone quarried would have been small. In any event, the practice ceased entirely in A.D. 135 following the failure of the Simon bar Kochba uprising against Roman occupation. After the abortive Jewish revolt, Jews were banned entirely from entering Jerusalem.

Before that, for the first twenty years after the crucifixion of Jesus of Nazareth (ca. A.D. 30), converts to the new faith of Christianity were drawn almost exclusively from the Jewish population of Judea (the area around Jerusalem governed by the Romans). Apart from their new spiritual beliefs, most of the daily lives of these Judeo-Christians, as well as their normal behavior, remained the same as before. They continued to respect rabbinical interpretations of the Laws of Moses, including dietary (kosher) rules, and they practiced circumcision. Burial practices too remained the same as before. The sense one gets from the New Testament Gospels of Jesus' crucified body being laid out in a freshly cut tomb meshes well with the picture of Second Temple period Jewish tomb furnishings.

THE JAMES OSSUARY PRESS RELEASE

For the last seven weeks of the year 2002 the James ossuary was on display at the Royal Ontario Museum in Toronto, Canada. It was seen by almost ninety-five thousand people. It was an unprecedented showing at this institution for what visually is a rather uninspiring and uneven oblong box. The attraction the box had for people is that it is a tangible relic. In spite of claims made by devout believers, there are scarcely any physical remains that can be attributed convincingly to the times of Jesus' life. Most of the symbolism that we take for granted in Christianity, like the secret sign of the fish or the image of the cross, were not formulated until more than a century after Jesus' death. Written accounts of Jesus may reflect eyewitness reports of his life, but most of the texts were composed several decades later, in Greek, not in Aramaic, the language of Jesus. Almost all of the hard copies that still exist were made even centuries later, and the first versions are often compilations of different originals. Whatever its association in terms of personages, then, the ossuary puts us in contact with an age when there were still people alive who, apparently, knew Jesus of Nazareth.

Following Lemaire, the James ossuary bears an inscription written in "formal Aramaic" of the first century A.D. that reads "Ya'kov bar Joseph akhui diYeshua" (James the son of Joseph brother of Jesus). A brother is rarely mentioned in an ossuary inscription, and so it was argued that this must have been a very special brother. That, together with the naming of the father as Joseph, gives us theoretically a reference to Jesus of Nazareth. When the original announcement was made by Hershel Shanks on October 21 that the ossuary had just come to light, it was presented as the earliest archaeological evidence for the existence of Jesus. The press release was followed shortly afterward by André Lemaire's *Biblical Archaeology Review* article, in which a photograph of the object and presentation of the inscription appeared. There was a flurry of activity on the Internet as the skeptics raced to air their doubts. The ossuary had belonged to an ordinary James, it was argued, not the special brother of Jesus. No one can deny that the names of Joseph, Jesus, and James were very common in Palestine at this time, so there needs to be extra proof that this was the ossuary of James the Just. The ROM became the focus for many of the criticisms once it was announced that the ossuary would be on display in Toronto.

There were the obvious detractors—those who followed the Catholic Church's position, claiming that Mary's virginity was perpetual and that Jesus therefore had no siblings (in spite of the fact that they are specifically mentioned in the New Testament). Some made mistakes because they confused this James with the apostle James, son of Zebedee, rather than James the Just. This confusion, for instance, had led to the erroneous suggestion that we measure the bones of James that are housed in the sanctuary of Santiago di Compostela in northern Spain to see whether they would fit into the box. But these bones, which had been spirited away to Spain from under the nose of King Herod, were those of the apostle James, not James the brother of Jesus.

For the most part, the comments of the lay audiences were derived from familiarity with particular biblical texts. But they often had only half of the picture. Many failed to make the distinction between when each of the Gospels was written; and few appreciated that Jerome wrote his influential commentary, arguing that the "brothers" and "sisters" of Jesus mentioned in the New Testament were actually "cousins," in the late fourth century. The following citations are a selection of references in textual scriptures to the family relationship of James to Jesus and his role in the early Christian Church in Jerusalem. Clement, bishop of Rome, wrote to James as "James, bishop of bishops, who rules Jerusalem, the holy church of the Hebrews."

Reference to Jesus as the firstborn of Mary:

"And she brought forth her firstborn son . . ."
(NEW TESTAMENT, LUKE 2:17)

References to James brother of Jesus:

"Is this not the carpenter's son? Is not his mother Mary? And his brethren James and Joses, and Simon and Judas?"
(NEW TESTAMENT, MATTHEW 13:55)

"Then after three years, I (Paul) went up to Jerusalem to see Peter, and abode with him fifteen days. But other of the apostles saw I none, save James the Lord's brother."
(NEW TESTAMENT, GALATIANS 1:18–19)

Reference to James as spokesperson and revered leader of the Christian community in Jerusalem:

"James, who was surnamed the Just by the Forefathers on account of his superlative virtue, was the first to have been elected to the office of Bishop of the Jerusalem Church."
(EUSEBIUS, DIED CA. A.D. 340, *ECCLESIASTICAL HISTORY* 2.1.2)

Reference to James as spokesperson and revered leader of the Christian community in Jerusalem:

"This same James, who was the first bishop of Jerusalem and known as Justus, was considered so holy by the people that they earnestly sought to touch the hem of his clothing."
(JEROME, A.D. 347–420, *COMMENTARY ON GALATIANS* 396.1.19)

Reference to the role of James as a pillar of the church:

"The disciples said to Jesus: We know that you will depart from us. Who is it that shall be great over us? Jesus replied: In the place where you are to go (Jerusalem), go to James the Just for whose sake Heaven and Earth came into existence."
(NEW TESTAMENT APOCRYPHA, GOSPEL OF THOMAS, LOGION 12)

Reference to martyrdom of James because he refused to deny Jesus was the Messiah:

"Convening the judges of the Sanhedrin, (Ananus) brought before them a man called James the brother of Jesus who was called the Christ, and certain others. He accused them of having transgressed the law, and condemned them to be stoned to death."
(FLAVIUS JOSEPHUS, A.D. 37–CA.100, *ANTIQUITIES OF THE JEWS* 20.9.1)

Perhaps surprisingly, the most common reaction was the expression not of disbelief but rather of amazement that Jesus had a brother, who actually was the leader of the mother church of Christianity in Jerusalem. But naturally, because it was the written words that purported to give us one of the earliest tangible associations with Jesus of Nazareth, it was the Aramaic inscription that faced the greatest challenges.

ARAMAIC WRITING

Of an inventory of almost 900 ossuaries in Israeli state collections, over 200 have inscriptions: 143 are inscribed in Aramaic script, 73 in Greek, 14 bilingually in Aramaic-Greek, 2 in Latin, and 2 in Palmyrene Aramaic. The different languages are reflections of the different countries where the Jews of the diaspora lived. This has led to the suggestion that some of the ossuaries found in Jerusalem belonged to people who wished to be transported after death to a final resting place in the holy city of Jerusalem. The local language of Aramaic clearly dominates the inventory.

Like Old Hebrew, Aramaic was a so-called Semitic language (based on the nineteenth-century classification of world language groups). *Semitic* was the term applied to those languages that were hypothetically derived from what Shem, the son of Noah, had spoken. Hebrew and Aramaic are closely related in language structure and word roots. Both languages are read from right to left, and they are written in a simple alphabetic script that is derived from the Phoenician alphabet of Canaan (as opposed to complex cuneiform signs, pictographs, or hieroglyphs).

With the dispersal of the Jews from the Kingdom of Judah in the First Exile period (587–539 B.C.), the use of Old Hebrew ceased except for those who maintained the religious texts. Jews in exile in Babylonia quickly learned to speak the common administrative and business language of the region—Aramaic, the everyday language of the Syro-Mesopotamian lands in the first millennium. With the return of the Jews to Jerusalem under Persian protection in 539 B.C., Aramaic continued to be the language of everyday communication. In the Dead Sea Scrolls, from as early as the fourth century B.C., many of the legal records were written in Aramaic. Jesus of Nazareth and the apostles spoke Aramaic. Then, following the spread of Christianity through the mission of Paul to the Gentiles, Greek increasingly became the language of the new religion.

Aramaic script is roughly similar to that of Hebrew, but the word for son (*bar*) and the form of the word for brother (*akhui*) used here on the James ossuary attest to its being Aramaic. According to experts who judge the inscription to be genuine, the general (paleographic) style of the letters places the inscription in the 20 B.C.–A.D. 70 time range. The shape of the *dalet* (*d*), *yod* (*y*), and *aleph* (*a*) narrow the time range down to roughly A.D. 50–70. The known date of A.D. 62 for James's martyrdom adds circumstantial evidence in support of this date.

But the initial public presentation of the ossuary was greeted with a flood of skepticism. The most influential at this point was Rochelle Altman, who boldly declared that the inscription was clearly written by two hands. Beginning at the right (because Aramaic is read from right to left), the first part of the inscription was judged to be crisp and clear—the letters sharply angular. By contrast, the left-hand part—with the critical "brother of Jesus" attribution—was said to be softer looking and more "cursive." Altman's observations were echoed by many. The left-hand part, in their eyes, was a later insertion. There were those who were ready to believe that it could have been an insertion made in the fourth century when pilgrimage to Jerusalem and the cult of saint worship became widespread. One could have suggested too that the same tampering for ulterior motives could have occurred during Crusader times when Christian attention to "the Holy Sites" reached a peak. The die-hard skeptics simply saw it as a modern forgery.

The Altman theory was to carry weight for some time, as others too were persuaded by the same line of reasoning. This was despite the fact that Altman added "proof" of the fake character of the inscription by pointing out that it had been carved in relief, not incised. And this was declared to be so expensive a technique that it negated the inscription's authenticity. Unfortunately, Altman was operating under an optical illusion, and the letters are incised, not excised. She simply read the photograph wrong. Clearly too, most others were deceived because they were looking at photographs or Internet images. Certainly, the two ends of the inscription had different appearances. But as we were able to observe later when we had a chance to look at the ossuary close up, this was because someone had cleaned the right-hand part of the inscription but not the left-hand part. The cleaning had removed some of the surface encrustation—what others have called falsely a patina—from down inside the letters. Those letters where a sharp tool has been used to clean them may even be judged to be slightly enhanced. So they look sharper than those of the rest of the inscription. Those on the left look softer and less angular—that is, more like a cursive script, and therefore of more recent date. But the soft look is due to the survival of the encrustation, which is a surface film built up through age.

Curiously, from a reading of the same published images, a completely opposite conclusion was drawn by Daniel Eylon, an engineer experienced in metal fatigue analysis in the airline industry. Eylon pointed out that he could see evidence of "wear and tear" in the left-hand part of the inscription—what he called "service scratches." The implications for him were that if something has been around for a long time, it gets scratched or nicked by being touched or moved. If someone deliberately adds something to the object, these scratch lines are interrupted. Eylon argued that the right-hand part of the inscription was suspect because the surface scratches stopped at the edge of the letters; the left-hand part of the inscription was ancient, because of the scratches that continued across the surface and through the letters. Interestingly, his interpretation was exactly the opposite of what others were suggesting. But even though he was closer to the truth, he had not taken into consideration the differential effects of the recent partial cleaning.

LABORATORY TESTS AT THE ROM

The *BAR* article had reproduced the report by the Israeli Geological Service stating that they had found traces of the same kind of patina (better called encrustation) inside the letters of the inscription as could be seen on the surface beside them. The implications were that the inscription had been there a long time to acquire this "film of age." When the ossuary was taken off display at the ROM in early January 2003, I invited a group of ROM researchers to examine it close up for the first time under high-powered magnification. In addition, some of the slivers that had come loose from inside the object when it was fractured in transit to the ROM were available for instrument analysis.

Under 60x magnification in the ROM laboratory, we were able to verify that there were indeed traces of encrustation inside the letters. But, significantly, where it had not survived was likely due to someone—probably fairly recently—using a sharp instrument to clean the inscription. The cleaning has been done carefully. Nevertheless, the end result is that the letters have been enhanced. The left-hand part of the inscription has not been touched. The so-called two-hand theory then can be dismissed on these technical grounds. Even some of the acute discussions that took place in the public domain concerning the apparent differences in the length of the letters at the two ends of the of the inscription can be disregarded as largely without foundation, because of the reality that some of them have been tampered with accidentally. Senior Aramaicists like André Lemaire and Frank Cross also judge the inscription to be legitimate on paleographic grounds. The little triangular notches on the top of the angular letters are said to be classic examples of formal first-century Aramaic.

Through a simple hand lens, the ROM team was also able to observe signs of aging of the inscription. There are minute lines running through the stone like very fine veins. This is because the stone is formed mostly of a dense and homogeneous mass of dead microscopic shell organisms (foraminifera) so typical of a chalk. But the deposits tend to be layered, and this allows what can be called a vein to form in the matrix. These veins are formed of calcite crystals, which are harder than the surrounding calcium carbonate. When exposed (as on the surface of the ossuary) the surrounding area erodes at a faster rate than the hard crystals in the vein, which is left as a "proud" line. Under magnification, the veins run consistently across the surface of the ossuary and through the incised letters of the inscription. While the hard parts and the soft parts in the stone have eroded differently, nevertheless the disproportionate weathering has occurred at a uniform rate. The implications are that (apart from where over-cleaning has been done) the inscription has weathered naturally, at the same rate as the adjacent parts of the ossuary.

There are three ossuaries in the ROM collections. On two of them, chisel marks are plainly visible on the largely undecorated ends. They represent marks left behind after trimming the stone roughly flat; only on the one long side are they sanded down to make a smooth surface. On this one long side, an overall red paint has been applied to the surface, and then a design incised through it. The process allows the shallow design to look stronger because the exposed stone stands out as a white line against a red background. A few rough brush strokes of paint have been applied to the rough ends. On the third of the ROM ossuaries, all of the sides have been sanded smooth, but there is still only a design on one long side. There is no trace of paint in evidence.

The James ossuary was originally sanded smooth too. Only on the inside can one see the faint, weathered traces of chiseling. The outside of the so-called back and lid were once painted, though only a few tiny flecks of what would have been an overall red paint coating remain. The flecks adhere to the pure white stone, and there has been no buildup of encrustation. Given the general weathering away of the paint, this implies damp conditions to cause the pitting, perhaps from moisture inside the ossuary. Any encrustation that had formed would have disappeared through surface spalling, as the damp stone weathered away. Soft limestone or chalk is especially vulnerable to erosion in acidic environments, and such weathering could easily occur from contact with ground moisture that was acidic due to decaying vegetation. The original surfaces of the ossuary are certainly pitted and worn, and it was cracked in antiquity. This became apparent during mending of the ossuary for its modern fractures. Yet while this weathering and ancient damage can be observed, the form of the ossuary was largely pristine.

From small shards that broke off from inside the ossuary when it was fractured in shipment, the ROM team has made some important observations. The insides of the crack were coated with encrustation. The bottom quarter of the ossuary inside was coated with a thick dirt-stained crust. A tiny piece of this crust was examined under the scanning electron microscope (SEM). Under the SEM one could see a sliver of the stone itself and several layers of encrustation formed as slightly irregular bands. The bands were slightly irregular in shape, and there were subtle color changes in each layer. This probable iron discoloration was so minute that it was not detected by the instrument. The varying colors of the layers, however, were particularly visible when using a "thin-section" of the material under a polarizing-light microscope. These minor visual differences in composition are convincing evidence that the crust is natural, that it had accumulated over a long period of time. They help contribute to making a fallacy of the idea of a "simulated aging effect" for the creation of the encrustation on the outside so favored by many of the skeptics. It is inconceivable that someone would spend this amount of time and effort to simulate the effects of aging on the inside of the ossuary.

Of course, a crust of this kind could also have been induced by using the ossuary as a planter for flowers, as has been the practice of some Jerusalem residents. The same explanation can also be given for the remarkably high phosphorous content of the thick crust on the inside, as opposed to that of the thin encrustation on the outside (as reported by the Israeli Geological Service). After all, plant fertilizer is phosphate rich. But in this case the weathering on the outside of the soft stone would likely have been much more severe. More plausible is the idea that the rich phosphorous content of the crust is derived from the leaching of the bones that were contained in the damp ossuary. The leaching was followed by recrystallization of the phosphorous from the bone as apatite minerals on the inside walls of the ossuary.

STAR-CIRCLE DESIGNS

Along the bottom of the ossuary, there is the trace of a decorative design, on the so-called back. It consists of three incised circles (two large, one small in between) containing compass-drawn, six-pointed stars. They can be seen only in a raking light, their traces are so faint. One explanation for the weathering of the design as opposed to the sharpness of the inscription—apart from the popular forgery theory—is that the ossuary had been previously used. Let's say that the bones of a family member had been housed in the casket for a half century or more in the damp conditions of a cave. This would probably have been enough to cause the surface of the ossuary to weather and the bones to disintegrate. According to this line of argument, the name of James was inscribed on the back of an old worn ossuary when it was used for housing his bones. We can counter the argument of those who say that this would have been inappropriate for the head of the Jerusalem church by pointing out that the community was small, its resources limited, and James came from a family of very modest means. Yet careful examination of the ossuary in the ROM laboratory has led to the conclusion that the inscription and decoration may be judged to have been executed at the same time.

The secondhand box theory can be dismissed by observing that the same preparation has been made for all four sides and the top of the James ossuary. Every side of the ossuary has been prepared with a groove around the edge, which acts essentially as a frame. Similar grooves run along the raised lips that accommodate the sliding lid. There is nothing in the use of the frame to denote which is the back or the front of the ossuary. To explain the buildup of encrustation but lack of pitting on the inscription side, one might argue that the ossuary was partly protected by being housed in a niche. Following this line of logic, the inscription was on the back of the ossuary, protected from weathering by virtue of being covered in fallen dirt.

The idea that the decorated side was the front of the box is substantiated by the fact that a large proportion of the known

Jerusalem ossuaries carry a design on one long side only. Of course, one must acknowledge that ossuaries with design are much more likely to end up in museums or private collections than plain ones. On the James ossuary the design consists of two finely incised, compass-drawn circles of three concentric lines each, with a smaller circle between them that is centered slightly above the other two. Weathering of the lines has obscured them, and their profiles have softened as though a scar tissue has developed along a razor cut. Inside the circles, six-pointed stars have been drawn. The device is easily achieved mechanically using a pair of compasses. The radius of the original circle is used to draw a second circle, whose center point is set on the circumference of the first circle. The two intersecting points of these circles now become the center points of the third and fourth circles, and so forth. The end result is a six-pointed star.

The use of a compass-drawn circle design is also a standard decorative theme. It has been customary among academics to label these so-called six-petaled devices as rosettes. Many suggestions have been proposed for their meaning in the past, but all have been discredited, or at least none has found widespread acceptance. As covered by Rahmani in his celebrated catalogue of Jewish ossuaries, suggestions have included the idea that they represent the eye of the deceased; that they represent a wheel symbolizing reincarnation; or that they represent a continuing use of the star of Ishtar, the goddess of procreation. So there is no academic consensus on what they mean.

Of course, they may have no meaning at all. Six-pointed stars set in a circle are a common decorative device in the architectural decoration of the entire region from the Levant to the Indian subcontinent in the first century A.D. As explained above, they are an easily drawn design. By overlapping the circles, using the same techniques, an infinite overall pattern of interlocking stars can be created. Compositions of this kind are seen covering palace walls, as executed in carved plaster work in Iran. Equally, in Herodian Jerusalem they appear as mosaics on a palace floor. So why would such a universal decorative device become virtually synonymous with ossuary use?

To appreciate the meaning, one must address the issue of symbolism in artistic expressions. Symbolism in design implies the use of a motif that may be quite common but that acquires particular meaning through direct reference to a special connotation. Something symbolic becomes special through association of meaning. The classic example is the swastika, which is a bent-arm form of cross design that can be documented in the art of the Middle East going back almost ten thousand years. But its adoption in the twentieth century made it exceptional, and to reproduce it now still results in charges of racism. A less politically charged symbol, but an equally recognizable one, can be cited for the uniform of the Detroit Red Wings hockey team. The red-winged blackbird, which is a summer migrant in Michigan and which lends its name to the team on ice, has a single plume of red on its otherwise totally black wing. Yet everyone knows that the double wing attached to a disc in red and white that adorns the Detroit uniforms denotes the Red Wings.

It seems highly significant that the star-circle is by far the most common decorative device produced on ossuaries. Of course, it may be that its use was synonymous with a funerary practice but without meaning. However, I would like to suggest that we can find a symbolic meaning for this universal decorative device when applied to ossuary use. The common use of stars on Jerusalem ossuaries could relate to their association with the idea of the coming of a messiah and the resurrection of the dead.

IS THE JAMES OSSUARY GENUINE?

As both a museum curator and a field archaeologist specializing in Middle Eastern cultures, I have quite different perspectives on questions of authenticity. Clearly if one is responsible for excavating an object, one may be sure that it is a genuine antique. Yet there are attested examples of excavated artifacts that turned out to be ancient forgeries. I have seen an apparently genuine Greek silver coin turn out to have a copper core. This fact of its being an ancient fake was discovered only when the excavated coin was cleaned by a conservator. In addition, I am familiar with an excavation in Iran where scholars have never agreed among themselves how to assign unequivocally a cultural attribution, or even date, to a decorated silver vase from the Iron Age. This can happen when an object is unique. Typological comparison—the principle of this looks like that—forms a major plank in an archaeologist's research platform. Of course, with the James ossuary we have ample typological comparisons for the overall sense of Second Temple period burial boxes found in Jerusalem. It is the inscription that is unique and therefore suspect in some eyes.

Museum curators tend to fall into two camps—those who are immediately suspicious of anything that looks like something they have never seen before, and those who (like me) are more suspicious of look-alikes. Given the highly developed skills and motivation of the forger to deceive, it makes sense that they read the same technical reports and catalogues as the academics. If professional archaeometrists conduct laboratory analyses on the composition of a silver object, for instance, they may find that the ancient silver contains a minute trace of gold that is imperceptible without the use of analytical laboratory instruments. Very soon after the report is published, the composition of the forged object will be doctored with an additive to make it read correctly if a laboratory test is conducted to test its authenticity. Furthermore, the forged item will tend to look very much like others that are known in collections. Antique dealers love to be able to pull out a catalogue and say, "Look, it's just like one at the Sackler." A forger tends not to play high-stakes poker and invent something odd because it doesn't sell. Yet it is equally true that artifacts manufactured at particular times in the past do tend to be topologically similar in general terms, which is why we have been able to pass judgment on the James ossuary, in spite of the fact that it has no excavation pedigree.

In our technical analysis of the ossuary while it was available to us in the laboratory at the ROM, there was nothing we found that would cast suspicion either on the authenticity of the object itself or on the inscription. Some of the evidence that came to light was quite circumstantial on its own. But these small pieces of evidence added together attest to authenticity. We rule out a modern forgery. Reputable specialists in first-century Aramaic inscriptions have attested to the authenticity of the inscription. If the inscription was partly an ancient forgery, added a century or two after James's burial, it is more likely that the forger would have attached to the name of Jesus the epithet of "Christ" or "Our Lord." After James, when the Christian church began to spread beyond Jerusalem, with the preaching of Paul, the Greek-speaking Gentile community became increasingly drawn to the idea of the supernatural character of Jesus, as the "Son of God," downplaying his humanity. The simple reference to Jesus on the James ossuary is a tiny piece of circumstantial evidence in support of its being a first-century casket.

Statisticians suggest that out of the known population of first-century Jerusalem, the combination of the three names cited in the inscription—albeit common individually—narrows the possibilities of the casket's occupant down to a very few persons. Of an inventory of almost 900 ossuaries, 19 carry the name of a Joseph, 10 that of a Jesus. There is also an ossuary known to have the name of Jesus son of Joseph inscribed on it. Statistically, the combination of the three names in the James ossuary increases considerably the possibility that this was James, the brother of Jesus of Nazareth. The rare reference to a brother indicates a very special relationship. Yet there is no proof that will ever come to light that can confirm that this James was the brother of Jesus of Nazareth. The argument would not hold up in a court of law as beyond a shadow of doubt. To take that step has to be a leap of faith. But it is exciting that such a simple stone box can take us back to a pivotal moment in the history of the world.

Some people ask how it is that such an item could have remained hidden for so long. Their doubts help fuel their skepticism. In this era of virtual reality we tend to think that we know everything. The James ossuary clearly demonstrates that we do not. We forget too that not much more than a century ago startling finds were coming to light in Mesopotamia that helped balance the pendulum that, due to Darwin, had begun to swing away from the idea that the Bible was historically accurate. Excavations at Nineveh, for instance, showed that it was a very real place indeed, not just the invention of a biblical author. And startling archaeological finds continue to come to light even in this century. This institution had on display recently an exhibition circulated by the Seattle Art Museum of bronzes from Sechuan Province in China. These bronzes are exceptionally striking, and they appear to have belonged to an advanced Bronze Age culture that we did not know existed before the chance exposure of the first of the bronzes in 1986. The James ossuary can easily be accepted as such a chance but real discovery.

A RESPONSE TO THE JUNE 2003 ISRAEL ANTIQUITIES AUTHORITY REPORTS

We've come a long way since October 2002 when there were many who suggested even the James ossuary was entirely a fake. Since the discovery of the star circles and the tests that were done on the shards that broke away on the inside of the ossuary while in transit, most can be comfortable with the idea that the box itself is a genuine ancient artifact. The IAA reports accept that position too. So we must concentrate single-mindedly on the inscription. Yet I would hasten to add that, in order to evaluate the instrument-derived findings, one must retain a holistic viewpoint as well. For some of the conclusions from the results of the tests may be explained in alternative ways, if one accepts the fact that we know precisely neither the environmental conditions of the ossuary's original context nor its recent history. We do not know exactly what has been done to the ossuary in the past twenty years that may produce instrument readings distorted from the norm. The Goren report openly accepts the idea that the James ossuary is in part deeply pitted in its lower section, a sign of exposure to considerable moisture.

I admit that I may have to state that I was wrong in my conclusion about the authenticity of the James ossuary (as presented in Keall, *BAR* 29, no. 4). I am open to the idea that I have been duped by an extremely clever forger. But I have yet to be shown any clear and unequivocal scientific evidence that definitively demonstrates that the inscription is completely false. In the end, we may still have to depend upon the credibility of Oded Golan and whether or not he will successfully defend his story or make a courtroom confession. We must bear in mind too that a collector may knowingly have forged pieces in his possession, even have forged them himself. But, equally, he may be in possession of genuine artifacts at the same time. So we must be careful to measure the scientific evidence about a single piece in isolation from the other pieces in the collection, however damning the character profile of the collector. Combining the reports on the Yehoash tablet and the ossuary in the same document smacks a little of deliberately imparting guilt through association.

I reiterate that one must observe that microprobe analysis (taking microscopically tiny samples and letting the instrument-derived percentages speak for themselves) is fraught with the danger that the results can be misread because they may not necessarily be fully representative of a norm. In the medical profession we are aware of the many times that cures for cancer or heart disease are proven to be false. Yet in these cases, thousands of laboratory studies can be assembled to provide a frame of reference for the new findings. In the case of the James ossuary, few parallel studies exist. Certainly, the Ayalon Report on the chemistry of the ossuary rock and patina referred to studies made on comparable Jerusalem ossuaries housed in the Rockefeller Museum. But I would imagine that none of those examined have had the same career as the James ossuary. And we are not told how many, to know whether the tests were statistically valid, which is an important factor in relying on instrument analysis.

One may suggest that the James ossuary may have spent some years in the polluted urban atmosphere of Jerusalem and Tel Aviv. Certainly, other ossuaries may have the same experience. But do we know whether the absorption rate for newly exposed soft rock (if the inscription was cleaned by Oded's mother) is different for rock that is covered with centuries of "rock varnish"? The point that I am trying to make is that for scientific data to be statistically valid, the physical history of the object must be the same as that of the others. Other anomalies in the case of James is that the ossuary was shipped twice for at least twelve hours in a low-pressurized freight cabin at probably thirty thousand feet, where it was exposed to a different atmosphere. What was the impact of that? (There are those, for instance, who believe that radiocarbon testing should not be done on a sample that has traveled by air freight because of the risk of a distorted reading.) The James ossuary was mended with polyvinyl acetate, including the middle part of the inscription. What is the effect of that substance on the oxygen isotopes in the samples taken? Distilled water was used to mix the fixative for the freshly broken cracks, in order to secure a better bond in the mending. What was the effect of that on the oxygen isotopes in the area of the mend? When filmmaker Jocobovici filmed the ossuary in the laboratory at the ROM, he used a water-based vapor-misting agent in the air to simulate smoke, in order to create a mystery mood. What was the effect of the vapor? Could it have had a different effect on the newly exposed letters of the inscription than on those where the rock varnish still remained?

While these may be individually trivial observations, there is one point where the Goren analysis can be largely discredited as scientifically invalid. If one trusts implicitly in readings produced by instruments, one cannot pick and choose which readings to accept and which to reject. Seven samples were taken from the patina of the inscription. Six of them produced anomalous readings, as measured against those of the "Judean chalk" of other ossuaries and other parts of the James ossuary. Yet the seventh sample—from the last strongly formed letter in the crucial word *Yeshua*—did match the expected reading for a Jerusalem chalk ossuary. Ayalon dismissed this reading on the grounds that likely a bit of the ossuary rock got mixed up in the sample. This is untenable from the methodological point of view. Trust the instrument or not, but do not dismiss the results when they inconveniently do not fit the theory.

We face the same challenge of how to interpret scientific data when it comes to the Goren report about the petrographic and mineralogical composition of the patina. The conclusion drawn is that the inscription was cut down through the original rock varnish coating and parts of the letters coated with a paste of chalk

dust that has a different microfossil composition from the coat-
ings in the other areas of the ossuary. It is suggested that the inscription coating may have been artificially produced through
either a hot-water application of the powdered chalk or through
heat treatment. But the evidence for this was largely derived by
observations from tests conducted on the Yehoash tablet, not on
the James ossuary. Again, from the scientific methodological
point of view, this makes a valid hypothesis but not a definitive
proof. If one presents as an alternative hypothesis (as suggested
in *BAR* 29, no. 4) that the first part of the inscription was sub-
jected to recent cleaning, what might the effects of that action
have been on the residues present? Furthermore, if the cleaning
has exposed a much earlier stage in the life of the coating's accumulation (through removing the top layer), is it conceivable that
the composition of it might be different from the last hardened
rock-varnish stage that survives in the second part of the inscription? To use a good lay term, are we comparing apples with or-
anges? In addition, referring again to the *BAR* commentary, what
explains the heightened calcite vein that the ROM team observed, which seems to imply weathering over a period of time?
Was this effect produced as a result of using some kind of
compressed-air tool to incise the letters? For cutting with a chisel
or mechanical vibra-tool would not result in this differential
weathering. As observed in the *BAR* commentary, the conclusion
drawn by the ROM team was that the there were sharp edges to
the letters, which could be the result of someone having cleaned
the inscription in recent times rather than the sharpness being a
case of the letters having been cut down through the ancient surface coating.

Finally, as a museum curator, I must address what one might
see normally as the psychological approach taken by the forger.
Generally speaking, the forger tries to fool the collector or academic by covering up the forged detail. As an example, two separate fragments from two identical but separate vessels may be
cleverly joined to look like one. At the ROM we have bought at
auction a pottery vessel made out of two vessels. The "host" object
was ground down on the inside to accommodate an ornate sherd

that was embedded on its interior. Artificial encrustation was pasted on the joins successfully to disguise the joins. Only when the item broke did we see the work of the forger. X-ray photographs of other objects has revealed that this was not a unique act. In other examples of forgery, for decades, completely new pottery vessels have been covered with the same encrustation, to simulate age. With regards to metal, artifacts can be artificially aged by subjecting them to acidic treatment, in order to accelerate the growth of corrosion. A cesspit is a good place to have this happen. But, for the most part, a forger hides the fabrication.

Why is the first part of the James ossuary inscription more clearly exposed, if it is the forged part? Why did the forger not apply much more artificial coating to disguise his work? It is a small point but one worthy of deliberation, as an attitude different from the norm. But the last line is that if we follow the IAA reports rather than the *BAR* commentary, we are left with the firm conclusion that at least the second part of the inscription is actually real, and this includes then still the critical wording that "the brother of Jesus" is named. And no one has disputed what a unique phenomenon it is to have a brother cited in this way in a Jerusalem ossuary inscription.

In the end, I conclude that so far I could be convinced that the inscription is fake only by a courtroom confession. So far, I repeat that I have not been given from the interpretation of instrument readings unequivocal evidence that the James ossuary inscription is false. I do admit that there are a lot of unanswered questions.

For more about Edward Keall, see www.rom.on.ca/neac/staff/ keall.
For more about the James ossuary exhibition as presented by Keall, see www.rom.on.ca/ossuary.

Acknowledgments

My thanks, first and foremost, to André Lemaire of the Sorbonne, without whom this book would not exist. I also thank the many scholars who have taught me about ossuaries, inscriptions, and James, including P. Kyle McCarter Jr., of the Johns Hopkins University, Father Joseph A. Fitzmyer of the Catholic University of America, Amos Kloner of Bar-Ilan University, and, of course, my coauthor, Ben Witherington.

For helping me as I groped in the world of statistics, I thank especially Joshua Frieman, as well as Roman L. Weil, Albert Madansky, M. Laurentius Marais, and Bernard Rosner.

For help on ancient coins and weights, I went straight to the source: Ya'akov (Yankele) Meshorer. Gracious, willing, and knowledgeable as always.

At the Biblical Archaeology Society, Molly Dewsnap Meinhardt selected pictures, wrote captions, directed research, and supervised the editorial process, all while serving as the creative managing editor of *Bible Review*. Amanda Kolson Hurley ably provided invaluable assistance to Molly and me, polishing the text, conducting research, and obtaining images. Steven Feldman, managing editor of *Biblical Archaeology Review*, helped prepare the original article on the ossuary for publication. Frank Sheehan designed charts and other graphics; Julia Bozzolo produced the map.

John Loudon at Harper San Francisco bravely took on the job of editing an editor; his capable assistant, Kris Ashley, kept us all on track.

Robert Barnett, Esquire, served as our agent in the cordial contract negotiations with our publisher. Kathleen Ryan, Esquire, pinned down details that we would never have thought of.

To all, my profound gratitude.

Hershel Shanks
Washington, D.C.
January 2003

To Laura Michaels Ice and Molly Dewsnap Meinhardt, without whose hard work and editing this manuscript could not have been delivered in good time and in good order. A special thanks must go to two fine scholars who I am honored to count as friends—Richard Bauckham and John Painter. Without your hard work on James, my portion of this book would not have been possible.

Philippians 1.3

Ben Witherington
Lexington, Kentucky
January 2003